GOD THINGS

ENCOUNTERS WITH JESUS
THAT TRANSFORM US

DR. MICHAEL M. PALOMPO
PROLOGUE BY: DR. WAYNE CORDEIRO

Copyright © 2011 Dr. Michael M Palompo
All rights reserved.

ISBN: 146627462X
ISBN-13: 9781466274624

Cover Design by Mark Palompo

TABLE OF CONTENTS

TABLE OF CONTENTS

DEDICATION

To Mona
My Love for a Lifetime
My Ku'uipolani

PROLOGUE
Dr. Wayne Cordeiro

I first met Mike Palompo when we were in our initial stages of pioneering New Hope in 1995. I knew he had been a long time staff person of Youth for Christ and now as the longest living youth pastor, he was ready to embark on the journey of a church planter. He was soon to leave for Regent College in Canada in pursuit of his graduate degree, so we were introduced to a brief friendship and then he disappeared for several years. His parting words rang familiar...

"I will return."

But true to his heart, he did, and with ink still wet on his diploma, dove into ministry. I knew he was committed because in everything he did, he started by throwing his heart fully over the line. An old Chinese proverb tells us: *"Never test depth of water with both feet."* But Mike did. He possessed a heart in hot pursuit of God's best, and it wouldn't be long before pioneering and shepherding a wonderful congregation in Mililani, Hawaii.

In 2009 Michael received his doctorate degree, and from his labors emerged a wonderful life manual, brimming with wisdom and counsel for any avid student yearning to discover more fully the ways of God.

Mike has himself been one such student, and with an apprentice's hunger for transformation, he has left behind fourteen mile-markers that will guide the reader along his journey. Despite more than three decades of faithful and successful ministry, he would identify himself, not a master, but a delivery person, ... a white-belted messenger of the vast truths contained in this book. Mike is not one to place himself among the elite. He has long since learned that the best group to be associated with are those who dwell beyond the servant's entrance.

"There," he would emphasize, "is where the greatest Servant of all has chosen to be found."

"For who is greater, the one who reclines at the table or the one who serves? Is it not the one who reclines at the table? **But I am among you as the one who serves"** *—Luke* 22:27 *NASV (Italics mine.)*

The Miracle of Transformation

God does not complete His transformation miracle in one fell swoop. We are often enamored by the instantaneous ones: on-the-spot healings, the sudden raising of a sick person, or the immediate wholeness restored to a leper. These momentous occasions make the front pages of our denominational magazines, missionary newsletters, and they make for rousing testimonials in any service. However, some of the best and most lasting miracles don't occur instantly.

They eventuate.

It is the metamorphosis of transformation that causes a butterfly to emerge from a caterpillar. The miracle process took place in a cocoon, insulated from the public view and protected from outside intrusion. Transformation is an inside job.

It is a Spirit-motivated invitation to *Likeness*.

I've seen it over and over again within the beautiful gates of New Hope, here in Honolulu Hawaii. Literally tens of thousands of ordinary lives destined for hopelessness are transformed by His grace and are now living trophies of His mercy.

Growing in Christ

Transformation is not an end in itself. It is the beginning of an adventure. It sets you moving forward ever progressing toward becoming what Christ appointed you for. And here in this wonderful treatise, *God Things*, author and pastor Mike Palompo unpacks the tandem responsibilities of the Holy Spirit in partnership with the student.

One important mile-marker is that of a student who hears His voice and responds. It's one thing to be hearing, but the barometer of transformation is in the *obeying*.

I travel the world teaching leadership principles from the Scriptures. One of the premier characteristics of a leader, I encourage, is the ability to *self-correct*. Unless one is able to come to his or her senses solely by the Spirit's promptings alone, the Lord will never be able to use them in broad ways. In fact, the most conspicuous mark that a person is ready to lead others will be by his ability to lead himself.

The prodigal son's story in Luke 15 is so poignant because he was able to self-correct. He didn't require the harsh rebuke of a supervisor or the nags of a desperate wife at the edge of divorce.

Self-correction is a mile-marker that implies maturity. It exhibits the prerequisite of a developed self-denial which comes only from repeated dying. It demonstrates a heart that has learned to be teachable, sensitive to the Spirit's nudges and vulnerable to His discipline. Without it, a person will perceive supervision and accountability as a penalty to be endured rather than a mentor to be welcomed. God prefers a healthy conscience to heavy consequences. The Holy Spirit is the rudder that will help us navigate the cross currents within our own hearts.

But will we be ruled by the rudder or ruled by the rocks? The choice is ours.

In each of us is contained the propensity to drift, and even in stormy times, the Holy Spirit is "hovering above the waters," offering a safe passage to a sheltered harbor.

But we must choose to obey and self-correct.

It might be in the cadence of your life when our balance favors overwork (or over-ministry 24/7) rather than rest and rhythm. He will speak. We must hear and self-correct.

It might be my sexual appetites that are beginning to gnaw at my heart, causing me to lose my bearings. It is precisely then that I must learn to steer courageously toward the sound of a Shepherd's voice.

It might be allowing the overgrowth of tasks to block out the face of the Son...

Transformation is feeling the Spirit of God peel back our flesh, our pride, or our stubbornness—a process that fillets our heart until it is *"laid bare before Him with whom we have to do"* (Heb. 4:13).

Transformation is permitting the Great Physician to scrub our souls until it bleeds a rich red, and now the cleansed wound is postured for healing.

But I caution you...

What you are about to read will change the way you see things. It will alter your sight. It will press you to move beyond the initial appearance of "men as trees walking." You will eventually see deeper things ... **God Things.**

When you do, keep your eyes open, for you are about to arrive at the ultimate outcome...

Simply Jesus.

Read on.

Dr. Wayne Cordeiro

Chancellor

New Hope Christian College

ACKNOWLEDGEMENTS

With gratitude beyond what human words can express:

To our New Hope Central Oahu staff—Earl Morihara, Glenn and Theresa Rosario, Lori Shimabukuro, Gary Lau, Pam Chun, Mark Palompo, Lei Olayon, Landon Ajimura, Amy Ke, and Jane Amano—our church council, and the hundreds of volunteers who comprise our NHCO ohana. "We don't go to church, we are the Church!" All God! You are the current God thing in my life!

To Wayne Cordeiro, my friend and mentor, and the New Hope movement—God thing!

To Mark Olmos and my friends from Hawaii Youth For Christ—God thing!

To my parents, Diosdado (Desi) and Angelina (Lina) Palompo, my sister, Leila Fregoso, my brothers, Jay, Ray, and Joe, and our whole family. You were the first God thing in my life!

To my wife, Mona, and our children, Mark, Rachael, and Caleb—God thing, up close and personal everyday, my treasures beyond measure!

To Jesus, my King, Savior, and Rabbi—my ever-present Friend—who transforms the normal (and abnormal) things of my natural life into supernal God things!

PREFACE

Jesus Christ is the alpha and omega of all Spiritual Transformation. I just wanted to state that upfront. As we will see there may be a host of reasons why we want our lives to change. But *God Things* will contend that Jesus is both the reason and the source of our transformation. The transformation we are dealing with in this book is not "self-improvement." It is not about taking principles from the bible and applying them to our lives in order to change ourselves. The Christian life is a principled one, but it goes way beyond principles to the very Person of Jesus Himself. It is about encountering Jesus—or more accurately, Jesus encountering us. The result is we will never be the same again, and neither will the world around us.

There are *good things* and then there are *God things*. The difference is God things are what God is doing, whereas good things are things people do in the name of God, but God probably had little to do with it. Sometimes God things occur as we go about doing good things. But what would happen if we intentionally set our sights on just doing God things?

One day the religious leaders confronted Jesus, "By what authority are you doing these things?" As He often does, Jesus answers their question with another question: "John's baptism: was it from heaven (God thing) or was it of human origin (good thing)" (Mark 11:30 NIV)? The religious leaders refused to take a stand. How about us? Would we be able to tell the difference between a God thing and good thing? Then would we have the courage to follow Jesus in the God thing? It is a critical point. Jesus refused to respond to their question because of their refusal to acknowledge that John the Baptist was a God thing. It would seem that refusing to acknowledge God things is a barrier to greater revelation of Jesus. "Then neither will I tell you where my authority comes from."

The Pharisees insisted on doing their good things. Jesus is only about God things. The reason? Only God things last. Jesus said, "Every plant which My heavenly Father did not plant shall be uprooted" (Mt. 15:13 NAS).

It makes me wonder about the current state of the Christian church in America. A little later we will take a look at some alarming statistics on the state of pastors in the US. In short, they are dropping out at a rate of 18,000 per year. Are we doing God things or good things? For 16 years I was a very busy youth minister. Ministry was my life. I spent all day doing some kind of youth ministry. Then at night I would meet my wife and we would go out and—you guessed it—do more ministry. A lot of good things happened. But looking back I wonder how much of it really mattered? Our marriage became strained. When we had children I felt like I spent more time reaching other people's kids than my own. But how can this be when Jesus said, "My food is to do the will of Him who sent Me and to accomplish His work" (Jn. 4:34 NAS)? The answer lies in doing God things, not just good things.

How do we transition from doing good things to doing God things? In order to identify God things, we first need to undergo a *Spiritual transformation*. Only a person who walks intimately with God can know the things God is doing. Only one who is in pursuit of Jesus first rather than serving Jesus can discern the things Jesus is doing. What we discover, however, is that even genuine Spiritual transformation is a God thing. We cannot change ourselves. This applies on an individual micro level to our personal lives, and it also applies on a macro level to community transformation. We want to reach our cities for Christ, but before that can happen Christ has to get a hold of us. So the first God thing we need to experience is the Spiritual transformation He is bringing about in our own lives, and that brings us to our current study.

Thesis of God Things

God Things contends for **encounters with Jesus** that first transform us (Spiritually) then the people around us (community).

In other words, there is a Spiritual transformation that takes place first in us that subsequently results in community transformation. The Transformation Scale, or t-Scale, summarizes the whole process. Imagine the cross: a vertical encounter with Jesus causes a horizontal encounter with Jesus that changes the world. Genuine transformation happens no other way.

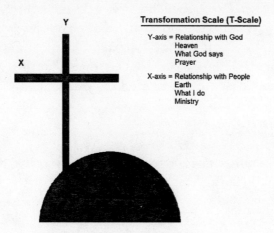

Walter Savage Landor once said, "What is reading but quiet conversation." Over the next few chapters, I invite you to join in on what I hope will be one of the most important conversations you've ever had. But it is not only between you and me. My prayer is that in some way beyond our imagining, our Lord Himself will somehow speak with you—that His Spirit might encounter you. Hearing His voice is critical to our transformation.

How many of us would agree that if we hear a good idea from someone—say, a preacher or a teacher—we have an *option* as to whether or not we will follow through? On the other hand, if it is something God told us to do, then we don't have an option. We are compelled to obey what God commands us to do. Hearing His voice and then stepping out in obedience to Him is at the heart of the Spiritual transformation process. This is why I pray that you will hear the Lord's voice in this conversation. If what you read is merely a good idea from some guy, then you have an option as to whether or not to do it. But if what you read is more than a good idea, and you discern by faith that it is the Lord speaking to you, then it is not just a *good* idea, it is a *God* idea. And you have no choice but to obey Him. How can you know for sure God is speaking to you? Suffice to say for now you will hear His voice. You were designed to hear the voice of God. You were born for this very purpose—that you might know and follow Him. Arriving at that place where you know that you know that you know that God is speaking *to you* is what Spiritual transformation is about.

GOD THINGS

Have faith—not so much in *your* ability to hear God but in *His* ability to get through to you. *God's ability to lead you is greater than the devil's ability to mislead you—or your ability to mislead yourself.* It is why Noah built the Ark, Moses set his people free, and Paul planted all those churches. They heard the call of God and were empowered to obey. That's when we start doing God things.

Discussion Questions

1. What's the difference between a good thing and a God thing? Provide an example in the bible of this distinction.

2. How can you tell the difference between a good thing and a God thing?

3. What is the process called that helps us become people who can tell the difference?

4. What is the thesis of this book?

5. What do you think the Lord might be saying to you as you read this preface?

INTRODUCTION

In 1998 I had just graduated with my master's degree from Regent College in Vancouver, British Columbia, when Randy Furushima approached me about teaching a course at a budding new bible institute called Pacific Rim (now New Hope Christian College). The New Hope movement in Hawaii was scarcely three years old, but God had already put it in the heart of our founder, Wayne Cordeiro, to start a school to train aspiring church leaders. "What would you like me to teach?" I asked Randy. "What do you want to teach?" (Answering a question with another question, I could see Randy was trying to be like Jesus.) I could've tried to be equally Christ-like and say, "What do *you* want me to teach?" But the answer was already clear in my heart that if I could teach anything, I would teach a course on Spiritual transformation. And so for the next decade I taught the Spiritual Transformation course at now New Hope Christian College, and still teach it as of this writing.

In 2009 Spiritual transformation was the subject of my doctoral dissertation at The King's University in Los Angeles, CA with Chancellor Jack Hayford. That required me to do a scientific survey of my former students of the Transformation class going back over a decade to see how they were doing. To my astonishment over 96% of them were still in active ministry and stated that the class had significantly influenced how they approached their ministries. God was confirming to me that we were on to something important in the training of church leaders.

This writing contains two broad sections. Part I is intended for everyone. My hope is that individuals, small groups, or congregations interested in a conversation on Spiritual transformation might find it useful. In the Appendix are excerpts taken from the dissertation and intended for my students in the Spiritual Transformation course.

During the decade of teaching the Spiritual Transformation course, we used two outstanding textbooks which I will forever recommend: John Ortberg's *The Life You've Always Wanted* and Klaus Bockmuehl's *Listening to the God Who Speaks*. *God Things* cannot improve on anything those two amazing authors wrote.

I am equally indebted to other writers such as Wayne Cordeiro, Richard Foster, Thomas Merton, Dallas Willard, and many others.

Close Encounters

There are three dates that stand out as moments Jesus encountered me. After these days, I would never be the same again: July 18, 1975, December 31, 1979, and March 3, 1994.

I was born into a traditional Roman Catholic home. So up until my 17th birthday I sincerely believed I had to work my way into Heaven through the rituals of the church. Then came the first of several unmistakable and life-transforming *encounters* with the Spirit of Christ. (Side bar for my non-charismatic friends: I was a conservative myself for many years, and immediately turned off by any mention of the Holy Spirit. But when you came to Christ, did you encounter a guy in a toga with long hair, a beard, who looked a lot like Jim Caviezel? Of course not. You met the Spirit of Christ. Like me you are more Pentecostal than you care to admit.)

It was on a Friday night about 11:30 PM on July 18, 1975. My high school friends and I had just returned from listening to Hal Lindsey (author of *The Late Great Planet Earth*) speak on the end times. That evening I watched as dozens of people streamed forward to the front of the Honolulu Concert Hall to (what I now understand) accept Christ into their lives. I had never seen anything like that in my Catholic Church.

I watched. But I was not one of those who walked forward.

Later that same night, we were at a friend's house playing cards. That's when Amanda asked, "Mike, did you want to talk with me about anything?" I later found out that Amanda was a Spirit-filled, Pentecostal Christian, who had some training in how to share the Gospel. "No, not really," I said. Five minutes later she grabbed me by the wrist and took me into the living room.

There she asked me what I thought of what Hal Lindsey had to say. I remember saying I thought it was interesting. Then she turned the conversation to Jesus. She explained the Gospel very clearly, but not in a way I had ever heard in the Catholic Church. "Mike, on the cross Jesus took all the punishment for our sin upon Himself *once and for all.* There is nothing more we need to do to earn or deserve eternal life. God gives us eternal life as a free gift when we enter into a personal relationship with Jesus."

It all made perfect sense. No more "Our Fathers," "Hail Mary's," or "Acts of Contrition" as penance for my sin. The cross now made sense. Jesus took away my sin *once and for all*. Her words were like a cool cup of water to someone who had spent a lifetime laboring to qualify himself for Heaven—and failing miserably. So when Amanda led me in a prayer to invite Jesus into my heart, I was no longer reciting a formula. This was not a ritualistic prayer to God. This was my own heart connecting for the first time to Jesus Himself. In that moment I knew my sins were forgiven once and for all. My life would now go in a new direction "all in" for Jesus. I had encountered Jesus. He had encountered me. I would never be the same person again.

It was a "point of no return." I cannot explain why, but when I received Christ into my life that night I dedicated *everything* of myself to Him. I was freed from religious work and now lived by the grace of God. I was on fire! Back then I would not have used phrases like "heard God's voice" or "encounter with the Spirit," but looking back that was precisely what took place. Instantly, I also went from depression to joy. An *emotional* healing had taken place in my life. I had been an asthmatic since childhood. But since that day the asthma attacks completely stopped. I was *physically* healed.

There with me that night was my best friend, Mark Olmos. I discovered that Amanda had led him to Christ the day before. Mark and I founded an on-campus student club together called the "John 14:6 Club." We spent our senior year at Radford High School leading as many friends as possible to Jesus. Later, that club would become Radford Campus Life and merge with Hawaii Youth For Christ.

That encounter with Jesus also sparked a mini-revival in my family. My brothers, sister, parents, cousins, nephews, nieces, and other family members all came to Christ. My sister, Leila, and her husband, Manuel, became missionaries in Mexico and continue to serve Jesus in their church in California. My brother, Jay, and his wife, Angeli, are co-founders of a new church, Island Grace, in Mililani, HI. Jay serves as the worship pastor. My brother, Ray, who is married to Lirio, is the Senior Pastor of Island Grace Church. My brother, Joe, and wife, Grace, have been outstanding Christian leaders for decades. My parents, Desi and Lina, (former religious Catholics like me) are excellent volunteers in both our churches. And there are a host of other extended family members who came to Jesus in our "Family Awakening."

The next significant Spiritual encounter in my life took place four years later during my last year of college. I was president of the Inter-Varsity Chapter at San Francisco State University. At the end of December 1979, a group of us flew to Urbana '79—Inter-Varsity's huge Missions Conference in Illinois. On New Year's Eve, no less a figure than Billy Graham gave the closing plenary address. Everyone knew Billy Graham as a powerful evangelist, but his mission that night was to call students to full-time ministry. As his message came to an end, I remember sitting on the edge of my chair with my head down and eyes closed, wrestling with the massive weight of that decision. Again, I would not have used this language back then, but the Lord showed up that night. I was graduating from college and stood at a crossroads. I felt this was again "one of those moments" that would determine the course of my life. Billy's voice rang out across the huge arena, "If God is calling you to full-time ministry for a lifetime, stand to your feet now." I remember Billy Graham speaking like it was yesterday. Although there were over 20,000 students in that arena, I felt as if he was talking to me. God was talking right at me. "Full-time for a lifetime? Are you kidding me? How could I make such a total commitment now?" But for some strange reason, my eyes still shut, I slowly rose to my feet in obedience to God. I could hardly believe what I was doing. I didn't want to open my eyes because I honestly thought I might be one of the only guys standing. The gravity of the call was so great, so radical. But to my surprise, when I finally managed to peak through one eye, there were thousands of us standing together. Of the 20,000 plus college students in the University of Illinois arena that New Year's Eve, there were easily more of us standing than sitting. It was off-the-charts amazing what God did that night. I walked away with a whole new course God had set for my life. I did not know how or where, but I was now committed to "full-time for a lifetime." The Spirit of Christ (not the language I used back then) had encountered me yet again, and I was determined to follow Him wherever He led.

I decided to join the full-time staff of Hawaii Youth For Christ in the Summer of 1980. One of my co-workers in the ministry was none other than my best friend, Mark Olmos. The ministry flourished, and from 1980–1996, we would help thousands of Hawaii teens find Christ. At its apex, we touched as many as 10,000 Hawaii youth annually with the Gospel of Jesus Christ, with over 200 of them making decisions in a year. Many of them continue to lead or serve in Christian ministries all across the state of Hawaii. Over the years, I have had individuals whom I could no longer recognize, come up to me and say, "I came to Christ in your ministry." Later, I will address a sad footnote to our ministry in Hawaii Youth For Christ, but that does not invalidate all the amazing things Jesus did all those years. In the history of the church in Hawaii, there had never been a youth revival like the one we saw in those Youth For Christ years.

I was content to do youth evangelism for the rest of my life. I married my wife, Mona (a YFC gal) in 1983, and we were raising two beautiful kids, Mark (born in 1986) and Rachael (1989). But then came my third major encounter with the Spirit.

In 1994 Mona and I were both struck with a sense of "holy discontent" in our spiritual lives. We began earnestly seeking God once again. "There must be more to God than this," we felt. For whatever reason—today we know it was the Lord's orchestration—we hungered for more of God. I had been a conservative, non-charismatic Christian for 19 years. I knew about the spiritual gifts, like the gift of tongues. But I was mature enough after 19 years to realize it was not about collecting gifts of the spirit as one might collect badges or baseball cards. My heart was, "Lord, if this will somehow draw me closer to You, then yes I want it."

I happened to be staring at a row of tall trees when I prayed this. And I noticed that a single leaf had detached from the very top of the tree in front of me. I looked to my right and there were no other leaves falling at that moment. I looked left and no falling leaves on that side either. There was just this one curious leaf falling from the top of this tree and it was heading straight for me. I know this sounds crazy, but I was wondering what was going to happen next. This leaf continued to tumble slowly right for me as if by some uncanny deliberation. Finally, as I stood perfectly still, it brushed ever so gently against my neck. Believe me, I know how this sounds. But long story short, I somehow felt touched by God in that moment—as if He were sending me a message that something was about to drop out of heaven and touch my life? That was in January of 1994.

In March, Mona and I attended a conference with Carol Cartwright at a local church in Hawaii. There Carol prayed the "baptism of the Spirit" over us. That night, nothing much happened. But the next morning, I began to pray out in a heavenly tongue I had never heard before. I know this was from His Spirit because a couple of times in the past I privately "tried" to speak in tongues on my own. "Shandala shandala shandala." No, that can't be it. "I-bought-a-toyota-but-I-shoulda-boughta-hyundai." No way. But this early morning at Moanalua Gardens Park in a heavy downpour, through my tears and worship, a heavenly speech I had never heard in my life came pouring out of me. At one point His presence was so powerful I asked the Lord to ease back His hand because I thought I was going to die.

A week later Mona experienced the same phenomenon. She had just dropped off our daughter, Rachael, at pre-school and was having devotions in the car. For her as well, the focus was not on tongues. But in the midst of worship, the Lord activated her prayer language. Again, a heavenly language poured forth continuously as the Spirit encountered her that morning.

In my first encounter with Jesus on July 18, 1975, I sensed Him say to me, "Once and for all" (Heb. 10:10) your sins are taken away. In my second encounter on December 31, 1979, He said, "Full-time for a lifetime" you will serve Me—my commissioning moment (Mt. 28:18-20). This time on March 3, 1994, as I received the spiritual gift of His empowering presence (Acts 1:8), I sensed Him say, "Happy Birthday." (My birthday was March 2.) Each encounter was supernatural and deeply personal.

My birthday gift in '94 was another course-altering experience. Becoming "charismatic" opened up a whole new range of possibilities I would never have considered before. Mona and I became friends with Wayne Cordeiro who was being led of the Lord to plant New Hope Christian Fellowship (a charismatic church) on our island of Oahu. We went to a spaghetti dinner at Aliamanu Middle School cafeteria in June 1995 where Wayne shared his vision for New Hope before about 100 people. He didn't have a sound system of his own, so he borrowed one that belonged to Mark Olmos and Faith Christian Fellowship. We became part of Wayne's nascent leadership team and had our inaugural service for New Hope Oahu on September 10, 1995, at Stevenson Middle School cafeteria. We were surprised to see 760 people attend that service. By that Christmas, New Hope had over 1,000 people on Sunday. By the time Mona and I left for seminary six months later in summer of 1996, the church was at 3,000. When we returned in the summer of 1998, the church was at 5,000. As of this writing New Hope remains the largest church in the state of Hawaii with over 10,000 in attendance and hundreds of people coming to Christ annually. My church, New Hope Central Oahu, has the distinction of being the first church plant, but Pastor Wayne has since birthed numerous daughter churches and extension campuses all over the world. On Easter 2011, approximately 32,000 people attended a New Hope church somewhere on Oahu. Nothing like this has been seen in Hawaii since Christianity first came to Hawaii's shores in 1820.

I'll never forget sitting in a staff meeting with Pastor Wayne and asking him, "How is this happening?" He threw up his hands and said, "I don't know." Granted Wayne is arguably the best communicator of the Gospel Hawaii has ever seen in modern times. The redeeming of the arts—song, dance, drama, and video—for worship and evangelism is clearly a powerful innovation that has reshaped the way Hawaii does church. And of course "Doing Church As Team" was an exponential force multiplier beyond the solo pastor having to do everything. Yet, there was still that sense that there was something—or Someone—else behind it all. On several occasions Wayne shared with us, "I will not touch the glory due to Jesus for all that's happening." Once again the Lord had led us into a God thing.

When I told Wayne that the Lord led me out of my 16-year youth ministry career in the summer of '94, he said he had a similar experience the same summer. He had been pastor of New Hope Hilo for 10 years when the Lord gave him the vision to start a new work on Oahu. Turns out that hundreds of people were getting that same call.

In my zeal to see Hawaii and other "nations" won to Christ, I sometimes forget the source of that zeal. As I pray for my friends and neighbors, I am reminded that God wants to reach them way more than I do. Jesus wept over Jerusalem and died at Calvary. What more proof do I need of God's heart? The current question then is, "What is God up to?" He said, "I will build My Church and hell is powerless to stop it" (Mt. 16:18 my paraphrase). So the key is to get behind Jesus and our ministry will be unstoppable.

When it comes to power to affect genuine transformation, I am a "zero." For it is not by (human) might nor by (physical) power but by His Spirit. But when I—the zero—get behind the "One" who is Christ the Lord, my zero becomes a perfect 10. When more zeros get behind the "One" then together we become 100; 1,000,000; 1,000,000,000 and more.

The key is to get behind the One and stay there. That's what this book contends for. God things are authentic works of the Spirit in our personal life and the lives of people around us. God things are not just good things. And not all good things are God things. A good thing is a human work done in God's name. To cooperate with God things requires a Spiritual transformation. But what is Spiritual transformation exactly? What is its purpose? We direct our attention to that matter next.

Discussion Questions

1. Can you identify a time or two in your life when you sensed that God encountered you?

2. What did He say or do in those encounters?

3. How did the direction or nature of your life transform as a result?

Chapter I

THE OUTCOME OF
SPIRITUAL TRANSFORMATION

"To fall in love with God is the greatest of all romances; to seek Him, the greatest adventure; to find him, the greatest human achievement."
— St. Augustine

"But we all, with unveiled face, beholding as in a mirror the glory of the Lord, are being transformed into the same image from glory to glory, just as from the Lord, the Spirit" (2 Cor. 3:18).

The Iceberg

Because only God can cause true Spiritual growth, our own transformation is a God thing. The iceberg is an elegant way of describing that there is more to us beneath the surface than we could possibly imagine. It really is true, "Transformers, more than meets the eye!" This is why Paul says the transformation process must happen from "glory to glory" or degree by degree. The Lord is the one who drops the waterline so we can see a little bit more about ourselves and cooperate with Him as He transforms that area. There is more to us in a *negative* sense in that we have psychological, emotional issues—matters of the soul—that need His transforming power. But if He were to show us all of that all at once, we would probably go into depression. So He orchestrates a divine timing for us to deal with our stuff. Simultaneously, there is more to us in a *positive* sense in that we have a greater potential for the kingdom than we could possibly imagine. But if He were to show us everything He had planned for us all at once, we would probably get scared off and run away. Or, we might get prideful over a vision that should have happened but never did because we got a fathead.

When we say *spiritual*, we don't mean becoming a psychic or a mystic. This is not a teaching about how to bend a spoon with your mind (sorry, you're not Neo) or how to have an out-of-body experience. We're discussing "Biblical Spirituality," not that New Age, Oprah mumbo jumbo. By *Spiritual* we mean the *Holy Spirit*. So we're really talking about "Spirit-ual" transformation—capital "S" as in Holy Spirit.

Transformation comes from the Greek word, "metamorpho." "Meta" means to "change." "Morph" means "form." Hence, change form or transform. "Metanoia" means to change one's "nous," or "mind." To change our mind about sin and to change our mind about Jesus lies at the heart of what it means to "repent." Therefore, transformation happens when repentance happens (and vice versa). Paul puts the two ideas together in this classic passage:

"And do not be conformed to this world, but be transformed by the renewing of your mind, that you may prove what the will of God is, that which is good and acceptable and perfect" (Rom. 12:2 NAS).

Did you catch that phrase "prove what the will of God is?" Being transformed is the will of God—a God thing. From glory to glory, degree by degree, we morph by allowing Him to change the way we think—transform our belief systems. Do we change *ourselves*? Christian Spirituality is not a do-it-yourself, self-improvement technique. Take a look at this:

"But an hour is coming, and now is, when the true worshipers shall worship the Father in spirit and truth; for such people the Father seeks to be His worshipers. God is spirit, and those who worship Him must worship in spirit and truth" (Jn. 4:23-24).

Underline "for such people the Father seeks." What's this? God is seeking. He loves everyone in the world (Jn. 3:16), but it seems He is especially after a certain kind of person. This is not my idea. These are the words of Jesus. Remember it was Jesus who gave us the visual of the Father *running* toward the prodigal son. This is the revelation Jesus wants us to know about our heavenly Father. What kind of person attracts the presence of God? Who are "such people" that the Father seeks? Those that worship Him in spirit and truth. Are you this kind of person? God wants to transform us into such people.

We were made in God's image. Within our corporeal form is a spirit that is very much like God's Spirit. You could say we are spiritually related to God. This is how we are able to relate to Him, worship Him, know Him, pray to Him, and speak with Him. The crazy thing is it also means He can relate to us. We were created to experience His presence in worship. We were designed to not only speak with Him, but—here it is—hear His voice. Our spirit was designed to relate to His Spirit. So making ourselves available to the Father is not so far-fetched after all. It is what we were *born* to do.

How does *metamorpho* happen then? How are our lives transformed? It does not happen by us attempting to change ourselves. This is a Spiritual transformation that can only happen by the presence and power of God. This kind of transformation can only occur by the work of God. What part do we play? Worship Him in spirit and truth. The spiritual disciplines we practice are not an attempt to self-improve or self-transform. They are not "religious work" to prove our worthiness to God or gain His favor. They are designed to help us worship Him in spirit and truth. And when we worship Him in spirit and truth, we become people the Father seeks. In effect we are not pursuing God; we are being pursued by God. We may think we are seeking after God, but when we worship Him in spirit and truth, He is seeking after us. Sometimes we wonder if God is with us as we study the word or worship Him in church. If we are worshiping Him in spirit and truth, we never have to worry about that; the Father is seeking after us.

With this in mind, Eugene Peterson has some wonderful definitions:

Biblical Spirituality: "The practice of paying attention to, responding to, and receiving the God who is revealed as Father, Son, and Holy Spirit. The intentional cultivation of prayer and obedience by the Christian community in response to the proclamation and teaching of the Word of God and as participation in the kingdom of God."[1]

Biblical: "An orientation and immersion in the large, immense world of God's revelation in contrast to the small, cramped world of human 'figuring out.' 'Biblical' in this context means living, imagining, believing, loving, conversing in this precise and richly organic context to which we are given access by the Old and New Testaments of the bible. It does not mean cobbling texts together to prove or substantiate a dogma or practice."[2]

Spirituality: "Living with the conviction that everything that God reveals in Jesus can be lived in and through the Holy Spirit, but only in and through the Holy Spirit. Spirituality is always primarily the work of the Holy Spirit. It is never learning a truth about God and then applying it to our lives. It is never learning how to do something right and then putting it into practice. Spirituality is the discipline of insisting that there is no such thing as mere doctrine or mere ethics. It all can be, must be, lived by and through the Spirit."[3]

To summarize we're engaging in biblical Spirituality. The bible is more than a book that teaches us some great principles for living, it is filled with examples of people who know God, talk with God, hear from God, and follow God. Spirituality in the bible is all about being led by, filled with, and empowered by the Holy Spirit.

The Ultimate Outcome
So why pursue Spiritual transformation? What is the *ultimate* outcome of Spiritual transformation?

The following are *not* the *final* outcomes of Spiritual transformation:

---

1   Eugene H. Peterson, "Lecture on Biblical Spirituality: Introduction," Biblical Spirituality 580, Regent College, Vancouver, BC, Spring 1998.
2   Ibid.
3   Ibid.

- personal character development
- godliness or holiness
- overcoming emotional issues
- ministry proficiency
- a better life
- a purpose-driven life
- better relationships
- happiness
- self-improvement
- spiritual power
- spiritual maturity
- Spiritual transformation is *not* the ultimate outcome of Spiritual transformation!

Don't get me wrong, all of these can be outcomes of Spiritual transformation, but they are not our *ultimate* outcome. So what is the outcome of Spiritual transformation?

Intimacy with God.

The greatest value in the kingdom of heaven is the love of God. Therefore, the ultimate reason for going through the Spiritual transformation process is intimacy with God. "And He said to him, 'You shall love the Lord your God with all your heart, and with all your soul, and with all your mind.' This is the great and foremost commandment" (Mt. 22:37-38 NAS). The entire bible is about walking intimately with God. Christian character, holiness, godliness, etc. are certainly important. But the purpose of our character is intimacy. The reason for our holiness is not so we can be seen as holy. It is intimacy with God. Evangelism and discipleship are incredibly significant. But the supreme motivation behind these is that others might love of God, and that evangelists and pastors might themselves experience His intimacy through their ministries.

Never confuse *fruit* with the *root*. "Seek first His kingdom and His righteousness, and all these things will be added to you" (Mt. 6:33 NAS). Jesus is showing us that there are fruit issues (what to eat, drink, and wear), and then there are root issues—or rather the root issue. All of life springs forth from an intimate relationship with God. When Jesus says kingdom and righteousness, He means our lives aligned with Him, His rule, His lifestyle. So too true character, godliness, and ministry effectiveness are by-products of an intimate walk with the Spirit. Seek first the root—intimacy with God—and He takes care of the fruit.

Notice we said that intimacy with God is the ultimate *outcome* of Spiritual transformation. We did not call it an *objective*. What's the difference? An "objective" may suggest we can go after this in our own power—a "good" thing. "Outcome" means it's a God thing. In other words, intimacy with God is not something we can pursue in our own strength. How many of us believe we have the capability to "achieve" a connection with God? Everyone from Nimrod (Tower of Babel) to Oprah (Eckhart Tolle) has tried. The whole point of the Christian faith is that we could never find God on our own. Jesus came to earth to tell us, "God is looking for us." The cross tells us that God's love for us is relentless. The Father is seeking. And good thing too because we were utterly helpless to get to Him. Here's the point: We must realize that intimacy with God is likewise a by-product. He is not something we can pursue as an objective. Intimacy with God is the ultimate outcome of *being loved by God*. The Father is seeking us. And He didn't just do that at our conversion. His Spirit continues to seek after us. And it is His relentless pursuit of us that transforms our lives. Our Spiritual transformation is a God thing not just a good thing.

Four Levels of Transformation

So God is in pursuit of us. He takes the initiative in our transformation. That's why we call it Spiritual transformation—because His Spirit is doing all the work. But what exactly is that work? Revelation. The Lord reveals who He is to us. We are His disciples (students) and He is our Rabbi. We know Jesus is our Lord and Savior, but in this moment would you acknowledge Him as your Rabbi and Teacher? Eventually, the Lord teaches us godly character and effective ministry, but before that He wants us to be intimate with Him. Intimacy means knowledge. But this is not "theology" which is the study of God, or knowing about God. This is intimacy, or knowing God. It's about how we *relate* to Him. Take a look at these four levels of relating to God:

LEVEL I	LEVEL II	LEVEL III	LEVEL IV
God is a Cop	God is a Judge	God is Love	God is Father
Minimum Required	Conform	Transformation	Intimacy
Egocentric	Legalistic	Liberty	Perichoresis
Focus on Self	Focus on Rules	Focus on Others	Focus on Trinity
Independence	Dependence	Interdependence	Oneness
Consequences	Commandments	Principles	Host His Presence
Bible as Consequences	Bible as Laws	Bible as Values	Bible as the Voice of God

Spiritual transformation is about progressing in the way we see and relate to God. At Level I you might see Him as a cosmic cop and our whole goal is to do just the minimum of whatever you think God requires of you. "Go to church? Ok, sure I'll go to church. There! Are you happy?" We're still pretty focused on ourselves. We want to be independent and do our own thing in church. You here the calls to serve in a ministry, but you figure if pastor ever brings it up, you will find a way to change the subject. You see in the bible consequences to avoid—like hell, for instance.

At Level 2 we've moved past trying not to get caught, but now we see God as a celestial judge. We're trying to conform to His rules and be as obedient and disciplined as possible in order to be approved by Him. The Christian life is like doing a vault routine at the Olympics and you're thinking, "All I need to do is stick this landing...Oh no! I did a little hop!" And God is up on the judge's stand making tenths-of-a-point deductions for every little infraction. You go to church but it is an unhealthy "dependence" on other Christians or leaders to make sure you do everything by God's law. You see church as a place of unspoken boundaries: "No drinking, smoking, swearing, or dancing allowed, but it seems that gossip, phoniness, self-righteousness, and hypocrisy are acceptable." You might feel judged by others in church, and you hope no one finds out "what you're really like." You serve in the children's ministry because, after all, your children are there and you should contribute your fair share. You see the bible as God's laws, and in the end you're hoping that you obeyed more of them than disobeyed. Then you will make it to that great medal stand in the sky.

At Level 3 this is where you actually might be a real Christian. God is Love but you tend to see your relationship with God as transformation as opposed to intimacy. It's a subtle point, but trying to be Christ-like is different from liking Christ. At this level you are trying to experience the full liberty in Christ that everybody talks about. At church your focus is more on other Christians than it is on Christ, so you have an interdependence on other believers. Obviously, we encourage people to experience this kind of fellowship. After all, this is why you joined a small group. You are looking for healing from hurts, habits, and hang-ups. But you are hoping that Rick Warren has the answer. Or maybe a pastor has some spiritual gift that will set you free. Conservatives lean heavily on the teaching pastor to be "fed." Charismatics are hoping to hear a rhema word from a prophet. What usually happens is once we are disappointed in the lack of immediate results we leave the church in pursuit of another church that might have the answer. Your focus is not on God but on others. It is on the church not Jesus, the bride not the Bridegroom. And of course, once you are more focused on someone's bride, you're in danger of adultery. Finally, you live by principles informed by the values you learned from the bible. At this point you might be saying, "Wait a minute, what's wrong with that?" Nothing. But for many years I focused more on the principles of God rather than the Person of God. There is a deeper level of relating to God, and it is the final level of transformation.

Level 4 is where we want to eventually get. God is our heavenly Father. I realize not everyone had a great relationship with his dad, but imagine ideally what that might look like and that's what this is. Our goal is not transformation but intimacy, and in the process we end up more transformed than we ever dreamed. We'll explain more in detail later what perichoresis means, but for now imagine the Trinity. The Father loves the Son who loves the Spirit who loves the Father and round and round they go for all eternity. God is the ultimate, loving relationship. Jesus, through His work on the cross, invites us into this Triune fellowship. Now watch this: We experience God's presence through the Holy Spirit who lives in every believer. The Holy Spirit is the third person of the Trinity. So if we are filled with the Spirit, where do we exist? In the fellowship of the Trinity! Lord, rid us of an academic understanding of what we just read to an intimate experience of that reality in our lives. In church we move from interdependence to oneness. Our focus is on what unites us not what divides us. Essentials are the important thing, not the non-essentials. So we work together as one to God's glory. We work everything out to stay one in Christ. We move from what benefit we may derive from loving one another, to unconditional love for one another. God the Father doesn't have many churches; He only has one. If He is my Father and He is your Father, then that makes me your brother. We continue to live by principles, but we also live by the conviction that the Spirit will personally lead us. We are hosts of His Presence in the world bringing a little heaven on earth everywhere we go. We get our value system from the bible, but we also hear God's voice as we meditate on the Scripture. We are anchored to God's word, but also led by His Spirit. How many of us want to get to Level 4?

If the imagery of God as our Father still troubles you, then think of Him as a perfect Friend. Jesus said, "No longer do I call you servants, but friends" (Jn. 15:15). Abraham was called a "friend of God" (James 2:23). Moreover, "Thus the LORD used to speak to Moses face to face, just as a man speaks to his friend" (Ex. 33:11). What an awe-inspiring vision to see you and God as the best of friends. That's Level 4.

We are praying to live out Level 4 Spirituality at our church, New Hope Central Oahu. Planting the church in 1999 was a huge, personal blessing for my family and me. "Doing Church As Team" the New Hope way was a new paradigm to doing ministry. It meant moving beyond a pastor-centered approach to the mobilization of the body of Christ. But here is the unexpected thing we learned: We discovered a greater sense of the *Spirit* in the church. As pastors humbled themselves to identify the work of the Spirit in others, we began to see a releasing of the power of the Spirit. What Jesus prophesied was coming to pass: "I will build My church and the gates of Hades will not overpower it" (Mt. 16:18 NAS). The greatest joy in ministry was not only watching the church grow, but watching the Father at work as Jesus said: "My Father is working until now, and I Myself am working" (Jn. 5:17 NAS). Jesus is working as Eugene Peterson quoted the poet Gerard Manley, "Christ plays in 10,000 places, lovely in eyes, lovely in limbs not His, to the Father, through the features of men's faces." It is awesome to experience the presence of the Spirit in one another at church every weekend.

What, therefore, is the *ultimate outcome* of Spiritual transformation? Intimacy with God.

Discussion Questions

1. How does an iceberg illustrate the human soul?

2. What is Spiritual transformation? Define biblical spirituality.

3. What are some examples of things that are *not* the ultimate outcome of Spiritual transformation? Why not? What is?

4. Describe the 4 levels of transformation. Why is the way we see God so important? How does our image of God affect the way we see church?

5. By faith what do you believe God said to you in this chapter? How will you step out and follow Him?

Chapter 2

THE PURPOSE OF
SPIRITUAL DISCIPLINES

"It is not the years of your life that count; it's the life in your years."
– Abraham Lincoln

Our most common prayers are probably of this variety: "bless the food," "traveling mercies," "watch over us as we sleep," or "please take away this headache." In other words, they are about living as long, comfortable, safe, and painfree as possible. But if we look at the lives of heroes in the bible—the prophets, the apostles, Jesus—they were anything but easy. Not that they were looking for trouble, but as they walked closely with God, that's when the drama began. The previous chapter was about intimacy with God as the outcome of Spiritual transformation. We learned that our transformation is totally a God thing. So does this mean we have no part in it? That we just kick back and let God do His thing? How do we *cooperate* with God as He draws us to Himself?

The answer—at least in part—has to do with Spiritual disciplines. There are so many ways to practice Spiritual disciplines incorrectly, so I urge you to tune in closely. Listen to the voice of the Lord once again. I did the best I could to teach this in this writing, but now may the Lord cause us to learn.

Here's the most compelling question as we think about Spiritual disciplines: How did Jesus walk in intimacy with the Father as a human being on the earth? An underlying assumption of this course is an understanding of kenosis as Jesus "emptied Himself" (Phil. 2:6) of divine power at the Incarnation. This is not Arianism which was the minority view at the Council of Nicaea (4th century) that Jesus was not God. (Jehovah's Witnesses are modern-day adherents of Arius.) Rather, Jesus is fully God and fully man, but in becoming human He emptied Himself of divine omnipotence, omnipresence, and omniscience. When He was born, Mary had to feed Him or He would starve. He didn't just divinely know everything about carpentry; Joseph had to teach him. He got sleepy, weak, tired, and hungry just like anybody else. If you whipped Him, He bled. If you nailed him to a cross, he died. He could be tempted in every way a man could be tempted, and had to choose not to sin. God is all-powerful, all-knowing, and ever-present. Jesus was amazing, but He wasn't any of those things. When He became a human being, He emptied Himself of divine power.

Some might be disturbed to hear this, but it's actually really good news. Jesus didn't "cheat" when He performed all those miraculous signs and wonders. He didn't toggle back and forth between being human and divine. So He wasn't in "human mode" when He was fast asleep in the back of the boat, then toggle to "God mode" when He calmed the storm. So how did He operate in the supernatural? Here it is: He was baptized in the Holy Spirit at the Jordan River at the beginning of His earthly ministry. He was the ultimate, Spirit-filled person. I like to think of Him as the prototype charismatic, demonstrating to us the full potential of the Spirit-filled life.

Because Jesus never sinned, He walked in deeper intimacy with the Father than anyone before or since. But the point is, don't sell yourself short! As we learn about Spiritual disciplines, we will learn what Jesus did to walk this closely with His heavenly Father. We will learn from the Master on how to do this.

Clearing a Pathway

Contrary to conventional thinking in the church, we do not become mature in Christ by applying biblical principles to our lives. Paul is clear, "God causes growth" (I Cor. 3:6). By themselves, Spiritual disciplines (solitude, silence, fasting, prayer, etc.) do not lead to Spiritual transformation. But here it is: *they can clear a pathway for our seeking Father.*

Spiritual disciplines are not about personal discipline. Christians are not like Shao-Lin monks who turn themselves into kung fu masters. Remember this is all about intimacy with Jesus from beginning to end. The Spirit of Christ saved us; the Spirit of Christ now brings us to full maturity. It was not possible for us to save ourselves; neither is it possible for us to cause spiritual growth in our own lives. So the disciplines are actually Spirit-ual disciplines not spiritual disciplines. The Apostle Paul said, "I planted, Apollos watered, but God was causing the growth" (I Cor. 3:6 NAS). The problem in the church is not difficulty believing in the supernatural but rather it is believing that some dimensions of spiritual life can be lived *apart* from the supernatural.

"Trust in the Lord with all your heart, and do not lean on your own under-standing. In all your ways acknowledge Him, and He will make your paths straight. Do not be wise in your own eyes; Fear the Lord and turn away from evil. It will be healing to your body and refreshment to your bones" (Prov. 3:5-8 NAS). Note that in v.7 Solomon says to "turn away" from evil. Spirit-ual disciplines are intended to help us "turn away" from evil and clear a path for God's healing and refreshment to come. We practice them to get ourselves out of the way so God can work. Spiritual disciplines help us say "yes" to God and His kingdom, and "no" to evil, darkness, and self.

I remember while I was in seminary I took voice lessons. No, I was not trying to become the next American Idol. I used to lead worship. But I had no formal training, so I was singing improperly. After leading worship I would lose my voice and spend the whole week recovering. That meant for days I could not talk. For a minister that's rough! We use our voices all the time. So my vocal instructor began to teach me how to sing properly, using my diaphragm more, and not over-projecting my voice. I never forgot what she said, "Mike, we need to get you out of the way, so you can sing." I had never considered that the rea-son I was blowing my voice out was because *I* was getting in my own way! The same thing is true for our spiritual lives. The more we train ourselves to get out of our own way spiritually, the closer we will draw to God.

Common Pitfalls

In his book, *Christ Plays in 10,000 Places*, Eugene Peterson identifies three clas-sic ways that Christians impede their own progress spiritually: moralism, gnosti-cism, and sectarianism. Morality is good, but *moralism* is the self-righteousness of the Pharisees. They turned morality into an idol. They created a life so good they no longer needed God. Their meticulous practice of the disciplined life led them further away from God rather than more dependent on Him. They were so blinded by their moralism, the Messiah walked amongst them and they didn't recognize Him. The purpose of Spiritual disciplines is not to create a life so good you don't need God. It is to grow more dependent on God.

Gnosticism, on the other hand, is the intellectual pride of some Greek phi-losophers. It suggests there is a special knowledge you can only get from them to achieve spirituality. Gnostics are gurus who have a secret discipline they alone can teach you. In today's church it can express itself as an elevated spirituality.

This "hyper-spirituality" creates elitism in the church. Conservatives might think of themselves as hyper-spiritual because their exegesis is superior to everyone else's in the church. Charismatics might regard themselves as hyper-spiritual because they have experienced more gifts of the Spirit than others. Gnosticism is the attitude: "I know something you don't so you should come to my seminar, attend my conference, or buy my book." Now you'll say, "But shouldn't we learn from one another?" Absolutely. The problem is not the sharing of knowledge. The problem is the elitism, the "one-up-manship," and the absence of humility. The purpose of Spiritual disciplines is not to make you a celebrity superstar of the church. It is to make Jesus the Superstar and make Him famous.

You can tell you're spiritual practice is going gnostic because this often leads to sectarianism. Christians splinter into various "religious clubs" based on doctrines or experiences, dividing the body of Christ. Fellowship is based on whether or not we agree rather than on unity in Christ. We shoot ourselves in the foot when we do this because we have so much to learn from one another. Jesus may have many congregations, but He only has one Church. At New Hope Central Oahu our motto is "anchored to God's word *and* led by His Spirit." Conservatives and charismatics downplay what divides them so they can learn from each other. (It works most of the time.) The purpose of Spiritual disciplines is not so you can create your own religious club of believers who agree with everything you say. It is to teach us how to be united with all Christians despite our differences. Imagine the richness of our fellowship if we all had this Kingdom mindset!

So according to Eugene Peterson moralism, gnosticism, and sectarianism are three common pitfalls in the practice of Spiritual disciplines. These are three typical ways we get in the way of what God wants to accomplish in us. And we should watch out for them.

What then *is* the purpose of Spiritual disciplines? Recall that the ultimate outcome of Spiritual transformation is intimacy with God. We are helpless to get to Him. But thankfully the Father seeks those who worship Him in spirit and truth. *The purpose of Spiritual disciplines, therefore, is not about us trying to get to Him, but rather to clear a pathway for the seeking Father to apprehend us.* When we avoid moralistic self-righteousness, gnostic intellectual pride, and sectarian disintegration; we are postured to receive our seeking Father. This is at the heart of Christian spirituality—the formation of a life that ever lives in God's presence. It was

God's intention from the beginning when He created us in His image. Mankind was to re-present the presence of God on the earth. But when we sinned we became separated from God and our re-presentation of Him became distorted.

So when we are restored through Christ into a relationship with God and become transformed from glory to glory by His Holy Spirit, into what exactly do we transform?

Intimacy, Identity, and Influence

Intimacy is the Spiritual formation of an authentic relationship with God as Father, Son, and Holy Spirit. Remember that word *perichoresis* we learned earlier? "Peri" means "around," as in perimeter or periscope. "Choresis" is where we get "choreography" or dance. Imagine the three Persons of the Trinity "dancing around" together in perfect rhythm and synchronization. The Father loves the Son who loves the Spirit who loves the Father and round and round they go for all eternity. They may be three Persons but they move as one in perfect unity. Now watch this: The Holy Spirit is the third person of the Trinity. So what happens when we enter into a relationship with Jesus and are filled with the Holy Spirit? Exactly! We gain access into the Trinity. We join in the dance. We can see now how intimacy with God goes way beyond religious observance or merely living by principles. We not only know God's law, we *know* God. At the heart of intimacy is knowledge. Through the proper practice of Spiritual disciplines, we clear a pathway for the Trinity to speak to us and direct our lives. Is such a life possible? It is not only possible, it is what God intended for us from the beginning.

Intimacy with God immediately begins to form identity. The Apostle John says, "But as many as received Him, to them He gave the right to become children of God, even those who believe in His name" (Jn. 1:12 NAS). John quotes Jesus as saying, "You are My friends, if you do what I command you. No longer do I call you slaves...but I have called you friends" (Jn. 15:14-15 NAS). Believers have a new identity in Christ as friends of God. Jesus goes on to say, "All things that I have heard from My Father I have made known to you" (Jn. 15:15 NAS). As friends of God we have a level of knowing (intimacy) that surpasses someone who sees himself merely as a servant of God. In fact it is as deeply personal as a father is to his children. The opposite of being a child of God is to be an orphan. Jesus says, "I will not leave you as orphans; I will come to you"

(Jn. 14:18 NAS). Many believers suffer from an "orphan spirit" which is the result of not receiving full adoption as a child of God. An orphan spirit does not live in total confidence of the Father's love and acceptance. Such a person might, for example, be jealous of another person's success. They might say, "What about me?" An orphan spirit lives with a sense of scarcity rather than abundance. To an orphan spirit God has limited resources rather than the cattle on a thousand hills. And they must fight for their piece of the pie before others take it all. So there is constant comparing between what he has and what others have. However, a person who has a full sense of adoption as God's child lives with a sense of abundance, rejoices in the success of others, and is completely content in what he has, knowing God will provide all His needs. The formation of identity, therefore, is a huge part of the Spiritual transformation process.

Intimacy with God forms identity in Christ that leads to Spirit-empowered influence in the world. Notice we did not first seek God's power for ministry. The first thing we seek is the "Face of God" not the "Hand of God." In Exodus 33 the Hebrews have rebelled against God and so here is what God says to Moses, "I will keep My word to you and give you the promised land, but My presence will not go with you because the people have sinned. Instead, my angel will lead the way." What does Moses do? His answer to God is, "Lord, if Your presence does not go with us to the promised land, then do not take us up from here" (Ex. 33:15). When Moses had to choose between the promise of God and the presence of God, he chose God's presence. Moses would rather be in a wilderness *with* God than in a land flowing with milk and honey *without* God. This should be our heart as well—the Face of God before the Hand of God. Now with the presence of God we have His power as well. Jesus said, "I will build My church and the gates of Hades shall not overpower it" (Mt. 16:18 NAS). It is our conviction that people do not build the true Church, Jesus does. So it is the presence of Jesus in the Church—His Spirit—that is the source of all true ministry on the earth. How many of us know that it is possible to do ministry without the power of the Spirit? Sometimes I wonder how many churches in America would keep on running just fine without the Holy Spirit. The point is if it is not a work of the Spirit then it is a merely human work and will have no eternal significance—a good thing, not a God thing. That is the kind of influence we want to have in the world. In the final analysis we are not here to carry out ministry but to cooperate with the Spirit of Jesus as He builds

His Church. So let me say it again, "The purpose of Spiritual disciplines is to get ourselves out of the way and clear a pathway for the seeking Father."

Intimacy with God forms *identity* in Christ that leads to Spirit-empowered *influence* in the world.

One way to understand Spiritual disciplines is that they help us go from the "lower room" to the "upper room." The lower room is our daily interaction with people. The upper room is the place in our spirit where we listen to Jesus. It is possible to operate on both levels simultaneously. On track one we are engaged in conversation with someone while on track two we are engaged with the Spirit. It's a way of praying without ceasing. Through our morning devotions we go upstairs to the upper room where we stay in tune to Jesus while interacting with people throughout our day.

The Church at Laodicea remains a classic, biblical example of a church that was *not* experiencing the manifest presence of the Lord in its day-to-day life. But the Spirit loved this fellowship too much to leave it in that state: "Those whom I love, I reprove and discipline; be zealous therefore, and repent" (Rev. 3:19 NAS). The spiritual condition of this church was such that Jesus was on the outside knocking to get in. Imagine that! A Christian church with Jesus on the outside is called "lukewarm." It was functioning like a church with its liturgy, ministry programs, teachings, and fellowships, but it did not operate as if Jesus was there with them. Do you know any fellowships like that? The presence of the Spirit is a historical fact, a biblical notion, a cultural tradition, but not an eminent reality. Jesus loved these believers too much to leave them that way. "Behold, I stand at the door and knock; if anyone hears My voice and opens the door, I will come in to him, and will dine with him, and he with Me" (Rev. 3:20 NAS). Jesus wants in! And once He's in, our lukewarm days are over.

There is a word I use to describe life in wondrous connection with the Lord—*Nexus*. No, not the shampoo. I got the word from a Star Trek movie where Captain Kirk and Captain Picard were teaming up to fight this mad scientist who was doing everything he could think of to get back into the "nexus." In the movie the nexus was this other dimension where a person experienced perfect joy, peace, and love—basically heaven. And this evil scientist was blowing up planets and killing billions of innocent people just to get himself back in there again. Well, the idea of the "nexus" got my attention. How many of us have experienced the intoxicating presence of the Lord and will do just about anything to get back in there again? It is the experience of being seated with Jesus in heavenly places (Eph. 2:6) as current reality while anticipating the fullness of heaven in the future someday. The nexus is what I experienced in each of my personal encounters with the Lord. It is what we can experience every day of our lives—albeit not as emotional or ecstatic every time.

This is what the Laodicean Christians were missing out on. Donald McCullough talks about how empty and boring church becomes without the presence of the Lord there:

"Visit a Church on Sunday morning—almost any will do—and you will likely find a congregation comfortably relating to a deity who fits nicely within precise doctrinal positions, or who lends almighty support to social crusades, or who conforms to individual spiritual experiences. But you will not likely find much awe or sense of mystery. The only sweaty palms will be those of the preacher unsure whether the sermon will go over; the only shaking knees will be those of the soloist about to sing the offertory."[4]

Well if you—like me—have had enough of "playing church," with its stale traditionalism, deadly complacency, and religious spirit, then listen for His knock on the door of your heart and let Him in. Catherine Kuhlman once said, "Don't grieve the Holy Spirit. He's all I've got!" That is what our ministries should be about. Church led by the Spirit is quite a different journey from the trivialized local congregation. Somebody once said, "Christian Spirituality is best done 'on the cliff's edge.' One more step and you've fallen over. One step back and the view is never quite as good."

The purpose of *Spirit*-ual disciplines is to "clear a pathway for the seeking Father" so we can experience access into His nexus presence. He is knocking on the door of the Church once again. Notice that Jesus is a gentleman and will not barge His way in. In the classic painting of Jesus knocking on the door of the Laodicean Church, there is no doorknob on the outside. It can only be opened from the inside. Would you welcome the Spirit of Jesus again into your life? You'll say, "I did that when I accepted Christ." So did the Laodiceans.

---

4   Donald McCullough, *The Trivialization of God* (Colorado Springs, CO: NavPress, 1995), 13.

The Christian life is not just an event, but also an on-going experience of His manifest presence.

In his wonderful book, *Windows of the Soul*, Ken Gire relates this profound story:

"A story is told of a carefree young girl who lived at the edge of a forest, where she loved to play and explore and take long adventurous journeys. But one day she journeyed too deep into the forest and got lost. As the shadows grew long, the girl grew worried. So did her parents. They searched the forest for her, cupping their hands and calling out. But there was no answer. In the gathering night the parents' search grew more intense."

"The little girl tried one path after another, but none looked familiar and none led her home. Her skin was welted from the switching of limbs as she pushed her way through the overgrowth. Her knees were scraped from the tripping in the dark. Her face was streaked from the tears she had cried. She called for her parents, but the forest seemed to swallow her words. After hours of trying to find her way home, the exhausted girl came to a clearing in the forest where she curled up on a big rock and fell asleep."

"By this time the parents had enlisted the help of friends and neighbors, even strangers from town, to help them search for their lost little girl. In the course of the night many of the searchers went home. But not the girl's father. He searched all night and on into the next morning. In the first light of dawn he spotted his daughter asleep on the rock in the middle of the clearing. He ran as fast his legs would take him, calling her name. The noise startled the girl awake. She rubbed her eyes. And reaching out to him, she caught his embrace."

"Daddy," she exclaimed, "I found you!"[5]

We seek God in our lives, but never forget that our heavenly Father is seeking— even more earnestly—for us. Through Jesus we see the Father's heart to find us.

The correct practice of Spiritual disciplines clears a pathway for the seeking Father. He then transforms us into those who help transform others. That's called ministry. But just as there is a right way and a wrong way to practice Spiritual disciplines, there is a right way and a wrong way to engage in ministry. We turn now to one of the greatest ironies in the Christian life: How ministry can harm our souls.

---

5   Ken Gire, Jr., *Windows of the Soul: Experiencing God in New Ways* (Grand Rapids, MI: Zondervan, 1996), 215.

Discussion Questions

1. What is the significance of the "kenosis," Jesus emptying Himself of divine power when He became human?

2. If Jesus emptied Himself of divine power, then how did He do all the works He accomplished on earth? How is this good news for us?

3. According to Eugene Peterson, how do moralism, gnosticism, and sectarianism impede our spiritual growth?

4. Discuss the purpose of Spiritual disciplines.

5. Articulate how the indwelling Spirit forms intimacy with the Trinity.

6. What is the relationship between intimacy, identity, and influence?

7. What does it mean to go from the "lower room" to the "upper room?" Why is this important?

8. What is the nexus? And how is this related to the problems in the Laodicean Church?

9. By faith, what do you sense the Lord saying to you in this chapter? How will you step out in obedience?

Chapter 3

HOW MINISTRY CAN HARM THE SOUL

"Men never do evil more completely and more cheerfully than when they do it for God."
— Blaise Pascal.

Serving the Lord in ministry is one of the most rewarding endeavors in life. How many of us know that God doesn't need us to redeem the world? But He involves us anyway so our "joy may be made full" (Jn. 17:13). True ministry is awesome! Becoming born again in Christ is bar none the most transformational experience in all of life. Immediately, we can't wait to tell others about Jesus. Often this happens automatically, with little training or motivation from others. Our hearts have been so touched by Jesus, we would do anything to help another person come to Christ. We invite people to church. We talk to the person next to us on the plane. We volunteer for a church ministry team. We become pastors.

Then somewhere along the way, something happens. It is very subtle actually. We don't notice the slight decline in the slope of the road before us. We always felt tired after a big ministry event. Nothing unusual there. We just catch our breath and bounce back the next day. There's no denying, however, it's not like before. But hey, this is for Jesus, right? So we suck it up and once again "lay down our lives" for Him. It's the least we can do after what He's done for us. But now something is wrong; we don't appear to fully recover anymore. We keep sucking it up. But our immune systems are low so we seem to always have a lingering cold. Our voice doesn't recover from preaching. We find ourselves uncontrollably crying for no apparent reason. We start thinking thoughts like, "Jesus' earthly ministry only lasted 3 years. I've been at this for 30!" Our motivation level is down and our cholesterol is up. Ministry might be on the rise, but so is your blood pressure. Your spouse is critical of the church and feels embittered at what ministry is doing to the family. Your children are struggling in their Christian lives but you have no time or energy to help them because of ministry demands. You feel like quitting.

Worst of all, you don't sense God's presence like you used to. Your private fantasy life is out of control. "Am I subconsciously hoping to get caught so I can get out of the ministry?" You feel like a hypocrite. "How could this happen to me?" you ask yourself. "I was serving Jesus. I was doing ministry." If any of this sounds familiar, you are not alone. Been there, done that, got the t-shirt.

In 1999 the 700 Club reported that the drop-out rate for Protestant Christian ministers is at an alarming level of 12 per day. Here are the main reasons:

- 38%   Burnout
- 80%   Isolation
- 37%   Marital Infidelity
- 80%   Job has negative effect on family

FASICLD (Francis A. Schaeffer Institute of Church Leadership Development) released their findings in 2007. Krejcir writes it has been compiling this data for over eighteen years and the results are supported by findings in similar studies. 1,050 pastors were surveyed at two pastor's conferences in Orange County and Pasadena, and a much larger sampling was involved in a Fuller Institute study in the late 1980's. Here is a sampling of findings reported by Krejcir in his article, "Statistic on Pastors."[6]

- 70% of pastors are so stressed out that they regularly consider leaving the ministry.
- 35% of pastors actually do leave, most after only five years.
- 100% of the 1,050 pastors surveyed had a close associate who had left the ministry due to burnout, church conflict, or moral failure.
- 77% felt they did not have a good marriage.
- 72% studied the bible only to prepare for a sermon (leaving 28% who are doing their devotions).

---

6   Richard J. Krejcir, "Statistic on Pastors." www.churchleadership.org. Francis A. Schaeffer Institute of Church Leadership Development (research from 1989 – 2006), c. 2007.

- 38% said they were divorced or currently in the process of getting divorced.
- 30% said they had either been in an ongoing affair or one-time sexual encounter with a parishioner.

In the summer of 2007 my mentor of 20 years confessed to marital infidelity that destroyed his ministry. The fallout from that revelation hurt a lot of people from my former ministry. There may be dimensions of that I may never recover from. It was far and away the most gut-wrenching thing I've ever had to go through. Here are some lessons learned from that experience.

First, we want to be sure that *what we do for Jesus* does not become more important than *Jesus*. Remember that the Great Commandment is to love God with all your heart, soul, mind, and strength. You'll say, "Of course, but what does that have to do with ministry?" Very simple: There is more to living in loving obedience to the Lord than doing ministry 24-7-365.

Second, is family a deterrent to our ministry or is family significant to your message? I remember a time in the early years of ministry when I didn't know how to navigate between family and ministry. I was so gung ho for ministry that I sometimes felt that family was getting in the way of ministry. Isn't that sad? As a young youth leader I wanted to reach more teenagers for Christ, and so I was gone almost every night a week at one outreach or another. And if we weren't doing outreach we were planning one. So I was hardly around. At the time, my wife and I had one child, Mark. And my attitude was, "Lord, my family and I are totally set apart for your glory, so being gone every night is totally justifiable." Boy, I couldn't have been more wrong. Then I remember one night coming home late after dinner as usual. Mark was riding around our cul-de-sac on his bike without his training wheels for the first time. A neighbor had taken his training wheels off for him, and he was whooping and hollering for joy as he was riding round and round our street. I caught just the tail end of that as I drove up from a ministry thing I was doing. I was happy for him, but it was kind of a wake-up call for me. "Why wasn't I there to take the training wheels off his bike for him?" Soon after that, I would figure out a very important truth: Our families are not a deterrent to ministry; they are part of our message. Our marriages don't get in the way of preparing for messages, they *are* the message we are giving the world. Our children are not a deterrent to our ministries. The quality of our relationship with them and the caliber of their lives are powerful testimonies to the world. There are many pastors in the world, but I am the only father my children will ever have. There are lots of ministers in the world, but I am the only husband my wife has. I like the sentiment of Andy Stanley. He says that if he is forced to choose between the church and family, he will "cheat the church." Amen.

Third, is my wife a bitter person or a fulfilled person? Obviously, ministry is not the sole cause of a spouse's bitterness or lack of fulfillment. The idea here is to listen to your spouse. What is she saying to you about the effect of ministry on the family? Stop. Listen. Discern what the Spirit is saying to you through your spouse. I'm not saying you should just do everything your spouse tells you. Look what happened to Adam when he did that. Instead, pray together and ask the Lord what to do and together obey Him.

Fourth, in a similar manner, listen to your children. Are you generally home for dinner? Is it a priority to watch their games, attend piano recitals, or go on a family vacation now and then? Or are you generally absent?

I don't claim to have a full understanding of what happened to my mentor. All I know is that was incredibly devastating on so many levels. I pray I will never inflict that kind of hurt on the people who look to me for leadership. By slowing myself down and taking time to listen to the whispers of the Spirit, I pray my demons can be held at bay and eventually expunged all together. There are more lessons from that pain which I will share later.

A Theory on Burnout

I want to reiterate we are called to serve. And it is one of the greatest privileges in life to serve Jesus on behalf of the people. God is a servant. Jesus did not come into this world to be served, but to serve. So Christians, like Jesus, are servants—ministers. But ministry can be a double-edged sword. How do we keep ourselves from burning out?

Part of the answer is *margins*. A margin is the difference between your capacity and your load. If the capacity of my car is 5 passengers, and I've loaded 3 people, then my margin is 2 (or 1 Samoan or 4 Filipinos). You get the idea. Each of us has a capacity unique to us. No two people are identical. We need to be aware of when our physical and emotional energies have reached their capacity. Knowing when our physical energies are waning is fairly easy to discern. But what about our emotional energy levels? This is an issue easily overlooked because we may not feel physically tired. We know our emotional energy has come to an end when we no longer care. Christians typically have great compassion for people. We know our emotional energy levels are low when our usual feelings of love and compassion are gone. That is when we know it is time to stop and rest.

How is it that we get tired of doing ministry in the first place? Didn't Jesus say that ministry was like food to Him? Shouldn't ministry energize us rather than deplete us?

Here's a theory on burnout.

Key passage: "They went out of the city, and were coming to Him. In the meanwhile the disciples were requesting Him, saying, 'Rabbi, eat.' But He said to them, 'I have food to eat that you do not know about.' The disciples therefore were saying to one another, 'No one brought Him *anything* to eat, did he?' Jesus said to them, 'My food is to do the will of Him who sent Me, and to accomplish His work'" (Jn. 4:30-34 NAS).

How is it that ministry burns us out when Jesus says it should be like food to us? That's because Jesus never said, "My food is to do *ministry*." He said, "My food is to do *the will of Him who sent Me* and to accomplish His work." Aha! So there's our answer. Jesus never said, "My food is to do ministry." He said, "My food is to do God's will." Just doing ministry busy work is never fulfilling. God is calling us to discern His will, not just make ourselves busy with ministry. It is possible then to do ministry that is *not* the will of God. Sometimes ministry is merely a good thing we are doing. But what we need to do is the God thing—His will.

Some of us need to do less ministry and more of God's will.

When does ministry cease to become "the will of Him who sent Me?" That is an excellent question. Remember, "Not everyone who says to Me, 'Lord, Lord,' will enter the kingdom of heaven; but he who does the will of My Father who is in heaven. Many will say to Me on that day, 'Lord, Lord, did we not prophesy in Your name, and in Your name cast out demons, and in Your name perform many miracles?' And then I will declare to them, 'I never knew you; depart from Me, you who practice lawlessness'" (Mt. 7:21-23 NAS). It is a frightening thing to consider that maybe what we thought was the will of God really wasn't. In this passage the ministers said, "Lord, we prophesied in Your name, cast out demons, and performed miracles! Doesn't that count as ministry?" Jesus said, "And you are? What you were doing there had nothing to do with Me. Don't let it hit you on the way out, guys." You see how important it is to keep our zero behind the One? These guys were performing miracles and it still wasn't a God thing. I don't know about you, but I find that stunning.

It wasn't just about *what* they were doing, but *how* they went about doing it. They had a supernatural edge to their ministry (who wouldn't want that?), but here it is: they practiced lawlessness. It was not what they were doing, but how they lived that turned Jesus off. No worship in spirit and truth here. And we know what that means: no seeking Father. Jesus shows them the door.

The Screwtape Letters is one of my favorites. In it C. S. Lewis wrote, "Brass is more mistaken for gold than clay is." What looks like ministry may not actually be the will of God. Brass sure looks like gold, but it is not the genuine article. General ministry has the appearance of God's will, but it may not be. Brass is a good thing. Gold is a God thing. Ministry is a good thing, but not all ministry is a God thing. Being Spiritually disciplined to go to the Upper Room to hear from God will help us discern His will. There are a million good things we could do, but there is a specific God thing which is His will for us to do. In ministry do not settle for brass. Go for the gold! Don't just do good things. Do God things.

Let me summarize our hypothesis on burnout: If doing the will of God only makes you stronger and provides nourishment to your soul, then burnout must be caused by *not* doing the will of God. Does that make sense?

Troubleshooting

Here is a troubleshoot list that might help us discern God's will in this arena:

- If you do not keep holy a Sabbath Day, you are *not* doing the will of God.
- If you are not building a loving relationship with your wife, you are *not* doing the will of God.
- If you are not building loving relationships with your children and training them up in the way they ought to go, you are *not* doing the will of God.
- If you are taking on way more jobs beyond your Spirit-directed assignment in the body of Christ, you are *not* doing the will of God.

- If you are acting like God's slave and not his child, you are *not* doing the will of God.

None of these constitute the will of God.

Mike, it sounds like you're saying we should live a balanced life. Is that right? Eugene Peterson offers the paradigm of "rhythm" over "balance."[7] When someone is playing a song too fast or too slow, we can tell immediately. In the same way, during the course of our ministries, we get the sense that the beat is too slow, and we should pick up the pace. At other times, we feel like the rhythm is too fast. There's no time for family. We come home and our kid has graduated from high school. The last thing you remember was not taking his training wheels off for him so a neighbor had to do it for you. That's when you know you need to slow it down. Your metronome is at 124 when it should be 72. It's not so much about balance as it is about rhythm.

Remember our hypothesis: If we do not do the will of God, we will burn out. We will eventually divorce our spouses and abandon our children. Then we will be forced to step down from ministry. Some pastors even give up on Christ. Let's not allow *what we do for* Jesus to get in the way of Jesus. You need to stop doing mere ministry and start doing the will of God. Doing ministry doesn't nourish our souls, doing God's will does. Don't settle for good things, repent and commit yourself to God things. Be Spiritually disciplined to go to Him daily. Prayerfully discern His leading in the Upper Room. Pay attention to the rhythm of your life and ministry and adjust. Determine today not to end up on the casualty list of those who dropped out of ministry because of what the ministry did to them. Do not allow ministry to harm your soul.

---

7   Peter Santucci, "In Sync: Interview with Eugene Peterson," The Life@Work Journal, Vol. 3, No. 6, 50.

Discussion Questions

1. Statistically, how has ministry harmed the souls of some pastors in America?

2. Can you relate a similar time when ministry had a negative impact on your life?

3. What is the author's hypothesis on burnout?

4. From C. S. Lewis' quote, discuss the importance of discerning between brass, the "good thing," versus gold, the "God thing."

5. By faith, what do you sense the Lord is saying to you in this chapter? How will you step out in obedience?

Chapter 4

THE DARK SIDE

"It is those we live with and love and should know who elude us."
– Norman Maclean

Remember our picture of an iceberg as representing our souls? Now imagine that the Holy Spirit lowers the waterline a bit to reveal a little more of the iceberg. Internally, we struggle. No one needs to tell us. No one else may know the specifics. But it is an irrefutable reality. We have a dark side. Anger, greed, laziness, envy, lust, gluttony, pride. Seven ways to sin—every one of them deadly. What we need is for the Lord to show us what to do about the beast within us. G. K. Chesterton once said, "Bedtime stories don't teach children to believe in monsters. Children already believe in monsters. Bedtime stories teach children that monsters can be killed." We know we have a dark side. We just need to know how the Lord can overcome our dark side.

I remember a family vacation once when we stayed at a friend's cabin that was right on the beach. Hawaii has the most beautiful beaches in the world. So we all enjoyed splashing around in the pristine blue water that afternoon. The next morning I woke up early to do my devotions on the beach. When I looked out at the water I was surprised to see how everything had changed. A once beautiful ocean was now replaced by jagged rock and coral. You see, the tide had gone out, revealing what was beneath the surface. Was this something new that just arrived that morning? No, it had been there all along. We just didn't see it during high tide. But now that it was low tide, the jagged rock and coral came to the surface. We're just like that. During high tide everything seems fine and we're all ok having fun. But at low tide, when we are tired, our jagged edges come to the surface. Our emotional energy levels have a high tide and a low tide too. At high tide Bruce Banner is doing fine. But at low tide the Hulk appears.

Defining the Dark Side

Definition of a Glaring Issue: A point of potential or actual disobedience in our lives that is usually not known or visible to others but is obvious (glaring) to us.

It is the opposite of a "blind spot." A blind spot is where our dark side is obscure to us, but obvious to others.

The most common glaring issues seem to revolve around money, sex, and power. How do we identify a glaring issue? It is a point of *disobedience* that has become very apparent and has a *strong hold* on us. If left unresolved this stronghold, or "glaring issue," could end our ministry career and devastate our family. Or, it has the potential of acting as a "gateway" to something more serious later.

Why is the Lord lowering the iceberg and showing this to you now? God's actions toward us are always motivated by love. He is not here to condemn us. He loves us and wants us to be free. And so the Spirit is revealing this issue to us now because He wants to lead us on a journey toward freedom. There is no condemnation. Showing us the truth about ourselves is the first step toward liberty.

McIntosh and Rima in their excellent book, *Overcoming the Dark Side of Leadership: The Paradox of Personal Dysfunction,* provide excellent, critical insights to the personal dysfunctions of leaders in the hope of understanding, discovering, and redeeming the "dark side." They do not see the dark side as necessarily demonic. Some issues may require spiritual deliverance from demonization, but others are a "dysfunction." We are all broken in some way in our souls. McIntosh and Rima suggest there was a "basic need" which was not satisfactorily met, causing a "traumatic experience" and a feeling of failure. This causes a sense of "existential debt" which the person attempts to pay through unhealthy behaviors during adult years. The interplay of basic need, traumatic experience, and existential debt result in the development of the "dark side." Think of the dark side as a kind of overcompensation or over-reaching caused by the need-trauma-debt experience.

In this paradigm the dysfunction is not something to be freed from but rather mitigated so it is not allowed to destroy the life and ministry of a leader. Interestingly, the authors contend that the dark side may also be used to accomplish positive results. Canadian Rob Angel felt he was an academic failure because of a spelling test he was unprepared to take in Washington State. Later on he would become the creator of Pictionary, a game of pictures not words, and made millions.

McIntosh and Rima contend for a five-step process to overcome and redeem the dark side: (1) acknowledge the dark side, (2) examine the past, (3) resist destructive expectations imposed by others, (4) practice progressive self-knowledge, and (5) understand identity in Christ.

Thorn in the Flesh

The next thing I want to tell you is not meant at all to discourage you but to encourage you greatly: We may *not* be completely delivered from our glaring issues this side of heaven. We take a very Spiritual approach to this topic and humble ourselves before the Lord who alone knows what is best for us. It may be the case that the Lord is setting you on a course of "spiritual healing and deliverance" and you will be radically set free from your demonic strongholds once and for all. I pray that is the case.

But take a look at this intriguing passage from Paul: "And because of the surpassing greatness of the revelations, for this reason, to keep me from exalting myself, there was given me a thorn in the flesh, a messenger of Satan to buffet me—to keep me from exalting myself" (2 Cor. 12:7 NAS). Paul talks about a mysterious "thorn in the flesh" from none other than Satan.

Why doesn't the Lord set him completely free from this? It is allowed to stay in Paul's life so that he will remain humbled before God and not exalt himself. I have to confess I do not totally understand the full dynamic of the Lord's interaction with Satan here. I suspect it might be similar to what is going on in Job. But I certainly can relate to glaring issues in my life that don't seem to completely go away. And I can see how they keep me totally focused and dependent on Christ.

Listen to me now, believe me later: We may not be completely freed from certain issues in our lives this side of heaven. But rather than be discouraged by that, allow it to draw us even closer to the Lord, more dependent on Him than ever. Let him teach us how to mitigate, or take the edge off, those issues so they don't destroy our ministries, lives, families, or marriages.

Through his struggle with his thorn in his flesh, Paul discovered a powerful secret. He experienced the strength of the Lord in the midst of his weakness. And he heard the voice of the Lord through his pain: "My grace is sufficient for you, for power is perfected in weakness" (2 Cor. 12:9 NAS). When Paul heard that, he did a complete 180 on all his weaknesses from that point on: "Therefore, I will rather boast about my weaknesses so that the power of Christ may dwell in me" (2 Cor. 12:9 NAS).

He went from asking God to take away his weakness to boasting in his weakness. For when he was at his weakest, he was strong in the Lord. Now that's a God thing! May the Lord redeem your journey with your dark side in a similar way. Like Paul, you could see it as a pathway to being strong in the Lord. In the end, we may discover that the goal was never moral "perfectionism," but rather a humble, on-going, lifelong dependency on the Spirit of Jesus.

Chains that Free Us

Please do *not* interpret anything I have said as license to sin. If you ever forget how seriously God takes sin, remember the cross. The Spiritual transformation journey is analogous to Joshua and the Israelites taking the Promised Land. The land is theirs but they needed to purge it of its previous inhabitants. Israel suffers to this day because it was not fully obedient to the Lord's command. That is what is happening to many believers today. Salvation is ours but there remains "pockets of resistance," or areas of the flesh in our lives that are not yet fully submitted to Christ.

The fact that we have these remaining "pockets of resistance" does not surprise God. As with Joshua, He is personally leading us to conquer our promised land. Remember Peter's denial? "Jesus said to him, 'Truly I say to you that this *very* night, before a rooster crows, you will deny Me three times'" (Mt. 26:34 NAS; cf. Mk. 14:30; Jn. 13:38). "And Peter remembered the word which Jesus had said, 'Before a rooster crows, you will deny Me three times.' And he went out and wept bitterly" (Mt. 26:75 NAS; cf. Jn. 18:27). Do you ever feel like giving up on yourself because it seems impossible to live the Christian life?

Think now for a moment on the implications of Jesus *knowing in advance* Peter was going to sin. Jesus prophesies to him the precise moment and the exact number of times he would sin. Jesus was not like, "OMG, Peter, I didn't see that coming! How could you?" Instead, Jesus also reassures him that he will recover and this will not be a deal-breaker for their relationship. And then He tells him he will be in a unique place to comfort the other disciples who will also need to recover from their falling away. Jesus redeems Peter's hurt so he can strengthen his brothers. If we keep following the Lord through our failures, He can recycle our pain to help others.

Our sin never catches God off guard. Again, this is *not* license to keep sinning. Rather, we are encouraged to never stop following Jesus. Like Peter, we will make it through. We may weep bitterly at times. But never give up on yourself because Jesus will never give up on you. Jesus knew that Peter loved Him. But maybe Peter wasn't so sure after all he had gone through. Jesus helped him with that too. After His resurrection, He made Peter say three times out loud, "I love you, Lord." Then Peter was ready to feed the sheep and minister once again. Do you see how the Lord orchestrated everything to cement Peter's bond of love for Jesus?

Earlier we were talking about ocean tides. A construction company was hired to build a large bridge across a bay on the east coast. As they were plotting out where to set the massive bases of the bridge, they realized that at the very spot where they needed to place one of the bases, the sea floor was unstable for some strange reason. When they sent divers down to see what was wrong, they discovered there was an old wooden ship sunk deep into the mud at the bottom of the bay. They tried dredging it out but that didn't work. What could they do? The blueprints called for the base to be planted right on that spot. Suddenly a young engineer came up with an idea. His plan was to tie chains around the old sunken ship and connect those to giant buoys on the surface. At low tide they would tighten the chains. Then as the tide came in, the gigantic buoys began to pry the sunken hulk from its watery grave. Then when the tide went back out, they tightened the chains again. As the tide returned, the ship was lifted again until it was completely free. The plan worked perfectly. They used the natural forces of the tide to pry that ship loose. And the bridge was built according to plan.

Normally we think of chains as a symbol of slavery. But in this case they are chains that free us. The reason? They keep us bound to Jesus. We may realize there are serious character issues sunk deep into our souls. They are remnants perhaps of an old, dead nature embedded within our minds. We've tried to set ourselves free, but it hasn't worked. We will need trusted Spiritual friends to help us. But most of all we need to "chain" ourselves to the Holy Spirit and allow His power to bring us to freedom. Just as the natural forces of the tide pried loose that sunken ship, so allow God's supernatural power to navigate us toward obedience. These are the chains that free us.

As I wallowed in pain over my mentor's moral failure, the Spirit uncovered a glaring issue *in me*—unforgiveness. I was so hurt I raged inside and wept bitterly. I kept replaying the evidence in my head over and over on a loop, condemning him. I had him on trial in my own heart. Then after about three years of not knowing how to forgive him, the Father spoke to my heart. "What would it take for you to forgive him? Do you want to sue him for everything he's worth? Put him in prison?"

"Yea, that sounds good," I thought.

"How about if I beat him for you? Torture him."

"Ok, that's going too far."

"What if I had him executed for his sin?"

"I think I know where You're going with this."

"For you see, I did all of those to my Son, Jesus, on *his* behalf—so he could be forgiven. I stripped Him of everything He owned and had him thrown in prison. I had Him whipped and scourged beyond human recognition. And I had Him crucified on the cross. And if my righteous wrath is now sated by Jesus' perfect sacrifice, do you not think that your imperfect judgment could be?"

I was in awe of what the Lord had said. It was not like God was going to let him get away with what he did. The Lord was saying that I needed to stop putting him on trial in the "lower courtroom" of my heart and appeal to His Supreme Court. And God will judge Him rightly. So I took my gavel in my hand, pounded it on my judge's stand and declared, "This court is adjourned." The Lord had set me free from my glaring issue, my unforgiveness.

Whether it's a glaring issue or a blind spot, we all have a dark side. When God shows us our dysfunction, He's not trying to embarrass us. He wants to set us free. He doesn't want this sin to impede our lives and ministries. He knows that when we sin, we discourage ourselves. We already feel unworthy of His grace. Sinning just confirms to us what we suspected all along—that we are worthless. "Who am I to call myself a Christian?" God knows we go through this. And He wants to bring us to a place where we know that we know that we know that nothing will separate us from Him. If we could do this ourselves, then we wouldn't need God, would we? That's why we call it a God thing.

Discussion Questions

1. What is the difference between a glaring issue and a blind spot?

2. Why is the dark side dangerous?

3. According to McIntosh and Rima, how was our dark side formed? How are we freed?

4. Do you think it is God's goal that we become morally perfect this side of heaven? Is God surprised by our dark side?

5. From the examples of Paul and Peter, what might be God's greater goal for us?

6. What are the "chains that free us?"

7. By faith, what do you sense the Lord is saying to you in this chapter? How will you step out in obedience?

Chapter 5

SOLITUDE AND SILENCE

"Let him who cannot be alone beware of community. Let him who is not in community beware of being alone."
– Dietrich Bonhoeffer

Here is what we've covered so far: We understand that the ultimate outcome of Spiritual Transformation is intimacy with God. Spiritual disciplines clear a pathway for the seeking Father to us. We see how ministry done apart from God's will can harm our soul. His Spirit points out glaring issues and blind spots in our lives that could potentially end our ministry careers, devastate our families, and distort our intimacy with God. In these next few sessions we will zero in on a few classical Spiritual disciplines that help us hear the voice of God. The first is solitude and its companion, silence.

Nexus Solitude

In Christian Spirituality we practice solitude to prepare us for transformative relations with people. We practice silence to prepare us to speak with others with transformational power.

Story is told of a weary clergyman who desperately wanted to meet with the famous psychologist, Dr. Carl Jung. "What seems to be the problem?" asked Dr. Jung. "Well," said the pastor, "I've been working 14 hours per day and I'm suffering from exhaustion. I'm ill-tempered with the other staff, and worst of all when I go home, I'm short with my wife and children. "I see," said the wise psychologist. "I am going to give you some instructions and I want you to follow them precisely, alright?" "Alright," said the clergyman. "Instead of working for 14 hours a day, cut back to 8 hours a day. Then spend your evenings alone by yourself. Do this for two days, then come back and see me." So the next day the clergyman worked for only 8 hours then went home to be alone in his study. That first evening he read a novel by Thomas Mann then played a little Mozart on the piano. The next day he again worked for exactly 8 hours, then retired to his study, played some Chopin, and fell asleep reading a novel by Hermann Hesse. Afterward he returned to his psychologist complaining, "I did exactly as you told me and I'm not getting any better!" "Tell me what you did," said Dr. Jung. "Well, let me see. On the first day I worked precisely 8 hours then went home, read a novel by Thomas Mann, then played a little Mozart. On the second day I again worked only 8 hours, then played some Chopin, and read a novel by Hermann Hesse."

"I see the problem," Dr. Jung said knowingly as he stroked his chin.

"What is it?" cried the clergyman.

"You don't understand", Jung replied. "I didn't want you to spend time with Herman Hesse, Thomas Mann, Mozart, or Chopin. I wanted you to be alone. I wanted you to spend time with yourself."

"By myself?" laughed the clergyman, "I can't think of any worse company."

Dr. Jung replied, "And yet this is the self you inflict on others 14 hours a day."

What is the self you are inflicting on others during the course of your day? Are you impatient? Angry? Controlling? Bossy? Shy? Withdrawn?

How many of us know that in Christian solitude we are by ourselves but not alone? I call it "nexus solitude" because our focus is the presence of God. Through solitude and silence we will help clear a pathway for the seeking Father.

Daniel is a superb example of someone with a heart for God's presence in solitude. Here's the context: King Darius had signed a law essentially forbidding anyone from worshiping anyone but him. Basically, you would be put to death for doing your devotions! But Daniel's time alone with God was more precious to him than his own life. "Now when Daniel knew that the document was signed, he entered his house (now in his roof chamber he had windows open toward Jerusalem); and he continued kneeling on his knees three times a day, praying and giving thanks before his God, as he had been doing previously" (Dan. 6:10 NAS). Daniel continued to worship God although it cost him the lion's den.

The supreme example of the value of solitude with God is Jesus Himself. "And in the early morning, while it was still dark, He arose and went out and departed to a lonely place, and was praying there" (Mk. 1:35 NAS). If Jesus, the Son of God, regarded solitude with His heavenly Father an indispensable discipline, how much more for us?

First and foremost remember that our ultimate outcome of Spiritual Transformation is the Great Command—intimacy with God. But we absolutely must not miss this either: Jesus did His earthly ministry in constant communication with His heavenly Father. "Truly, truly, I say to you, the Son can do nothing of Himself, unless it is something He sees the Father doing; for whatever the Father does, these things the Son also does in like manner" (Jn. 5:19 NAS; cf. 5:30; 6:38; 8:28; 12:49; 14:10). As we can see, this was Jesus' modus operandi in His earthly ministry. Many ministers live in a world where they are expected to "take initiative." What strikes me about Jesus is how *little* initiative He takes in ministry. In solitude He *waits* on His heavenly Father to initiate ministry. Then He moves in consonance with His Father's will. Over and over again He revealed that He was receiving on-going, up-to-the-minute updates on what to do in ministry from the Father. On earth Jesus only did what He saw His heavenly Father doing. He spoke what He heard His Father speak. Now catch this: as disciples of Christ we learn from His example and do ministry on earth exactly the same way. Jesus prophesied and promised that we would do "greater works" than He (John 14:12). No matter how you interpret what Jesus meant by "greater works," one thing is for certain: they would have to be a work of God not flesh—a God thing. Through the Holy Spirit within us we too can receive on-going, up-to-the-minute updates on what the Father is doing and—here it is—cooperate with Him in building His kingdom on earth as it is in heaven. Again, we need to do less "ministry" and do the Father's will instead. In solitude Jesus was not just trying to "get away from it all." I'm not saying He wasn't resting. However, His ultimate reason for practicing solitude was to begin His day in the presence of His heavenly Father, discern what He was doing, then minister in perfect choreography with Him. Ministry—indeed all of life—is supposed to be a beautifully orchestrated dance between the Father, Son, Holy Spirit and us. We have all seen dance wonderfully choreographed, like synchronized swimming or my favorite, Jabbawockeez on America's Best Dance Crew! When we are filled with the Holy Spirit of Jesus, we are brought into the choreography of the Trinity as He builds the kingdom on earth as it is in heaven. As we fulfill the Great Commission, the Lord says, "I am with you always even to the end of the age" (Matt. 28:20 NAS).

Nexus Silence

About 99% of the time spent in solitude is time spent in silence. I call it "Nexus Silence" because its purpose is not just refraining from talking but to tune in to the voice of God. In his book *Listening to the God Who Speaks*, Klaus Bockmuehl describes Jesus as a "Great Listener." I found that really intriguing. Often when we think of Jesus we see Him as the greatest preacher who ever lived. Even his enemies recognized the authority in His voice and feared Him. Not many regard Jesus as a "Great Listener." Bockmuehl is right. This is what characterized His time of solitude with the Father. To be thorough we should point out that scripture says, "In the days of His flesh, He offered up both prayers and supplications with loud crying and tears to the One able to save Him from death, and He was heard because of His piety" (Heb. 5:7 NAS). Doubtless this was a reference to His prayer in the Garden of Gethsemane. But what about all the other times He awoke a great while before daybreak?

We know that prayer is having a conversation with God. Now let's say you were a big martial arts fan, and you wanted to be the best martial artist you could be. One day you win this drawing for one hour of free kung fu lessons from Jet Li. So you get just one hour of free lessons from one of the greatest kung fu masters alive today. When you see him are you going to do most of the talking? Of course not. I think you might ask him one question like, "Mr. Li, what are your top 3 secrets to being a great kung fu master?" Then give him 59 minutes to do all the talking. Meeting with Jesus in solitude should be just like that. We are His disciples and He is the Master. Do you want to learn to discern the Father's will? He is the Master. Do you want to learn to pray? He is the Master. Do you want to know how to live in obedience? He is the Master. If being the best disciple we can be is our goal, then we should ask our one question then spend the balance of our time listening for the answer. Believers need to understand prayer more as cultivating a listening heart rather than talking to God.

How can we know that God is speaking to us? Here is a hint: God sounds exactly like the bible. Wayne Cordeiro in his book, *Divine Mentor*, gives a powerful perspective on turning to biblical characters as mentors. He regards David, Jeremiah, Peter, Paul, and John as some of his best friends, mentoring him in the ways of the Lord. This is cultivating a listening heart, and a heart that truly listens is an obedient one. The Latin root of the word "listen" is *oboedīre*, to obey. This is why the bible journaling discipline done in moments of solitude and silence is a powerful one. It gives us an opportunity to ask the Master our one question, then give Him the balance of the hour to teach us the answer. But we must sit silently and listen.

The Taoist philosopher, Chuang Tzu, once said, "The purpose of a fish trap is to catch fish. Once the fish is caught, the trap is forgotten. The purpose of a rabbit snare is to catch rabbits. Once the rabbits are caught, the snare is forgotten. The purpose of words is to convey ideas. When the ideas are caught, the words are forgotten. Where can I find a man who has forgotten words? He is the one I would like to talk to." Have you ever watched TV and listened to a person who obviously has no clue what he is talking about? There are few things in life more annoying. On the other hand, every now and then, we will come across a person who is an absolute delight to listen to. His words are carefully chosen. His demeanor is laced with humility and love. Jack Hayford and Wayne Cordeiro come to mind. Profoundly, both of these men place a huge premium on solitude and silence in the presence of the Master.

By contrast ill-chosen words can destroy another person: "So also the tongue is a small part of the body, and *yet* it boasts of great things. Behold, how great a forest is set aflame by such a small fire!" (Jas. 3:5 NAS). In Proverbs Solomon points out how rambling words lead to sin: "When there are many words, transgression is unavoidable, but he who restrains his lips is wise" (Prov. 10:19 NAS). In fact he seems to be saying there is a positive correlation between the amount of words and how much we sin! So if many words lead to sin, few words—silence—leads to piety and wisdom.

In silence the Master teaches us the proper way to speak: "If I speak with the tongues of men and of angels, but do not have love, I have become a noisy gong or a clanging cymbal" (1 Cor. 13:1 NAS). In silence we learn to root our speech in love, so it is not a noisy gong or clanging cymbal.

Solitude and its counterpart, silence, are powerful disciplines in the practice of biblical spirituality. In solitude we say "no" to human relationships for awhile, and say "yes" to relationship with God. In silence we say "no" to words for awhile, and say "yes" to listening to the words of God.

Discussion Questions

1. Describe the self you inflict on others.

2. What are nexus solitude and nexus silence? What is their purpose?

3. Why and how are they significant to life and ministry?

4. What do we learn from the examples of Daniel and Jesus?

5. How does bible journaling help us hear God's voice?

Chapter 6

WORSHIP IN SPIRIT AND TRUTH

"Some things are understood not by grasping but by allowing oneself to be grasped."
— Karl Rahner

"True worshipers will worship the Father in spirit and truth, for such people the Father seeks to be His worshipers. God is spirit, and those who worship Him must worship Him in spirit and truth" (John 4:23-24 NAS).

We've been talking a lot about how worshiping in spirit and truth is absolutely vital to intimacy with the seeking Father. So we need to ask the Lord to teach us now what that means. We get the word "spirit" from the Greek word πνεῦμα (pneuma). In John 4, this is not a reference to the Holy Spirit, but rather to us as spiritual beings. Humans are not bodies with spirits, we are spirits with bodies. Our spirit is the non-physical or non-corporeal part of who we are. In other contexts this word could be translated "wind," "breath," "life," or "soul." It may be invisible, but it is real and palpable to us. It is the seat of our emotions, will, passion, mind, intelligence, and so much more. It is the true essence of who we are as human beings. Long after our physical bodies die, our spirits will live on into eternity. We are generally described as having three dimensions: body, soul, and spirit. With our bodies we relate to the physical world. With our souls we relate to ourselves. With our spirits we relate to God.

John 4:24 tells us, "God is spirit." Literally, the Greek says "pneuma ho theos" or "spirit is God." Placing the word spirit in front like that may be a Greek writing device to add emphasis to the fact that God is spirit. So it's kind of like, "Spirit! is God." In worship we connect with the Spirit of God through our own spirit. We're using our minds, emotion, and will. We can do this all the time 24-7-365, even while we sleep. Lots of people in the bible heard from God in dreams. When Gen. 1:26-27 says we were made in the image of God, it means we were patterned after His spiritual likeness. So we were designed to relate to God. We do this so naturally and seamlessly, we are sometimes hardly aware we're doing it. Just as we were given eyes to see light, we also have spiritual eyes to see the Light (Jn. 9). We have spiritual ears to hear His voice (Jn.10:27). We can "taste and see" that the Lord is good (Ps. 34:8), and so on. All of us have spiritual senses along with our physical ones. Worshiping Him in spirit is what we were born to do. Later, when we discuss the function and form of worship, I will show you how we cease worshiping in spirit and that's where worship starts to go weird.

The word "truth" in the Greek is αλήθεια (aletheia). Jesus talks about the "true worshipers of God" worshiping Him in spirit and truth. To worship God in truth, therefore, means being a true worshiper. That is, there is nothing false or insincere about your worship, no pretense or phoniness. A true worshiper has integrity. Integrity comes from the same root as the word "integer," as in whole number. Worship in truth is to worship God with your whole heart. "In truth" also means to worship God according to the Truth. Jesus is the Way, the *Truth*, and the Life. No one gets to the Father except through Him (Jn. 14:6). So to worship in truth means to worship in and through Christ. Yes, only believers can worship in spirit and truth. His death on the cross was the perfect sacrifice to bring us through the veil and into God's holy presence. We can't access the Father any other way. Because of Jesus nothing can separate us from God now. By His blood our spirit is made pure and given access to His Spirit. What many don't understand is that our souls may still have emotional wounds and our bodies will still get sick and die, but our spirit is perfectly whole in Christ. Jesus, who is the Truth, transforms us into true worshipers of God.

Now that we have an idea of what "spirit and truth" means, let's talk about "worship." Regarding worship, I would like to focus on two things: (1) the distinction between function and form, and (2) the proper function of worship.

Function vs. Form

The *function* of worship is the act of true worship—the behavior of rightly and correctly worshiping the Lord. *Form*, on the other hand, refers to the way or style we use to worship. Form would entail everything from whether or not to raise your hands to whether or not to use guitar and drums in worship. The biblical principle is that there is no freedom in the function of worship, but great freedom in the form of worship. *Function is sacred, form is not.*

That Christians will worship God is non-negotiable. Exodus 34:14 states, "For you shall not worship any other god, for the Lord, whose name is Jealous, is a jealous God." Not only is there clear instruction to worship Him, God is specific that we ought to worship Him and Him alone. "Worship the Lord with reverence, and rejoice with trembling," states the Psalmist (Psa.2:11).

On the other hand, there is great latitude given to *how* God can be worshiped. Throughout Scripture there is tremendous variety as to the way God's people worship Him. People worshiped God in different positions: bowing (Psa.138:2), standing (Psa.135:2), lifted hands (Psa.134:2; 141:2). The bible records that these were practiced in combination such as in Nehemiah. "And Ezra opened the book in the sight of all the people for *he was standing* above all the people; and when he opened it, all *the people stood up*. Then Ezra blessed the Lord the great God. And all the people answered, 'Amen, Amen!' while *lifting up their hands*; then *they bowed low* and worshiped the Lord with their *faces to the ground*." (Neh. 8:5-6, NAS) Different locations: the temple (Psa.138:2), mountains (Lk.9:28), houses (Dan.6:10; Acts 1:14), the belly of a fish (Jonah 2:1)! Different instrumentation: trumpet, harp, lyre, timbrel, stringed instruments, pipe, and cymbals (Psa.150:3-6). Sometimes they sing (Psa.9:2). Sometimes they cry (Psa142:1). Sometimes they tell of God's greatness (Psa.145:6). Sometimes they shout (Psa.145:7). Sometimes they dance (2 Sam.6:14). And so on. The point is that there is tremendous freedom with regard to the form that worship takes.

It may interest you to know in our main passage in John 4, the Greek word for worship is προσκυνέω (proskuneo). The early history of this word is debatable, but it could literally mean "to kiss." Proskuneo also has a sense of going "prostrate" before God. This is why we see the practice of falling on your knees and kissing the ground in some religions. In Christian worship there are certainly tender moments when our heart is to kiss the face of our heavenly Father or collapse in adoring veneration before Him.

Understanding the distinction between function and form is crucial to right worship. Function is sacred; form is not. Does this mean that worship in church may take any form? Because congregations don't naturally think of the distinction between function and form, we get all hung up on the wrong thing. So leaders need to teach and train our people. Then we carefully discern and ask the Lord to lead us. If someone starts dancing like crazy in front of the church, then they might become the focus of our attention rather than Jesus. On the other hand, if we are all sitting there stiff as a board, that's probably not good either. I used to go to a church where it was all right to lift one hand up in worship, but not two! Do you see how weird we get? The pastor and worship leader must understand the difference between function and form, and free up our congregations to worship in spirit and truth. Invite the Lord to help you. He will show you the way.

When the Samaritan woman of John 4 spoke with Jesus about worship, she was focused on the form issue. "We Samaritans worship on this mountain while you Jews say it should be in the temple." When churches argue over things like hymns versus praise songs, organ versus guitar, or whether or not to have hula, those are all issues of function. They are important issues, but they are secondary. When we make the form of worship more important than the function, that's when churches go weird. Function is sacred, form is not. Jesus steered her away from the form of worship to its vital function.

Proper Function

Proper function means the true worship of God. To worship God properly requires two things: (1) An accurate understanding of who God is, and (2) a clear understanding of how to approach God.

To worship God properly, we must first have an accurate understanding of who He is. Worship is essentially ascribing the correct value to God. So when we have an accurate understanding of who God is, we can't help but worship Him. We marvel at His attributes: holy, loving, self-existent, immutable, infinite, unified, omniscient, omnipotent, and omnipresent. The more clearly we see Him, the more we are in awe.

J.P. Moreland describes God as the "maximally perfect being." That is, God is not only the greatest being in existence, He is the greatest being *who could possibly* exist. This is the correct value of God. There is none higher, none greater, and none wiser. A being greater than God is inconceivable. When we get that, worship becomes our reflex response. If our God were not omnipotent, omniscient, and omnipresent, then He would not deserve our full worship. The Jesus of Mormonism, for example, was once a man who attained deified status. He had a beginning, which would mean he was created. I once walked into a Mormon church in my neighborhood and after talking awhile, I finally realized they were not talking about the God who created the universe. So I asked them, "Who do you believe created all of existence?" Their answer: "We don't know." Personally, I would not worship that Jesus. Instead, I would reserve my total worship for the God who created heaven and earth, the Lord of lords, King of kings (Rev. 17:14), and God of gods (Ex. 15:11). *He* would be the One who deserves my total worship.

Therefore, in order to worship God truly (proper function), we need to have an accurate understanding of who God is. That said, how many of us would agree that our human brains will always fall short of understanding fully who God truly is? That's why the best worship of all is when we run out of descriptions because our language and vocabulary fail to convey the totality of His majesty. Gregory of Nyssa, a 4th century Cappadocian monk, once said, "Concepts create idols; only wonder understands." There is a special kind of knowing that expresses itself as a sense of awe. You come to a place where you realize, "God, you are so beyond me and so amazing and so awesome. I could never fully conceive who you are. So with my mortal limitations, I don't just worship who I conceive You to be, but who You conceive Yourself to be." Like Paul we cry out in our human limitations and declare, "Oh, the depth of the riches both of the wisdom and knowledge of God! How unsearchable are His judgments and unfathomable His ways" (Rom. 11:33 NAS)! We know enough of God to blow us away. Just watching His back pass by as we hide in the cleft of the rock is enough to make us tremble. Beyond that, we relinquish control over trying to grasp fully who He is. Karl Rahner, a German theologian, could not have said it more eloquently: "Some things are understood not by grasping but by allowing oneself to be grasped." How many of us realize that trying to understand everything about God and worship may be a form of control? When David danced with all his might before God (2 Sam. 6:14), his wife thought he was a fool because she didn't grasp what he was doing. David, on the other hand, was *being grasped* by the wonder of the Lord. He probably in his mind didn't get it all either, but he let go of the need to understand everything. Obviously, we've made a pretty strong case here for understanding accurately who God is in order to worship Him truly. But we also need to know that when it comes to God, we will not comprehend Him fully any more than an ant could understand us. Don't let your need to first understand everything hinder you from worshiping Him wholeheartedly. Let go of your need of control, and allow yourself to be gripped by the awesomeness of the living God who is a consuming fire.

True worship, therefore, comes from apprehending—and being apprehended by—who God is. Secondly, true worship is about how to approach Him. In the Old Covenant, the sacrifice of animals represented the need for atonement through the shedding of blood. Because of the sin of mankind beginning from Adam and Eve, we could no longer freely gain access to the presence of the Lord without a plan of redemption. Adam and Eve were forced to leave His presence. Once a year (and only once a year) on the Day of Atonement, the high priest (and only the high priest) was permitted to enter into the Holy of Holies (God's presence) in the temple. All this to say, if we try to approach a holy God any other way but His Way, we're dead.

In the New Covenant, mankind received from God the fulfillment of that plan through the death and resurrection of Jesus Christ. No longer would God's people need to sacrifice bulls and goats (Heb. 10:4), for Christ, the Lamb of God, became the perfect sacrifice for our sin. At the crucifixion, the veil which separated us from the Holy of holies, was torn, signifying that we can once again access the presence of the Lord. Now, through Christ, nothing separates us from God. This presents some incredible opportunities for worship.

While journaling one day, I was awe-struck by the truth of Hebrews 7. I discovered an uncommon Greek word found only in this chapter—ʾρκωμοσία (horkomosia), which means "oath." When we are asked to swear an oath, we're typically told, "Place your left hand on the bible and raise your right hand. Do you swear to tell the truth, the whole truth, and nothing but the truth *so help you God?*" In other words, we don't swear by our own imperfect name, we swear by God's name. But what would happen if God Himself swore an oath? He would make that oath by His own perfect and righteous name. Hebrews 7:20-28 speaks of the "Oath of God." Referring back to Psalm 110:4: "The Lord has sworn and will not change His mind, You are a priest forever." The Hebrew word for swear is "shaba" which comes from the number seven, the Hebrew number of completeness and perfection. Ok, that's enough background. Here's what Hebrews 7 is saying. The priests of the Old Covenant were appointed by law. They were imperfect and temporary, a mere shadow of what was to come. Now we have a new High Priest—Jesus Christ. God swears an oath (horkomosia) by His own righteous name, the name that is above all names. He binds Himself seven times (shaba) with this oath. This is for all time and He will never change His mind. God solemnly swears: Jesus is the perfect High Priest who ushers us into His presence perfectly. Awesome. We do not approach God's presence in worship the way *we* think we should. We approach Him by His own perfect Way.

Spirit and Truth

"True worshipers will worship the Father in spirit and truth; for such people the Father seeks to be His worshipers" (Jn. 4:23 NAS). When we are apprehended by what worship truly is, we are blown away. No human ritual, ceremony, liturgy, or form could ever draw us into His presence. It is by the *hand* of God that we see His *face*. It is the gracious gift of the Father through the Son. True worship is a God thing!

Now tune in closely. Scripture is clear that God is omnipresent. That is, He is present everywhere all at once. Have you ever wondered how that is so? Augustine once stated, "As the soul is to the body, God is to the universe." When we see an object, we do not say, "My eyeballs saw that." We appropriately say, "I saw that." There is a soul or spirit dwelling within our mortal bodies. And that soul is present everywhere within our bodies all at once. With respect to our bodies, our soul is omnipresent. So in the same way, God is present everywhere with respect to space in general.

However, this is not to say that God is *detectable* always. On the contrary, for the most part He remains hidden. But when worship is taking place in spirit and truth, He becomes manifest. This is called the *manifest presence* of the Lord. God does indeed inhabit the true praises of His people (Ps. 22:3).

The prophet Jeremiah envisioned a day when the Lord would be found by His people. In a message to the exiles, he states, "Then you will call upon Me and come and pray to Me, and I will listen to you. And you will seek me and find Me, when you search for Me with all your heart. And I will be found by you, declares the Lord." (Jer.29:12-14a) That day has arrived in

Christ. Through the completed redemptive work of Christ, the Lord may now be found by His people.

Remember the Church of Laodicea (Rev. 3). That's the Christian church that left Jesus outside knocking and waiting to be invited in. How is it possible that an omnipresent God is not present in the Laodicean church? Very simple. Because of their lukewarmness, He was not detectable, or manifest.

Would the Lord have any reason to be standing outside of your worship service? Experiencing the manifest presence of God in worship through Christ is our awesome privilege as His children. His Nexus Presence is what we long for. I find it fascinating that soon after Jesus explains true worship to the Samaritan woman, He chooses to reveal His identity to her. "I know that the Messiah is coming...He will declare all things to us," she says (Jn. 4:25). Jesus said to her, "I who speak to you am He" (Jn. 4:26). He had been with her all along, but now He was revealed.

I'll never forget Easter Sunday morning, April 16, 1995. I couldn't wait to wake up and meet with the Lord. I sensed the seeking Father was eager to see me also. In fact, as excited as I was to see the Lord, I felt *He* was *more* anxious to see me. I couldn't seem to wash up and get dressed quickly enough. There was an instant awareness of the Lord as I went to prayer. I played Handel's Messiah "Worthy is the Lamb." And with tears streaming down my face, I worshiped the One who alone is worthy of all my love and adoration. I detected the manifest presence of the risen Lord in that room. Jesus Christ truly is risen. As His Spirit connects with our spirit, we have the capacity to experience His detectable, manifest presence in real time. May that be the case for you, dear friend. May you experience firsthand what it means to be in Nexus Worship—the manifest presence of the risen Savior. When we all get to Heaven, there will be no more evangelism. But worship of the Lord will go on for all eternity. The Church must be characterized as the locus of God's manifest presence on the earth. And His disciples should hunger and long for Jesus more than anything else. Worship Him in spirit and truth. Now *that's* a God thing!

Discussion Questions

1. What is the distinction between God's omnipresence and His manifest presence?

2. What is the difference between function and form in worship?

3. What is the significance of worshiping in spirit and truth?

4. How could the church become more focused on true worship versus the form of worship?

5. By faith what do you sense the Lord is saying to you about your personal worship times with Him? How will you step out in obedience today?

Chapter 7

FASTING

"Ask me not where I live or what I like to eat...Ask me what I am living for and what I think is keeping me from living fully for that."
— Thomas Merton

One of the most common excuses I hear is, "I just don't have enough time for devotions." Fasting is an excellent discipline to help us find more time with the Master. I am not discounting the possibility that going without food has some spiritual benefit, but think of it this way: In the ancient world they didn't have fast food restaurants, instant coffee, microwaves, or just-add-water Ramen noodles. Eating a meal was a long, arduous, time-consuming process. It began with first going out and hunting some game, then field dressing it, then starting a fire, and roasting it. If you wanted bread you would have to bake it from scratch yourself. There was no plumbing, so you had to go out to the village well to fetch water. All of this took the better part of your day. So how do you get a little extra time to be with the Lord? Don't eat! You save time not just because you skipped a meal, but because you didn't have to *prepare* one. These days going without a meal still saves time, but perhaps there are other things that take up even more of our time? This is why it makes sense to fast from TV, video games, sports, or just about any time-consuming activity in our lives.

Fasting from food is also a great way to train ourselves to say "no" to our flesh and "yes" to God. Our flesh is a big baby. When it doesn't get something it starts crying like a spoiled child. Saying "no" to our flesh through fasting teaches us to say "no" to anything our bodies crave. The same discipline we learn saying "no" to chocolate chip cookies is the same discipline we use to say "no" to greed, immorality, and other sins. But it's not just about saying "no." As we fast we say "yes" to the word, worship, prayer, meditation, journaling, and other ways to be with Jesus.

No

In *Christ Plays in 10,000 Places* Eugene Peterson eloquently describes the importance for Christians to learn how to say "no" (askesis) and "yes" (aisthesis). We train our minds to say "no" to sin and disobedience. The Greek *askesis* is where we get the word ascetic. We take up our cross. We crucify the flesh. We clear away the debris in our lives. After 911 over 185,000 tons of debris cluttered Ground Zero. It took months to clear away. It is John the Baptist in the wilderness saying, "Repent!"

Peterson calls this "The Road:" "Now when Jesus saw a crowd around Him, He gave orders to depart to the other side. While on the road a certain scribe came and said to Him, 'Teacher, I will follow You wherever You go.' And Jesus said to him, 'The foxes have holes, and the birds of the air *have* nests; but the Son of Man has nowhere to lay His head.' And another of the disciples said to Him, 'Lord, permit me first to go and bury my father.' But Jesus said to him, 'Follow Me; and allow the dead to bury their own dead'" (Mt. 8:18-22 NAS). While on the road, Jesus taught us to say no to our flesh.

Yes

Christians also train to say "yes" to obeying Jesus. It comes from the Greek *aisthesis* which is where get the word aesthetics. We are transformed by God's beauty. From crucifixion we move to resurrection. Once the debris is cleared we can now start building the Church. It is the Apostle John on Patmos saying, "Behold the Lamb of God." We are transformed into whatever we say "yes" to.

Peterson calls this "The Mountain:" "And some eight days after these sayings, it came about that He took along Peter and John and James, and went up to the mountain to pray. And while He was praying, the appearance of His face became different, and His clothing *became* white *and* gleaming" (Luke 9:28-29 NAS).

NO	YES
Askesis (Ascetics)	Aisthesis (Aesthetics)
The Road	The Mountain
Submission	Transfiguration
Take up your cross	Follow Him
Crucifixion	Resurrection
Deliverance	Healing
Flesh	Spirit
Clear away debris	Build the Church
John the Baptist	John the Apostle
Repent!	Behold!

So here is a picture of the biblical, spiritual discipline of askesis and aisthesis: On the one hand we are saying no to sin and the things of this world; on the other, we are saying yes to obedience. We embrace the seeking Father who runs to us. When we fast we say "no" to lesser things and "yes" to God things.

Discussion Questions

1. What is fasting and what is its purpose?

2. What does it mean to say "no" (*askesis*) and "yes" (*aisthesis*) to God?

3. How does this Spiritual Discipline train us for obedience?

4. By faith, what do you sense God is saying to you in this chapter? How will you step out in obedience?

Chapter 8

SABBATH

"Going to sleep is an exercise in faith; for while we are slumbering, we allow God to take back control of the world for awhile."
— Michael M. Palompo

We place little value on rest: How many times have we said proudly, "Oh gosh, I'm sorry, I can't make it. I'm busy that day." Or, "I have so much to do this week!" It's almost as though we feel there's something wrong with us if we have some spare time. For instance how many times have you heard, "No, actually I'm totally free that day?" Or, "I plan to rest on that day, so I left it completely open." Or even rarer still, "I plan to spend that day with the Lord."

Ask yourself, "Do I rest for the purpose of recuperating to prepare for more work on Monday morning?" Or do I rest to set aside work to focus on the Lord? Ok, I admit those questions are a total set up so we can talk about the value of Sabbath.

Too many of us live frantic lives filled with stress and anxiety. I like Jesus' example when Jairus, the synagogue official of Mk. 5:21-43, calls on Him to heal his daughter. I can just imagine the Apostles going into crowd control mode: "Alright, everyone, please move aside. Messiah coming through! We have an emergency situation." So they are making their way through the crowd when Jesus suddenly stops for no apparent reason. Can you just see Peter saying, "Master, what's the hold up? We need to get going." "Somebody touched Me," Jesus says. "What? Of course somebody touched you. They're pressing in on you from every side!" "No, this was different. I felt a power surge come from me as if...just as I thought. You!" Just then everyone's attention focuses on a woman discreetly backing away, desperately trying to go unnoticed. "It was you, wasn't it?" Jesus asks. Realizing she had been found out, she confesses that she had indeed been healed. "I knew You were in a hurry, Lord," said the woman, "so as You were passing by, I secretly reached out and touched the hem of Your garment. And look! I'm healed! It's a miracle!" The bible says that Jesus not only stops to find out who it was that "stole" the healing, He ends up listening to her entire store. Now *that* is an unhurried Person. And what about Jairus' daughter? She was resurrected.

Workaholics Anonymous

There are quite a few Asians in Hawaii. (I'm one of them.) And Asians sometimes have a pretty warped work ethic. My good friend, Kenton Lin, is Chinese, and I asked him one day to describe his Asian work ethic:

"Money, wealth, status. We compare ourselves with the Joneses (or in this case the Wongs). It is ingrained in the Asian culture. All work points to these things, rather than the Creator who gives us our worth. We work hard to have million dollar homes. We work hard so our sons and daughters can go to Yale. We work hard so no one will look down on us. We work hard so others can see how hard we work. We work hard so others can see we have 'the ideal life'—a big house, a large family, a successful family, children who are married, children who are doctors and engineers, who themselves have million dollar homes, and drive a Mercedes. These are things that measure who we are."

Wow. It sounds really mental, but unfortunately it is all too commonplace in Asian cultures.

For a state world-famous for its leisure, it may shock you to know that many people in Hawaii suffer from workaholism. How do you know that you might be a workaholic?

1. You work 7 days a week.
2. You feel guilty when you rest.
3. When you rest, you are thinking about work.
4. Your work and your self-esteem are one.
5. If you had to choose between spending time with family and doing work, you choose work.
6. There is no time to appreciate what you've accomplished, only time to work.

That we work hard is *not* the problem; the problem is we do not know how to rest. Sabbath rest is built in to the design of creation. Here is some of what the bible says about the Sabbath discipline.

Qadosh

First, it is a time to rest from our labors. "Thus the heavens and the earth were completed, and all their hosts. And by the seventh day God completed His work which He had done; and He rested on the seventh day from all His work which He had done. Then God blessed the seventh day and sanctified it, because in it He rested from all His work which God had created and made" (Gen. 2:1-3 NAS). God gave the principle of Sabbath to the ancient Hebrews. To the Jews the word "qadosh" was a very important word; it meant sanctified or "holy." According to this passage, what was the first thing God declared holy, or qadosh? Was it an altar? Was it a person? No, the first thing God declared holy was a day—the Sabbath Day. A block of time was declared set apart exclusively for God's use and purposes. Jewish theologian Abraham Joshua Heschel gives us some insight into the Hebrew understanding of the meaning of Sabbath.

> "The meaning of the Sabbath is to celebrate time rather than space. Six days a week we live under the tyranny of things of space; on the Sabbath we try to become attuned to *holiness in time*. It is a day on which we are called upon to share in what is eternal in time, to turn from the results of creation to the mystery of creation; from the world of creation to the creation of the world."[8]

We were designed to take a break from all our creating in order to give attention to our Creator. There are reasons, however, why practicing the Sabbath might prove difficult for some. First, like many Asians, this might go against our upbringing. We may have grown up all our lives not being taught that it was all right to take a day to rest. If this is you, then before you can experience Sabbath rest, God requires you to repent! You will need to repent (Greek, *metanoia*: "change your mind") from the idea that taking a day for Sabbath rest is unacceptable. You will need to come to grips with the idea that God made us to work six days and rest one. So obeying the Lord in the area of Sabbath will require repentance.

Second, it will require faith. What do I mean by that? Consider this: when the Sabbath arrives in the course of each week, chances are we will *not* be finished with work. There will still be things left undone on our to-do list.

8   Abraham Joshua Heschel, *The Sabbath* (New York, NY: Noonday Press, 1951), 10.

In that moment we will face a choice. Do we keep going and try to finish our work? Or do we stop and have a Sabbath? Will my supervisor understand? Is it irresponsible for me to stop now? So many contingencies. For some of us the most spiritual thing we can do is go to sleep. When you think about it, sleeping takes faith. It means you will be out of commission for a few hours and have to trust God to manage things. Only His Spirit can lead the way. For believers in the New Covenant, the observance of Sabbath is never a legalistic rule. But it may require us to have faith.

Third, we might think resting is a sign of laziness. It may be something ingrained in us from childhood. If our parents saw us playing around instead of doing our homework, we may have heard them say, "Get back to work, you lazy kid!" For me it was usually followed up by, "Do you want to end up being a garbage collector when you grow up?" But later on in life, we actually become pretty disciplined people. (I said many of us, not *all* of us.) So much so we could work 12, 14, even 18 hours a day and get up the next day and do it all over again. In these cases we would need to repent from the workaholism and listen to the Lord. Observing the Sabbath requires obedience.

Finally, as with anything involving obedience to God, the devil opposes our observance of the Sabbath. There may be a demonic strategy at work here. The enemy knows he is powerless to stop the advancing kingdom. So instead of coming against us, he uses our own momentum against us like a judo expert. He goads us into over-committing ourselves. Perhaps he deceives us into perfectionism under the guise of excellence. Or, we need to keep winning people to Christ because the time is short and it's all so very urgent. Whatever the case, he leads us to believe, "It's all for God's glory, don't stop! Keep going!" This is a very common problem with pastors because a pastor is never quite sure when he's working and when he's observing the Sabbath. Think about it. What would an average person do on the Sabbath day? Go to church, read God's word, and maybe spend an extended time praying and worshiping the Lord. For many pastors that's what they do everyday! So a pastor may need to figure out how *not* to do those things on his Sabbath day. To be obedient we will need to resist the temptations of the enemy who dupes us into thinking we can never stop working.

Sinkholes

I used to live in San Francisco. I remember watching the news and seeing a huge crater in a neighborhood where there used to be a home. What happened? It's called a sinkhole. In many places there are underground rivers that flow beneath us. Sometimes one of these subterranean rivers will dry up leaving a long, unstable cave in its place. Then what happens is the cave collapses and everything on the surface suddenly gets sucked into the earth. Vehicles, pets, road signs, even entire homes get swallowed up. It's like something out of a movie, except it is tragically real. Our spiritual lives can be just like that. The Holy Spirit flows through our lives like a living stream overflowing in abundance. But then we get cut off from the Lord somehow. Perhaps we simply neglect to spend time with Him in solitude, silence, or sabbath. Our internal river dries up in our spirit. It is unnoticeable at first because it is something completely inward. But eventually, things on the surface begin to collapse. At first, we get sideways with special people in our lives. Then a vital ministry folds. Finally, our marriage and children get swallowed up.

By contrast, observing the Sabbath is emotionally and spiritually healthy. It helps to keep the living streams of the Spirit flowing strong in our souls. The classic story of St. John the Apostle and the Hunter illustrates this: One day a hunter came back from the field and saw St. John by his home playing with doves. Curious, he stopped to ask the aged Apostle why he was doing that. St. John (being Christ-like) answered with a question of his own. "When you return home from a hunt, do you keep your bow strung or unstrung?" "Why, unstrung, of course," answered the hunter. "Why do you unstring your bow?" continued St. John. "If I keep my bow strung, it will lose its tautness and become weak," explained the hunter. "That is why I play with doves."

When we observe the Sabbath, we will need to rest from the thought of labor. "Remember the Sabbath day, to keep it holy. Six days you shall labor and do all your work, but the seventh day is a Sabbath of the Lord your God; in it you shall not do any work" (Ex. 20:8-10 NAS). The problem with some people is their Sabbath day is actually a planning day for work on Monday. Again, not to be legalistic, but this is not resting. The biblical pattern is to rest one day out of seven. We do not rest on Sunday only for the sake of work on Monday. In God's eyes, we are not his beasts of burden; we are His children!

The Sabbath is a special day for God to spend with His kids. I recommend we do something different from our regular labor. In other words, play! Now the wonderful thing about this is that it does have a transformational effect on our work. Again, we are not doing this to prepare for work. But ironically, if we truly obey the Lord in observing the Sabbath, we will become more energetic and more productive workers. Have you ever noticed how for a child, there's no distinction between work and play? Imagine feeling so mentally and emotionally rested that you can't wait to go to work to have fun! Ministers especially need to catch this principle of allowing the—here it is—restfulness of Sabbath pervade the workplace. This is more powerful and valuable than we can possibly imagine.

We no longer have to run on empty. When we come to Christ our whole concept of work is transformed. My wife hates it when I drive around with the gas gauge just above empty. She says, "Mike, if you run out of gas, I am not going to help you push!" I always say, "Don't worry, honey, I can drive all the way to the other side of the island and back on that amount of gas!" After it goes down to empty it still has a couple of gallons of gas in reserve, right? I have actually run out of gas twice because of this. Once while my wife was in the car with me. Don't laugh, most of us do this with our lives. We allow ourselves to get physically, mentally, emotionally, and spiritually drained and empty. Sometimes I think our favorite theologian is Jack Benny. We're tired, exhausted, on the verge of burnout, and we pull into a gas station and say, "One dollar, please." And I can just see Jesus go like this: (Puts hand on cheek like Jack Benny used to do.) Sabbath days are an opportunity to pull in, not for self-service regular, but full-service premium. The Lord checks under the hood, kicks your tires, checks the oil, and wipes the windshield. We drive away with our tank full of premium unleaded fuel…with Techron even. Then we go to work, and it's not drudgery because we work for Christ. Our hearts are full. We have the energy to care, to do a good job, to go an extra mile, to go beyond the call and do more than what supervisors expect of us. If we approach work like that we will be the last person laid off and the first person promoted.

One Way or Another

Now let me tell you a very important secret about the Sabbath. Turn in your bible now to 2 Chron. 36: 20-21. "And those who had escaped from the sword he carried away to Babylon; and they were servants to him and to his sons until the rule of the kingdom of Persia, to fulfill the word of the LORD by the mouth of Jeremiah, until the land had enjoyed its Sabbaths. All the days of its desolation it kept Sabbath until seventy years were complete" (2 Chron. 36:20-21 NAS). What happened was the people of God were disobedient to the Lord, particularly in breaking the Sabbath. So the Lord judged them by exiling them to Babylon. Now what happened in the land after they were exiled? The bible says, "The land enjoyed its Sabbath." Here's the point: we will take a Sabbath... *one way or another.* We may have to be sent into exile first, but eventually we will Sabbath. Have you ever noticed how if we keep working without stopping what eventually happens to us? We get sick. Do you know what you are doing when you're sick? Observing the Sabbath! One way or another, we will take a Sabbath.

Sabbath, Shabbat, Shut Up!

So how do Christians today experience Sabbath rest? Coming to God's house is an obvious great start, but it doesn't stop there. Rest in Christ. Take a look at these two passages. First Jesus says, "For the Son of Man is Lord of the Sabbath" (Mt. 12:8). But earlier He said, "The Sabbath was made for man and not man for the Sabbath" (Mk. 2:27). So which is it? Is the Sabbath day for the Lord or is it for man? A Christian's Sabbath needs to center on the Lord of the Sabbath. But don't do what the Jews did and turn the Sabbath into legalistic bondage. They actually made laws on every kind of work you couldn't do on the Sabbath. So it got to the point where Jesus was healing on the Sabbath and the Jews condemned Him because He was performing "work." How crazy is that! But they were also hypocrites because if their family donkey fell into a ditch they would not hesitate to get him out. Jesus wants us to follow Him into Sabbath rest. Think of it like this: Jesus, the Lord of the Sabbath, gives each of His friends a precious gift—a special day to be with Him. The Sabbath was made for man, not man for the Sabbath. God gives us this day to bless us with His rest. On the cross Jesus said, "It is finished" (John 19:30). Nothing more is necessary to bring us into His rest. In Him we have the Shalom of Yahweh—perfect peace.

So practically speaking what do Christians do on their Sabbath day? You could begin your day in nexus solitude and nexus silence. Then go to the house of God for worship, fellowship, and listening to the word of God. Afterward, perhaps give some attention to your family. Maybe you could do something fun together—anything but work. Then as I mentioned earlier, perhaps the most spiritual thing you can do is sleep. Take a nap!

Sabbath. Shabbat. Shut up!

On my Sabbath days sometimes I like to watch shows about nature. Once I was watching National Geographic and I saw this fascinating documentary about these beetles that live on the Skeleton Coast in Africa. It's called the Skeleton Coast because it is an actual coastline with a beach that leads into a desert as it pushes inland. In other words, it looks like a really big beach. Needless to say fresh water is scarce. But a certain beetle that lives there has come up with an ingenious solution to the water shortage problem. Early in the morning it will crawl out onto the sand and bow its head. It actually looks as if it's praying. While it does this dew begins to form on the beetle's back. As the drop of dew gets larger and larger, it eventually flows forward to the beetle's mouth because his head is tilted down. And the beetle drinks its ration of water for the day. Each day he needs to do this to stay alive. Can you imagine what would happen if he overslept one morning? Yike!

God declares a portion of time holy (qadosh) unto Himself. Then as the Lord of the Sabbath, He authorizes that this day be given to each one of us. On this day we bow our head in the sand and pray. We rest. We wait. We re-create. Sabbath. Shabbat. Shut up! Suddenly the living streams of His Spirit begin to course through our spirits once again. *God, our Creator, reminds us we are human beings, not just humans doing.*

Discussion Questions

1. Could you be a workaholic? Do you display any symptoms?

2. How would you summarize God's heart regarding the Sabbath? How important is it to Him?

3. What happens if we don't Sabbath?

4. Practically speaking, what would need to happen in order for you to Sabbath? Repent? Obey? Have faith? Resist temptation?

5. When is your Sabbath day?

6. By faith, what do you think the Lord is saying to you about keeping holy the Sabbath day? How will you step out in obedience?

Chapter 9

STUDY

"I want to know the thoughts of God. The rest are details."
– Albert Einstein

As we watch the news these days, how many of us have said, "We've lost our minds!" Politics are a mess. Terrorists are blowing themselves up. And we're too busy watching reality TV. Actually, the problem is we *have* lost our minds! When we walk away from God, we lose our minds. We lose our capacity to reason. We lose objectivity, rationality, and logic. How does God Himself describe an intimate relationship with Him? Love Him with all our heart, soul, *mind*, and strength, and our neighbors as ourselves (Mt. 22:37-40; Mk. 12:30-31; Lk. 10:27; cf. Deut. 6:5). The Spiritual discipline of study helps us cooperate with the Spirit as He renews our minds to love Him.

The Empty Self
In his book, *Love Your God with All Your Mind,* J. P. Moreland identifies the "Seven Traits of the Empty Self" as one of the greatest barriers to loving God with our minds. Much like the Greek character, Narcissus, such a person perishes from self-absorption. According to mythology, Narcissus was so vain he fell in love with his own reflection in a pond and died of starvation. Interesting that his best friend was another mythological character named Echo.

Now compare the "empty self" of Narcissus with Ezra's "emptying of himself" in order to engage the word of God: "For Ezra had set his heart to study the law of the Lord, and to practice it, and to teach His statutes and ordinances in Israel" (Ezra 7:10 NAS). Ezra's commitment to the word of God forms our basis for the Spiritual Discipline of Study. Wayne Cordeiro would often say, "If you're wondering what the voice of God sounds like, He sounds like the bible!" Yes, God speaks to us Spirit to spirit. That is what Job, Abraham, and Moses did before they had the Scripture. It is what the Apostles did in order to write the Scriptures (Jn. 14:26).

<u>7 Traits of the Empty Self</u>

1) Totally Consumed by Self

2) Big Babies: controlled by infantile cravings

3) Narcissistic: manipulate relationships to suit own needs

4) Couch Potato: passive life

5) Live by Feelings: sensate

6) Unable to Develop an Inner Life: only style & image matter

7) Hurried and Busy

By J.P. Moreland
Love Your God with All Your Mind, pp. 88-92

What we're contending for here is not the kind of inerrant, infallible, authoritative inspiration that gave us the original autographs of Scripture. Recall the end of the book of Revelation: "I testify to everyone who hears the words of the prophecy of this book: if anyone adds to them, God will add to him the plagues which are written in this book; and if anyone takes away from the words of the book of this prophecy, God will take away his part from the tree of life and from the holy city, which are written in this book" (Rev. 22:18-19 NAS). I know the Apostle John is referring to his own prophecy, but we simply don't want to go around saying, "Thus saith the Lord."

The God Card vs. The Cardboard God

One of the classic abuses of Pentecostals is using the "God card." That's when we go around saying, "God told me this and God told me that." True story, I met a woman in church who told me, "God told me to divorce my husband and marry another guy." Her husband was an old guy and the new guy was a handsome Filipino guy. No, not me. A different handsome Filipino guy. The trouble was she used the God card. Since God had spoken to her, no one could dissuade her. She ended up divorcing her husband and living alone.

When we use the God card we close ourselves off from the rest of the community of saints. Yes, God speaks to us, but He speaks to *all* of us. If you're on to something, you will more often than not receive a confirmation from other trusted saints in the body of Christ. It is always good to ask for confirmation. If we sense the Lord speaking to us, ask Him to confirm to us what He is saying. There is nothing wrong with that. Asking for confirmation does not mean you are doubting or lack faith. On the contrary, our intention is to know that we know that we know that the Lord is directing us. For when we know, we are determined to step out in obedience. When I received my calling from the Lord to "full-time for a lifetime," I got a call asking me to come on staff with Hawaii Youth For Christ. That was my confirmation.

Our journey is always one of faith not sight. When Peter stepped out of the boat, he did not know for sure he would not drown until after he stepped out in obedience. But it could not be his will, it had to be Christ's will. That's why Peter said, "Command me to come out to you" (Mt. 14:28). Peter could not will himself to walk on water. It had to be the will of God. The only reason he could do it was because Jesus said, "Come." This is actually at the heart of what it means to pray in Jesus' name. Is it His will? So for example, when we pray healing on someone, they will be healed according to the will and timing of the Lord, not ours. We cannot heal anyone any more than Peter could walk on water. Only Jesus can heal. Believe it or not, sometimes taking away a person's "thorn in the flesh" is the not the best thing for them. It could cause them to be less dependent on the Lord, not more dependent. So hold off on using the God card because it cuts us off from listening to others. You don't have papal infallibility. (I'm not sure if even the pope has papal infallibility!) No one has the corner on hearing the voice of God. That's why we need to be surrounded by a Spirit-ual community. They will help us confirm God's will for us.

Our sister who wanted to marry the handsome Filipino guy also made another classic mistake. God will not ask us to do something that contradicts what He already said in the bible. God opposes divorce (Mal. 2:16; cf. Mt. 19). And He's not ambivalent about a lifestyle of divorce and remarriage either (Luke 16:18). So the best way to discern what God is saying to us is by staying anchored to God's word. His written word will lead us to His living Word.

Not to be outdone by the Pentecostals, some conservatives have an aberration of their own. They would never use the God card. But their dysfunction is on the other side of the spectrum. God has ceased speaking to His people altogether. In their experience there are no prophets, no miracles, no healing, and definitely no tongues. He used to do all that before in the bible days, but not anymore. So God is reduced from being a personal being who interacts with us in real time to a two-dimensional character found only in history. You know those life-size, cardboard stand-ups of movie characters we sometimes see at the movie theatre? They're there so you can take a picture next to Thor, Captain America, or Jack Sparrow. I used to think that way. God gave us His commandments and principles in the bible. He died for us on the cross to forgive our sin. Now it was up to us to live for Him. It was up to us to fulfill the Great Commission. The Holy Spirit was given to illuminate the scripture not empower our lives. That's how I used to think about God. These particular conservatives would never use the God card; they're problem is believing in a cardboard God.

From Genesis to Revelation

One of the great benefits of the study discipline is a heart that loves the *whole* word of God. The psalmist proclaims, "I rejoice in your word like one who finds a great treasure. I hate and abhor all falsehood, but I love your law. I will praise you seven times a day because all your laws are just. Those who love your law have a great peace and do not stumble" (Ps. 119: 162-165 NAS). And it is a love for the entirety of Scripture.

How often do we pick and choose our favorite verses a la carte? Sometimes Christians are guilty of "selective hearing." Kind of like my son, Caleb. Sometimes when I tell him to take a bath or do his homework, I have to repeat myself over and over again before he does it. In Hawaii we say, "He make like he get deaf eah" (deaf ear). On the other hand, all I have to do is whisper, "Anyone want to go to McDonald's?" and no matter where he is in the house, we hear, "I do! I do!" It's called selective hearing. Christians do that when they focus only on the passages that inspire them the most or support their beliefs.

Nothing wrong with having a favorite verse. But we need to study the whole council of God from Genesis to Revelation. Some conservative Christians do not know what to do with passages that talk about healing, miracles, or spiritual gifts. Similarly, some Charismatics will only step out in obedience when they "receive a prophetic word," ignoring what God has already revealed in His written word. So both sides gravitate toward the passages they agree with the most. We all need to be more like Jeremiah who said, "Whether it is pleasant or unpleasant, we will listen to the voice of the Lord our God to whom we are sending you, in order that it may go well with us when we listen to the voice of the Lord our God" (Jer. 42:6 NAS). Whether it is pleasant or unpleasant, we abide by His word.

From Written Word to Living Word

Finally, as with all Spiritual Disciplines, our final destination is always God Himself. Study of the written word leads us to love the living Word. "In the beginning the Word already existed. He was with God, and He was God...So the Word became human and lived here on earth" (Jn. 1:1, 14).

Here's an important question: How does comprehension of the written word lead to being apprehended by the living Word?

As we study the word, it is essential to remain in a state of humility before the God who brings greater revelation. Only then are we postured in our hearts to truly hear His voice. One concern with those who study and grow in knowledge is arrogance. Love for the word without love for God (and others) leads to hubris (1 Cor. 8:1; 13:4). In other words, we are going in the wrong direction if our bible discipline makes us cocky about how much bible we know rather than grateful to know God. This is a subtle point but it makes a huge difference in how we communicate to others what God has revealed to us. A greater knowledge of God should lead to reverence and worship not conceit and pride. Mere academic study in the flesh leads to arrogance; the Spiritual discipline of study leads to awe.

Perhaps the greatest mind of the 20th century was Albert Einstein. Time magazine declared him the person of the century. Not year. Century! In the last 100 years Einstein stands out as making the most significant contributions to mankind. His formula $E=MC^2$ explained the connection between matter, light, and energy, giving us nuclear power. What was the secret to his genius? Einstein once said, "A spirit is manifest in the laws of the universe in the face of which we, with our modest powers, must feel humble." There is our answer. The greatest mind of the 20th century beheld the universe and *stood in awe.*

I once saw a picture of Einstein standing on a beach. And he was watching a sunset. Most watch sunsets and think, "O, how beautiful." But Einstein figures out $E=MC^2$! There's a kind of awe that simply evokes an emotional response.

Then there's the kind that leads us to the deepest levels of truth and reality. The capacity to say "wow" is the opposite of the empty self. To behold something greater than yourself and stand in utter amazement is the doorway to unlimited knowledge. The universe we live in is awesome. God is awesome. If we are ever bored studying God's word, it's not because the word is boring. It's because *we* are boring! Einstein once said, "He who can no longer pause to wonder and stand rapt in awe, is as good as dead; his eyes are closed." Einstein harnessed the secrets of the atom not by comprehending but by being apprehended.

We might think that through our study of God's word, we will finally comprehend God so we can impose His will on the rest of mankind. I've noticed that those who approach the bible this way end up bringing division to the body of Christ. As a result we gather in congregations according to whom we agree with rather than Whom we adore. Obviously we're all for accurate exegesis of God's word. But I will be the first to acknowledge that I certainly do not understand the *full* counsel of God's word. No human being does. Suddenly, the Scribe stands up and yells, "But God will never contradict His word!"

I am confident God will never contradict His word, *only my interpretation of it.*

In my personal, doctrinal journey I have gone from Roman Catholic to Baptist to Nazarene to Pentecostal. So you could say I'm a Roman Bapta-Naza-Costal. Now our church aspires to going from denominational to trans-denominational. I have come to a point where I realize that the complete answer to knowing God does not lie in merely acquiring more knowledge of God. When our search for God is limited to knowing more *about* God, then we may not truly know Him. In one sense I could say I know *about* my wife, Mona, because I have a collection of pictures of her and lots of information about her history, background, etc. But there is another kind of knowing that comes from getting married, going on a honeymoon together, and spending decades loving one another. Words fail to describe fully that kind of knowing. It is not something to grasp, but rather an experience that grasps you. When our words fail to capture all that we are experiencing of God and we are left with a powerful sense of wonder, there is a profound level of knowing going on there. In that moment we do not just know *about* God, we have come to know God. We know we are practicing the Spiritual discipline of study correctly when the by-product is not arrogance but a sense of awe. We have gone from comprehending the written word to being apprehended by the living Word. We go from information and inspiration to Spiritual transformation. And that's a God thing!

This concludes our discussion of classic Spiritual disciplines. I chose to focus on solitude, silence, worship, fasting, Sabbath, and study. Obviously, there are others. Noticeably absent is the discipline of prayer. But I hope you were able to catch my strategy: Each discipline mentioned here postures us not just to speak to the Lord, but more significantly, to listen for His voice. We must understand the times and know what to do. So I tried to discern which disciplines would be most helpful to us in the 21st century.

From classic Spiritual disciplines, we move on to a hugely important area when it comes to intimacy with God—our relationships with people. How many of us know that our relationships with others can either improve or impede our relationship with God?

Never forget: "And the second is like it, love your neighbor as yourself."

Discussion Questions

1. Do you have any traits of the "empty self?" If so, which ones alarm you? Contrast that with Ezra's "emptying of self."

2. Describe the problems that come from using the "God card" and believing in a "cardboard God."

3. Discuss the importance of loving the whole council of God from Genesis to Revelation.

4. How do you go from comprehending the written word to being apprehended by the living Word?

5. What was the key to Einstein's genius? How does this relate to the Spiritual discipline of study?

6. Describe a sense of awe. Why is it important to our maturity?

7. By faith, what did the Lord say to you in this chapter? How do you intend to obey Him?

Chapter 10

SEXUAL IDENTITY

"Be sure you put your feet in the right place, then stand firm."
– Abraham Lincoln

It might seem random that in a book about intimacy with God we find a huge section on relationships. But remember that our symbol for Spiritual transformation is the cross (t-Scale). God is in the vertical, but He's also in the horizontal. One person said, "I love Jesus, it's people I can't stand!" We see that in the church all the time. But in God's heart that's an oxymoron. Like jumbo shrimp, government intelligence, a little pregnant, or half dead, it doesn't exist. The closer we get to God, the more we love people. When we truly have the heart of God, we will love our families, care for orphans and widows, and reach everyone for Jesus.

So far we've been dealing with Spiritual disciplines that we generally practice in solitude before God. By ourselves we don't have much problem avoiding sin. Our problems begin as soon as we start interacting with people. The right practice of solitude prepares us for relationship. The right practice of silence prepares us to speak. The right practice of Sabbath prepares us for work. In these next two sessions, we will discuss Relational Disciplines: Sexual Identity (pre-marital and marital disciplines) and Spiritual friendship.

A Relational Discipline is a Spiritual Discipline practiced in Spiritual fellowship with another whereby we anticipate together the leading, filling, and empowering presence of God.

I don't need to tell you there's a withering assault on Christian values going on in our country. If you're trying to stay a virgin until marriage, you will get zero back-up on the average public high school campus. A long time ago, three young Jewish boys found themselves in the same situation. Their names: Hananiah, Mishael, and Azariah (Dan. 1-3). They were uprooted from their homeland and thrust into exile in a pagan, anti-God environment. They were stripped of their citizenship, their culture, and even their names. They were forced to take on new identities: Shadrach, Meshach, and Abednego. So everything on the *outside* changed, but they remained true to the Lord on the *inside*. They were three friends who committed themselves to *take a stand for God* together in a hostile environment. When they were told to eat pagan food, they *took a stand for God* and refused. When they were told to bow before the king's statue, they *took a stand for God* while everyone else bowed. Now they were threatened with execution by immolation, but they still *took a stand for God*. While in the midst of the fire, God shows up. They had taken a stand for Him at every turn. *Now Jesus would take a stand for them*. He became manifest in the fire right beside them, shielding them with His supernatural presence and power.

Like Shadrach, Meshach, and Abednego we need friends who will help us take a stand for Jesus in a hostile, anti-God environment, and not bow to the pressures of the world. We may go through intense, fiery persecution. But as we do, watch how Jesus shows up and takes a stand for us.

The Ultimate Theory of Everything

It may not sound "spiritual," but God is all about relationship. You could say relationship is my "Ultimate Theory of Everything" (UTE). God's entire universe is a complex array of things working intricately and elegantly together in relationship. Human beings are no exception. Indeed, human beings are *exceptional* among God's connected creation. We are the only ones spoken of in the bible who have the distinction of being made in the image of God. So there is something unique and very special about us, distinct from plants, animals, planets, and stars. There is an Intelligent Designer. The best way to understand how we were designed is to know the Designer.

Mass confusion exists in America today over sexual identity. We have men with men and women with women. We have married men going after the wives of other men. We have unmarried men and women living together. We have men who marry multiple wives. We have men who dress like women. We have men who become women, and women becoming men. We have parents who refuse to identify the gender of their child so it can decide later what it wants to be. We have desperate housewives going after the gardener. Dogs and cats living together, mass hysteria!

The root cause of our sexual identity crisis is we have ignored our Designer. And when we no longer know our Maker, we use a do-it-yourself kit. So here's our grand strategy behind forming our sexual identity: get to know *God*. The better we know God, the better we know ourselves. And the opposite is true: The less we know God, the more sexually messed up we'll be. Do you see the disconnect between saying we know God and being dysfunctional sexually?

So let's take it from the beginning. We were made in God's image. So what's God like exactly? The Christian concept of God is He is one God with three Persons: the Father, Son, and Holy Spirit, also known as the Trinity. He is not three gods. He is one God with three Persons. Don't try to figure all that out right now because you won't. This is God's self-revelation in the bible. For centuries the Christian Church has known this, but avoided talking about it because it's confusing. But we need to know a little about it, so we can understand ourselves. My advice is for now don't try to grasp it, but be grasped by it (because it's about to get worse). But be encouraged, once we are grasped by the truth of what God is, understanding what we are becomes amazingly clear. Watch this: God is not just a personal, relational God. *God, in His very being, is Relationship.*

God is Family unto Himself. The intrinsic nature of God-is-Family goes like this: The Father loves the Son and the Spirit, Who in turn love the Father and one another. But keep in mind this is all happening within the singular being of God, not three separate beings. Because God is one, the three persons of God all function in a perfectly unified, choreographed dance. For all eternity even though He is one God, He has existed as perfect love, never alone and never lonely.

This God, who is Himself Family, created fathers, mothers, husbands, wives, sons, daughters, grandparents, and everything else that has to do with family. The bible says God made us in His image. That means *we* are deeply relational. God is the eternal, ultimate, loving relationship. And when He designed us, He used His own nature as the blueprint. Understanding this about the intrinsic nature of God is absolutely huge. That's why I call it the "Ultimate Theory of Everything" (UTE). If we get this, we will take a quantum leap toward understanding why we are the way we are. Why do we long to be in love with someone? Why do we long to be loved by someone? Why can't I just "get over her?" Why am I so attracted to her? The UTE will answer all your questions.

"Then God said, 'Let Us make man in Our image, according to Our likeness; let them have dominion over the fish of the sea, over the birds of the air, and over the cattle, over all the earth and over every creeping thing that creeps on the earth.' So God created man in His *own* image; in the image of God He created him; male and female He created them. Then God blessed them, and God said to them, Be fruitful and multiply; fill the earth and subdue it" (Gen. 1:26-28 NKJV).

The formation of sexual identity is not just about figuring out our sexual orientation. It is about prayerfully asking, "God, what is Your design for me sexually?" How did God design human beings to relate to one another sexually? Why is it such a powerful drive? How does He want us to live? What Spiritual disciplines can we practice to hear His voice and obey His will?

The issue of sexual identity is a crucial one because so many ministers experience moral failure in this area. It is probably the number one way that pastors screw up (no pun intended....Ok, I did intend it). Given the number of moral failures, one could argue that a minister (me) is not the best person to ask about this question. So we will ask the Lord instead. The Genesis passage above gives us the basis for our understanding of biblical, sexual identity. Let's take it one step at a time.

Heterosexuality is God's plan for human beings. "In the image of God He created him; male and female He created them." God designed human beings to be heterosexual. Just like the old joke, "God created them Adam and Eve, not Adam and Steve." I know that's cheesy, but it's an unforgettable way to put it. Men have their special equipment from God and women have theirs. We need to humble ourselves before the reality of that design. God also didn't create them Adam and Eve, Cindy, and Jennifer.

Not Good on Purpose

In Genesis 2 the bible elaborates further on the creation of the first couple. In short it says that as God made the earth, sun, moon, plants, animals, etc., He looked at all He had created and said, "That's good!" Then after He created man after His own image, He again looked at all He created, but this time He said, "Wow, now that is *very* good!" (Gen. 1:31) To be accurate God didn't say that man by himself was very good, but that creation with man as co-ruler and co-creator with God was very good. So everything is moving along nicely and the world is a perfect place...except for one thing.

God looks at Adam one day and says, "Adam, what's wrong? Why the long face?" Now of course Adam's loneliness comes as no surprise to God. After all, He was the one who made Adam in His own image. This is radical: Adam is a *single person* created in the image of God who is *three Persons* in one. Human beings are single-person beings made in the image of a being who is intrinsically a living Relationship. I ask you: what happens when you create an *individual* being using the blueprint of a Trinitarian Being? Exactly. You get loneliness—not just a casual, superficial feeling, but a profound, existential yearning. You have a single person who longs for relationship from the deepest recesses of his soul because that's the way he was designed. Can anybody relate to this?

Now I need your full attention to catch this next point: *When* in the Genesis story did this take place? Was it before or after sin came into the world? *Before.* "And the LORD God said, '*It is* not good that man should be alone; I will make him a helper comparable to him" (Gen. 2:18 NKJV). Remember we said that God created everything and said, "It is very good." But in this perfect world we find one thing that is *not* good. We're not saying it's evil. It is simply not good. And because there's no sin in the world, it's *not good on purpose.* Adam is lonesome. Being incomplete is not immoral. Adam is in a perfect relationship with God, yet he is still lonely. I'm going to say something now that you may not grasp. If so, just be grasped by it:

There is a dimension to our sexual identity that not even a perfect relationship with God will satisfy.

"What?" cries the angry religious mob, "that's blasphemy! I am complete in Christ. Stone him!" Listen, you are complete in Christ. Yet how is it that Adam, who has not sinned—therefore in a perfect relationship with God—needs a wife? Can you see that this is not a question of anything being *wrong* with Adam? It is a powerful statement from the Lord on the way we were *designed.* Our longing to be in a relationship is not evil. We were created to be attracted to the opposite sex. If you have any guilty feelings about that, you can stop condemning yourself now. So if Adam was in a perfect relationship with God and still felt lonely, can you imagine what happens to those of us who have an *imperfect* relationship with God? Adam was in a perfect relationship with God and he's already got issues. For the rest of us, that's complicated by our sinful nature. No wonder we are so dysfunctional. Our issues have issues!

I hope this truth brings some measure of peace to you. Single brothers, it is not wrong for you to be attracted to the opposite sex and long for a meaningful relationship with a woman some day. Single sisters, there is nothing wrong with hoping to have a husband one day and living happily ever after. God designed us precisely for that. When you lie awake at night hoping that some day you will find true love, know that it was God who put that longing in your heart. He is the eternal, ultimate, loving relationship. And He patterned you after Himself.

Beware of a "Victorian spirit" in the church that thinks sex is dirty. It is not always deliberate, but sometimes the church seems to convey that if you are physically attracted to someone that must automatically mean you are a sinner. That is sheer nonsense. That said, this doesn't mean we can become licentious. We can't jump from relationship to relationship rationalizing, "This is how God made me." So how can a young person keep his life pure? The old-fashioned way: by keeping it according to God's word (Ps. 119:9). Here are some practical Spiritual disciplines for singles discerning God's will for them regarding marriage.

Celibacy and Chastity

Celibacy and *chastity* are two immensely misunderstood and under-appreciated words in society these days. Celibacy means you are unmarried and abstaining from sex—and that includes anything physical that could lead to going all the way. Everyone must go through a season of celibacy in life. Paul refers to some in the Church who have the gift of celibacy and remain single their entire lives for the sake of Christ (1 Cor. 7:7). But the majority of us will go through a *season* of celibacy before eventually getting married. "For this is the will of God, your sanctification: that you should abstain from sexual immorality" (1 Thess. 4:3 NKJV). Chastity means purity or virtue. Chastity is God's will for us for our entire lives, whether we are single or married.

Celibacy and chastity are two powerful Spiritual disciplines during our premarital years. Each year my church, New Hope Central Oahu, performs a "Virtuous Reality Ceremony" for our singles. Paul says, "And do not be conformed to this world, but be transformed by the renewing of your mind" (Rom. 12:2 NKJV). When a person comes to Christ, He puts it in his heart to be pure. They will get zero help from the world to live pure. So in our "Virtuous Reality Ceremony" I want them to know they have an entire church fellowship in their corner, praying for them and cheering them on with all our hearts. During this ceremony they receive a purity ring from their parents as an inspiring reminder of their commitment to virtue. The Virtuous Reality Ceremony has established a Christian counter-culture in our church among the young people. I am not saying they are perfect, but they stand together to honor God and one another.

Their aspiration is to one day give their purity ring to their spouse on their wedding day saying, "Before I knew you, I was faithful to you." We are so proud of our young people for taking this stand.

What follows is the teaching I give at our Virtuous Reality Ceremony each year and forms the basis for the Spiritual disciplines of Celibacy and Chastity.

To live in God's Virtuous Reality, we first need to understand that He has called us out from the world. "You adulteresses, do you not know that friendship with the world is hostility toward God? Therefore whoever wishes to be a friend of the world makes himself an enemy of God" (Jas. 4:4 NAS). God is not talking about staying away from non-Christians. He is talking about not living according to the *values* of a world that does not know God's will. When we live by the world's values this is called *worldliness,* and it is the opposite of life in the kingdom of heaven. It is the opposite of God's Virtuous Reality. The bible is saying that as Christians we have now become friends of God. But know this: if we have become friends with God that puts us at odds with the world. Now that Jesus Christ is our savior He now becomes our Lord, and that means *we no longer conform to the world, we transform it.* But we won't make a difference in the world unless we first allow the Lord to transform us. "And do not be conformed to this world, but be transformed by the renewing of your mind" (Rom. 12:2 NKJV).

So that means Christians need to re-think everything we thought about boyfriends, girlfriends, and the whole dating scene we learned from the world. As Yoda once said, "You must unlearn what you have learned." God designed us to be attracted to the opposite sex, but we can express that attraction the wrong way. We were designed for relationship, but we can get into a wrong relationship. We could be with the wrong person at the wrong time. We might be with the right person doing the wrong things at the wrong time. What the Lord wants is for us to be with the right person doing the right things at the right time. The Lord is not giving us a new set of rules, but rather a new way to think. So let's listen now to the Holy Spirit, and allow Him to renew our minds. Only then will we be able to live in His Virtuous Reality and transform the world.

Worldliness leads to all the problems we see in the world today—teen pregnancy, STDs, abortions, etc. All too often we see in the Church the exact same problems we see in the world. The reason is people in the church are using the exact same dating practices they learned from the world. In the world the common sequence of events is body, soul, and spirit. We are attracted to a person's body and get physical. Then we get to know their soul and become friends. Then we find out about their spiritual beliefs last. In God's Virtuous Reality, the proper order is the exact opposite—spirit, soul, and body. Our first priority is to discern if we are compatible spiritually. Then we become soul mates. Then after marriage our bodies become one.

I've been a pastor now since 1999. Before that I was a youth minister for 16 years. I know, I'm a really old guy. But age has the benefit of spending a lot of time observing people. How can I put this graciously? Christians suck at relating to the opposite sex.

One of the biggest challenges for Christian young people is knowing how to go from single to married and remain obedient to God in the process. Remember God's will: "For this is the will of God, your sanctification; that is, that you abstain from sexual immorality" (1 Thess.4:3). How do we go from single to married and still do the will of God?

We date like the world. But we can't put all the blame on our youth. The church hasn't taught them any other way. If we date the world's way, we end up with the world's problems. As Josh Harris would say, we need to "kiss dating good-bye." Single ladies, God's will for you is to have a husband not a boyfriend. Single men, God's will for you is to have a wife not a girlfriend. So as Beyoncé would say, "You need to put a ring on it!" God's will for you is not a fleeting romance or a one-night stand, but love for a lifetime in marriage.

Does that mean that we ban boyfriends and girlfriends at our church? No. We don't want a legalistic culture. Instead, we give the Spirit space to form virtuous convictions within the hearts of our singles. Besides, we cannot honestly say the bible forbids boyfriend-girlfriend relationships (because it doesn't). But we can say this practice is *unwise*. I've discovered that if we come down hard and say, "Thou shalt not have a boyfriend until you're 25 years old," then young people will simply hide and go behind your back. (At least, that's what I did when I was a teenager.) So the best is to keep an open dialogue.

When my son, Mark, wanted to have a relationship when he was a sophomore in high school, here is how I approached it. I said, "Mark, you can go out with this girl, but stay open to the Lord. As soon as your relationship with this girl gets in the way of your relationship with God, then you need to ask the Lord what to do about that." He agreed. Within a few weeks, they were no longer together. I knew my son loved the Lord, but I also knew he was inexperienced in relationships with the opposite sex. So mother and I needed to pray that the Lord would form *virtuous convictions* in him, and God was faithful. The Lord's standards for holiness are the highest the world has ever seen: "But I say to you that whoever looks at a woman to lust for her has already committed adultery with her in his heart" (Matt. 5:28 NKJV). God is all about what is going on in our hearts. We teach that to our teens, but the Lord has to be the one who forms the *conviction* to live it out. If we are totally committed to making Jesus Christ the Lord of our lives and we are completely honest with ourselves, then it is extremely difficult to maintain a boyfriend-girlfriend relationship without a clear end game. More on this when we talk about Christian courtship.

It's called the "Law of Diminishing Return." Christian boyfriend-girlfriend relationships put themselves in an impossible situation. God's design is that we would be powerfully attracted to one another, but we know God says save sex for marriage. So we tell one another, "We will just hold hands and that's all." This lasts for a while, but the physical attraction is just too strong. Holding hands doesn't have the same *return* that it used to. The thrill of holding hands has *diminished.* The Law of Diminishing Return leads you to kissing. You know God says save sex for marriage, so you promise each other not to take it any further. But now kissing doesn't give you the same *return* that it used to. You want to keep taking it further because the Law of Diminishing Return is driven by our design. So we take it further and further. Light petting leads to heavier petting until we inevitably go all the way. We were designed to go all the way. We weren't made with brakes. (Married couples have a word for all this preliminary stuff—foreplay!) Only a superhuman effort will keep us from falling into sin. Most of us are only human. This is the reason that boyfriend-girlfriend relationships are *unwise.* The best way to avoid the Law of Diminishing Return is to avoid putting yourself in this situation in the first place. Remember Jesus' standard of "lust in our hearts." If we were honest with ourselves, we would realize we were in sin long before we went all the way.

But wait, there's more. Boyfriend-girlfriend relationships are unwise for another compelling reason. God wants our marriages to last a lifetime. "What God has joined together let not man separate" (Mt. 19:6 NKJV). In high school what typically happens in boyfriend-girlfriend relationships is we get together for a few weeks, get sideways with each other, break up, and find somebody else.

We might do that repeatedly until we find someone we decide to marry. Now here's the interesting thing: When that day comes we vow to stay together "until death do we part." We swear we will never break up. The trouble is we haven't been training ourselves to do that throughout our dating lives. In fact, we've been doing the exact opposite: we have taught ourselves that when a relationship doesn't work out, we break up, and find somebody else. It should come as no surprise that the divorce rate is where it is. We're only doing what we've trained ourselves to do all our dating lives. Just because we put on a tuxedo and a wedding gown doesn't make us a different person. We're still the same person with the same worldly convictions on the inside. And wherever we go, there we are!

Is there another way to do this? Absolutely. How do singles who love the Lord with all their heart find the love of their life without compromising their faith? We have seen that when the church is ineffective in teaching God's way, young people default to doing it the world's way—with disastrous results! So here's my best shot at this challenging issue.

The key principle is the *timing of God*. Scripture has a couple of words for time. Chronos has to do with tracking *time*, while kairos has to do with *timing*. Jesus told the Apostles, "It is not for you to know times or seasons which the Father has put in His own authority" (Acts 1:7 NKJV). The word for "times" here is *kairos*, which is God's appointed time. There is a kairos time for relationship, and only God knows when that is. In Adam's case there was a kairos time to introduce him to Eve. If you think about it, God could have created them both at the same time, but He doesn't. Maybe God wanted to spend some quality one-on-one time with Adam first before he got married. (Looks like it wasn't enough!) At any rate Adam probably had that lonely feeling for a while, but what could he do? It's not like he could go to church or a bar to meet somebody. He would need to wait on God's timing. Creating Eve from Adam's rib is powerful on multiple dimensions, but I simply point out that it was totally a God thing. Like we said, Adam had no choice. But we too can insist on God's timing and God's choice. Philosophers call the creation of Eve *ex nihilo*, "out of nothing." In other words, this relationship did not come about because Adam felt lonely and started chasing after girls. God chose the perfect girl for him, and brought her to Adam at the time of His choosing. He can do the same for each of us. We can have an attitude that prays, "Lord, lead me to the person *You* want me to marry, and let it be at the time of your choosing."

So let me set the stage with what we know so far. God exists as the eternal, ultimate, loving relationship; and the blueprint He used to design human beings was *Himself*. The deep sense of longing we feel for relationship is all part of being made in His image. Even if we were in a perfect relationship with God, we would still feel lonely just like Adam did. But it is not God's plan for us to jump from relationship to relationship. That trains us for divorce. His plan is that we experience love for a lifetime in marriage. The Law of Diminishing Return says that we need to time this just right. We were designed to go all the way in marriage. So we wait on both God's *choice* and *timing*. How do we know if we're ready for marriage? And how do we find Mr./Miss Right? Keep going.

Here is the game plan that my wife, Mona, and I used to follow the Lord as He brought us together. By the grace of God, we've been married since 1983. It goes without saying that we are not perfect. It is our prayer that these guidelines will help you discern God's leading for you so you too can experience love for a lifetime. These are principles based on God's word. But they are also intended to keep us mindful of His personal guidance in our lives.

Am I Ready for Marriage?

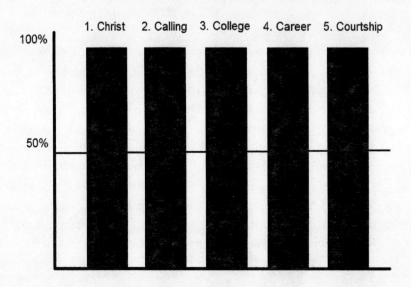

The Five C's to Marriage

There are 5 major decision areas in our lives: Christ, Calling, College, Career, and Courtship. Those may not be the best headings for what they actually represent, but what can I say, they all start with "C." The plan is to teach our youth to take these issues on in this order: Christ, Calling, College, Career, and then finally Courtship. Doing it in this order is not a rule. And life is rarely this nice and orderly. But by doing this we stand the best chance of going from single to married God's way without compromise. It gives us time to wait on the Lord for His choice and His time. Again, I understand that in the real world, we're all in different places; but if I wanted to teach a solid game plan to our youth, this would be it. We all know the old saying, "The best laid war plans change as soon as we meet the enemy." But it's still better to have a plan going in to battle versus no plan at all. At the end of this section we will give ourselves a score on each of the major areas: Christ, Calling, College, Career, and Courtship.

(1) Christ

Earlier I asked, "How do we look for Mr./Miss Right?" That was actually a trick question. Sister, do not look for Mr. Right, *become Miss Right!* Brother, do not look for Miss Right, *become Mr. Right!* Instead of trying to be married, young people should focus on *becoming marriageable.* Ask yourself this question, "Would anyone want to marry you in the current state that you're in?" How about this, "Would you choose yourself as someone you'd like to marry?" Chances are most teens have a long way to go by way of character development. That is precisely what we're contending for in this stage.

The first and foremost decision we'll ever make in life is the decision to follow Christ. Who we marry is our second most important decision. Mona and I have three wonderful kids who all love the Lord: Mark (born 1986), Rachael (1989), and Caleb (1998). We prayed for each of them as soon as we found out Mona was pregnant and haven't stopped praying. As soon as they could complete a whole sentence (which was when they were about three), I led them in a prayer to accept Christ into their lives. My Christian birthday was July 18, 1975, so I picked July 18 as the Christian birthday for all my kids. Hey, why not! I figured it was a good day for me. I knew they would eventually grow up and make up their own minds, but I wanted them to have a solid foundation to make that decision. No question there is always the prayerful journey in the Spirit for each child where "Christ is formed in them." And that is the bulk of what this season is all about. In short it is not just about the decision to become a Christian, but about the critical Spiritual Transformation process of forming a Spirit-to-spirit relationship with Jesus. *Christ-like character* is critical. Don't spend your time looking for Mr./Miss Right, *become* Mr./Miss Right by becoming more like Christ. Learn to pray and hear God's voice so He can guide your future. Study the Scriptures and adopt a biblical worldview. Build strong relationships with other godly young people who share your values of celibacy and chastity. Grow passionate in your love for God, and learn to worship passionately. And as you pursue God in all these areas and wait on Him, He will reveal the next area to you. The first C in preparing for marriage is "Christ." The second is "Calling."

(2) Calling

Now that you see the importance of a strong relationship with Christ, now we need to discern what "ministry assignment" He wants you to accomplish. The first area dealt with *who we are in Christ*. This area deals with *what we do for Christ*.

As I mentioned earlier, I gave my life to Jesus in 1975 and then in 1979 received God's call to *full-time ministry for a lifetime*. Not everyone's journey is the same. It may not be a typical clergy type ministry. It may be a marketplace one. But guaranteed God will call you to something. There's a practical reason for discerning this first before getting married. The bible says Eve was a helper suitable to Adam. In other words, they complemented one another in everything God called them to do. The same is true for us. If you're called to "suffer for the Lord in Hawaii," then the Lord will hook you up with a helper suitable.

There is no question that God still calls His children into ministry today. This is quite different from "picking a ministry that looks interesting" and trying it out. We are contending for the calling of the Lord discerned in prayer. If joining a ministry was *our* idea then we can quit as soon as we get bored with it. Or we get sideways with the leader and leave. Or it becomes too time-consuming, inconvenient, or hard. But if we were *called by God* we have no choice but to see it through to completion. Doing that ministry becomes a function of *obedience* to the Lord not personal preference. There is a stark difference between picking a ministry we like and obeying the Lord in the ministry He's calling us to. Our first C is "Christ." Our second C is discerning our "Calling" before marriage.

(3) College

This has to do with the broad category of completing our educational goals. This requires all sorts of qualifiers because I realize not everyone plans to get a college degree.[9] I just call it "College" because it starts with C. Some go to tech school while others become journeymen in a trade. My only point is to know the educational goals God wants you to accomplish and complete those. You don't want to find yourself in a position where you have to drop out of school because of pregnancy. Again, knowing that it is God's directive is crucial. If you are in college to make your parents happy, you will not be very motivated to complete it. But if you discerned that it is *God's will* for you to be there, then completing it becomes a function of obedience to Him. Now you *have* to finish! If you haven't picked up on it yet, that happens to be the way we approach all of life. Pray and ask the Lord for His will, then obey God. My recommendation is to finish school first before getting married. (Get your MS before your Mrs.) Keep in mind that I'm Asian and I'm probably speaking out of my culture here. Is it possible to be married and go to school at the same time? I suppose so, but it will be more difficult financially and a huge challenge to focus on studying. College is tough enough without a family, and many end up dropping out because of pressures at home. So before you get married, don't be a fool, stay in school! Discern God's will for your educational goals and obey Him. It is often in college that we settle on a possible career. College is a great time to discern God's will for your future career. What passions are running through your soul? What gifts, talents, and abilities has He blessed you with? Humble yourself before the Lord and ask Him what He designed you to do for Him. (1) Christ, (2) Calling, and (3) College. Our fourth C is "Career."

---

9   My personal opinion: before you write off pursuing higher education, you should first pray and wait on the Lord. These days a bachelor's degree is almost as common as a driver's license. Once again let the Lord guide you. Let's say you don't get the full ride to Harvard or Yale. I don't see anything wrong with attending a community college for two years before paying the big bucks on tuition. And if you're considering a secular college, watch out for the seriously liberal agenda that has taken over many schools. Make sure God is calling you to these schools before you attend. They could wreck your Christian faith with their weird values. These schools are still good for the hard sciences—medicine, law, engineering, etc. But stay away from courses like Women's Studies, La Raza, and Humanities where they spread their liberal agenda. Generally, an excellent Christian school such as New Hope Christian College (shameless plug) would be an excellent choice for Christians seeking to grow in Spiritual formation, character, and academics.

(4) Career

A college degree is still pretty good preparation for a career. I know we like to point out exceptions like LeBron James or Andrew Bynum who started their NBA careers straight out of high school. But chances are you ain't them! The issue here is money. Before you get married, you need to have a steady cash flow. Coming straight out of college my ministry supervisor gave me some very wise advice which I am grateful for to this day. He said, "Mike, before you get in to a serious relationship, devote one year of undivided attention to establishing your ministry." I still went out on casual group dates with my friends, but I didn't start a serious *courtship* in that first year. It was one of the smartest things I have ever done. Serving the Lord full-time requires lots of prayer and concentration, and I was still learning tons about ministry in my rookie year. Would it have been against the bible to get married in that first year? Of course not. But with my total concentration on ministry, my learning curve was steeper and I became a far more effective Christian leader. The ministry flourished and the Lord blessed us with resources. Now listen carefully: Many young couples naïvely say, "We don't need money, we have love!" Unfortunately, love won't by groceries or pay the rent. You need a job. And not just flipping burgers at McDonald's. You need a steady cash flow to support your wife and future children. Wisdom says do this first before getting married. Discern God's will for your career and obey Him, and everything else will be provided for you.

Here are some important considerations in choosing a career:

(1) *Spiritual:* Have you prayed and asked God which career He wants you to have? Does it fit in with God's call on your life?

(2) *Priorities:* Will the demands of this job interfere with my commitment to God and family?

(3) *Passion:* Would you do this job even if you didn't get paid?

(4) *Financial:* Does it pay enough?

Before we move on to our last C, let's do a quick mental scorecard. Give yourself a score on each one of the first four: Christ, Calling, College, and Career. If you have a strong relationship with Christ and solid Christian character you are above 90% on the "Christ" column. If you know your Calling in life discerned through prayer and confirmed in the Spirit by trusted, mature believers around you, put yourself above 90% in the "Calling" column. If you have completed your educational goals which, by faith, the Lord set before you, then mark yourself at 100% in the "College" column. If you are at least a year into your career with a steady income you can live on, then give yourself a 100% in the "Career" column. The average teenager, however, usually has a scorecard that looks something like the one below:

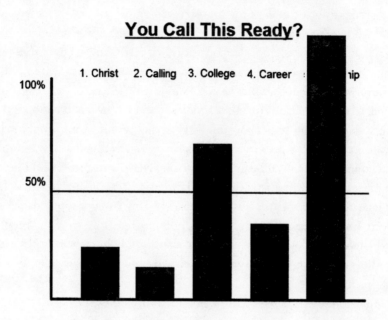

As you can see this teenager's relationship with Christ and character development are below 25% because he's still young in the Lord. All he knows about his Calling is, "It has something to do with God, right?" Educational goals are better because he should graduate from high school in a year or two, but his Career is unknown. On the other hand, his relationship with his latest girlfriend is through the roof! They plan to get married after graduation and live off "love." As we have seen time and time again in America, this is a recipe for disaster! This is where we get high divorce rates, unwanted pregnancies, and STD's. Dating the world's way is a proven failure. There is overwhelming evidence of this all around us. Waiting on *God's choice* and *His timing* for a spouse is wiser, more successful, and way more fulfilling.

In contrast with this teenager, if you are operating at 90% plus on each of the first 4 C's then you are ready for the 5th and final C!

(5) Courtship

I remember when Mona and I went on a date early on in our relationship, I said to her, "Mona, I want you to know that I am dating you for the purpose of maybe marrying you some day." Needless to say, she was stunned to hear me say that! I didn't say it very well back in those days. What I meant was I wasn't just dating for fun. I was in an attitude of discerning if God might be bringing us together. After she came to, she figured out what I was trying to say. And now looking back she actually appreciated the honesty. She never had to wonder about my intentions. I wasn't proposing to her on the spot, but neither was I fooling around and "playing the field." A lot of guys do that and most sisters have no idea what a guy is thinking when they go out. I was seriously praying for God's will for us, and she was grateful to know that from the outset.

The Christian courtship process is an intentional, prayerful process of discerning God's will for marriage. It is not a random, trial-by-error game of trying to get hitched. If your parents are mature Christians they will be invaluable to this process. Include them. Certainly, other mature Christian leaders in your life should be involved to help you discern God's will.

Again, we're assuming you have the first four "C's" operating in the 90% range. So you're running the race for Jesus with all your heart. Here's the cool thing. What you do now is look left then look right. And you see who is running the race for Jesus just as hard as you are. During our Hawaii Youth For Christ days there were literally dozens of "eligible" single bachelors and bachelorettes in our fellowship. It was a Christian single's dream. When you're running hard for Jesus, you find like-minded brothers and sisters running beside you. They have the same heart for Jesus as you. They have a similar calling. And they are roughly in the same life stage as you. Now one of these might be your future spouse.

This is where it gets very exciting. We need to ask the Lord to really lead us because there is no set way that two people discover one another. And that is part of the adventure! Who says God isn't romantic? There is quite a bit of drama here because you're sticking your neck out risking rejection and all that stuff. After my opening line with Mona she could have said, "Don't call me, I'll call you." The first time I met Mona she was one of the college leaders in the camp group I was leading. No, I didn't say she was one of the teen girls in my camp group. I said she was one of the college-aged leaders in my camp group! At the time I had no idea I had just met my future wife. How romantic!

For starters here are three quick guidelines: (1) Never be alone, (2) never get physical, and (3) never fall in love. (I'm using the word "never" for emphasis.)

Never be alone. When you go out stay in groups. Don't even drive in the car alone. That's when trouble starts. Remember how we're designed. Our sexual urges do not come with brakes.

Never get physical. Don't even start. Remember the Law of Diminishing Return. Besides, as soon as you start getting physical, you no longer get to know the person on the inside. The relationship deteriorates to something superficial. During our YFC days before seeing Mona on a regular basis, I actually went out on "group dates" with other sisters in Christ. I am so glad I never got physical with any of them because they went on to marry other guys. I could've been fooling around with somebody else's (future) wife! OMG! And some of those guys were my brothers in Christ. Can you imagine what being at their wedding would've been like? Awkward!

Never "fall" in love. The average guy "falls" in love about 5 times a day. When he gets on the bus to go to school, he sees a cute girl: "I love her." In first period he sees a different girl, "No, I love her." At recess he sees another girl, "Now I love her." At lunch and on the way home he falls in love two more times. Girls are not that different. As soon as a cute guy says "hi" the typical teenage girl has already set a wedding date and picked out the names of their kids. This is that normal longing for a relationship we were talking about which comes from the way God designed us. A real love relationship, however, takes careful discernment. And it's based on deeper values than just looks. Don't confuse the two. Never fall in love.

Step two is to go through some kind of pre-marital study series. Mona and I went through *Before You Say I Do* by H. Norman Wright and Wes Roberts. Many people believe they should get engaged first before going through a pre-marital study. The reality is some people go through a pre-marital study and *change their minds* about getting married. That's not good if you're already engaged, sent out invitations, and ordered your wedding dress. So I strongly recommend a "pre-engagement" series to help you discern compatibility. It is always better to know that you have "irreconcilable differences" *before* you buy rings and put a down payment on a reception hall.

Step three: Set a wedding date. Once we discern that your relationship is truly a God thing then take out your calendars and set a date. Do not let this linger for years and years. Our human design needs to see light at the end of the tunnel. Practically speaking, setting a date means finding a wedding location. No location = no wedding date. So decide on a location and check their availability. I do not recommend a long engagement. Mona and I were engaged for eight months and that was long enough. You do not need to plan an expensive wedding. I would shoot for meaningful over fancy. Save your money for a new house and get married in a church instead of an expensive hotel. I'm not opposed to a nice wedding, but you're not William and Kate. Mona and I had a beautiful wedding at her church and a meaningful reception at the Chief Petty Officer's club in Pearl Harbor. (It's like a nice restaurant.) Instead of using the financial gifts from our wedding to pay for the wedding, we used them to make a down payment on our first townhome. So set a date, don't spend too much, and have fun! Many people put way too much emphasis on their *wedding* and way too little emphasis on their *marriage*.

In conclusion getting married God's way is like waiting for the traffic lights to go from red to green. If a young person doesn't yet know Christ, the light is red. When you give your heart to Christ and become mature in Christian character the light turns green. You head up the street until you reach a red light at an intersection called "Calling." When the Lord reveals His calling on your life, green light. You drive to the next street that will help you prepare for your calling, and that's called "College." When you graduate the light turns green and you follow the Lord's leading to "Career." You stop there until you're reasonably established with a steady income. Once that happens, God gives you the green light to date seriously. When the Lord introduces you to your helper suitable, then Courtship begins.

The Five C's are actually a powerful process of Spiritual Transformation. Everything we learned at every intersection will serve us well in our future marriage. Remember, that was God's will for us all along. He is the eternal, ultimate, loving relationship. And He wants us to live happily ever after to His glory.

For every Christian single waiting on God for His choice and His time, be encouraged by these hopeful words from President Ronald Reagan. He said this to thousands of Christian teenagers at a huge youth conference back in the late '80's:

"I'm sure that each of you believes that someday you'll find someone to fall in love with, and you will; and sometimes you may get frustrated, and yes; finding the right one may take longer than you thought, but don't worry. It will happen. For each of you out there some place is that someone. It's important for you not to pay any attention at all to those who say that promiscuity is somehow stylish or rewarding. You know that when you meet that person and meet them in marriage, that you will be true to each other. Well, did you ever stop to think: you can start being true to that one special person now."

At the end of our Virtuous Reality Ceremony, the young people make this final pledge:

"Now because of my love for Jesus, I make this commitment to God, my church, my family, friends, and myself—and if God wills, my future spouse and my future children—to live a virtuous life, to be sexually pure from this day to the day I enter a biblical, marriage relationship. I do this to honor God, honor my parents, respect others and to accept God's very best for myself, those I love today, and those I will love tomorrow." Our dream is to see our young people on their wedding days say to their bride/groom: "I was faithful to you before I even knew you." That's righteous. But it's also romantic!

Then parents present a purity ring to their child, and the church gathers around to warmly congratulate and encourage our young people.

A word to those who think it's too late for them. I realize that in this day and age just about everyone has a sexual history. Our churches are full of people whose hearts have been broken, relationships shattered, divorced, remarried, and divorced again. Others abandoned marriage and lived promiscuously. Some have children from many different partners. Can you see that this happened because God was not invited to be Lord over your life? It is not too late to open the door of your life and make Him Lord. It doesn't matter how bad you think your life has been. Our God is an expert at redeeming broken lives. He creates universes in His spare time. Don't you think He can bring order to your world? Don't wait another minute. Start obeying Him now.

Celibacy and *chastity* are two pre-marital Spiritual Disciplines the Church needs to recover in this day and age. Like Shadrach, Meshach, and Abednego, we take a stand for God in a hostile environment. Although we may go through a fiery assault on our values, we look for the Spirit to make a personal appearance just when we need Him. Virtuous Reality is a first step for a new generation of young people who refuse to live the world's way. It not only urges them to take a stand, it shows them where to put their feet.

Discussion Questions

1. Why are there chapters on relationships in a book on Spiritual transformation?

2. How is today's society like the time of Shadrach, Meshach, and Abednego? How should Christians respond?

3. What is the Ultimate Theory on Everything (UTE)?

4. Why do human beings have such a profound sense of longing for relationship?

5. From Genesis what is the biblical view of our Sexual Identity?

6. Discuss the Spiritual disciplines of celibacy and chastity.

7. Discuss how the world's values in boyfriend-girlfriend relationships do not help us achieve God's plan of love for a lifetime in marriage.

8. Discuss the Five C's as an alternative to the world and pathway to God's best.

9. By faith, what did the Lord say to you in this chapter? And how do you intend to step out in obedience?

Chapter 11

DISCIPLINES FOR MARRIAGE

"We mistakenly pursue a happy sex life as if it were a goal, when it is actually the by-product of a higher pursuit."
– Michael M. Palompo

Now let's talk briefly about marriage. The Apostle Peter shows us the connection between our intimacy with our spouses and our intimacy with God: "You husbands in the same way, live with your wives in an understanding way... and show her honor as a fellow heir of the grace of life, so that your prayers will not be hindered" (1 Pt. 3:7 NAS). A bad marriage impedes our capacity to connect with God.

God's design for marriage is one man and one woman loving one another for a lifetime. In order to glorify God in ministry, Christian leaders must have healthy monogamous, heterosexual relationships. Here are some practical guidelines on how to keep Christ in the center of our marriages. We know that marriage is a gift from God, but have you ever considered that it is a Spiritual discipline? Remember our definition of a Spiritual Discipline: a practice that clears a pathway for the seeking Father.

Here's where we find ourselves today: People have issues with monogamy and heterosexuality. Men in particular are not monogamous by nature. And the rise of homosexual activism brings tremendous confusion to an already confusing issue. The challenge of entering into a monogamous, heterosexual relationship for a lifetime should make us keenly aware of our need for the presence and power of God. There is joy unspeakable on our wedding day when we say, "I do." But there should also be a serious, humble prayer from deep in our spirit, "God, we need you now more than ever!"

The "practice" of marriage can be a supernatural experience where we get to see God transform us into monogamous, heterosexual beings. When we watch the movies the good guy always gets the girl in the end, but we never find out what happens next. What happens to Prince Charming and the Fairy Princess 20 years and 30 lbs. later after they've raised 5 kids? By contrast, in real life that is when the great adventure is just beginning. Marriage as a Spiritual discipline will transform us more than any other experience in life, if we know how to cooperate with God. So let me give you my best shot at understanding the Spiritual discipline of Holy Matrimony.

First, we need to understand the "shape" of marriage. The diagram below gives us the overall picture. Marriage is a love triangle (but not like how you see on TV). It is a Spiritual dynamic between God, the husband, and the wife.

The Shape of Marriage

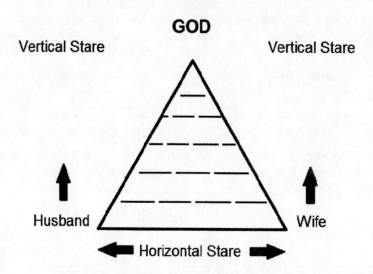

Horizontal Stare vs. Vertical Stare

One of the most common problems in marriage is seeing all the issues your spouse has and trying to change them. Marriage is the most intensely intimate of all human relationships, so you're going to get to know one another real up-close and personal. A wife stares at her husband and thinks: He's such a slob, why doesn't he clean up his mess? He doesn't help around the house. He comes home late every night for dinner. He only pays attention to me when he wants sex. A husband stares at his wife and thinks: She's spending too much on shopping. She doesn't keep house. Why is it she always has a "headache" at exactly the wrong moment? When husbands and wives focus on each other this way, they are engaging in the "horizontal stare." But how many of us know we cannot change each other?

The only One who can transform your spouse is Jesus. So instead of trying to change one another horizontally, the answer is for both husband and wife to look *vertically* to God. The diagram above illustrates the Spiritual discipline of keeping our eyes fixed on Jesus, the Author and Perfecter of our faith. Who is the Author and Perfecter of our faith? It's not us. Only Jesus can transform your spouse. Paul says, "He who has begun a good work in you will complete it until the day of Jesus Christ" (Phil. 1:6 NKJV.) Who began a good work in your spouse? Not you. Who will complete it? The same One who began it. That is the hope of every husband and wife. But if we want to see that happen, we must relinquish control over trying to change our spouse and instead pursue our *own* Spiritual Transformation. It's called the "vertical stare" at Jesus.

Each day in devotions, we behold the Lord Jesus. John says, "We beheld His glory, glory as of the only begotten of the Father, full of grace and truth" (Jn. 1:14). Jesus came so we could behold the invisible God. As we encounter Him in the word, we are in awe of His glory. We welcome His real-time, detectable Spirit, and we are blown away by His grace and truth. We fall short every day, yet graciously He loves us still. We feel unworthy of His acceptance, but His truth breaks through: "I accepted you before you were acceptable. I loved you while you were unlovable. It is my gracious, loving acceptance that will transform you. And that's the truth." When we focus on Him, His empowering presence transforms us. We become like Him: love, joy, peace, patience, kindness, goodness, gentleness, faithfulness, and self-control. We are not trying to change our spouse. That is an exercise in futility. But through the vertical stare, we are transformed.

When both husband and wife repent from the horizontal stare and commit themselves to the vertical stare, something awesome happens. Take a look again at our diagram. As the husband draws closer to God he becomes more like Him, illustrated by him moving vertically up toward God. At the same time his wife is also focused on the Lord and vertically progresses upward. Now as both ascend vertically, look what happens to them horizontally. They draw closer to one another! The closer they draw to God, they get closer to one another. Why? They are becoming more like Jesus. And wouldn't want to be married to someone whose character is like the Lord? The husband is becoming Mr. Right for his wife. And she is becoming Miss Right for him.

When our hearts are transformed by the power of the vertical stare we are a totally different person. The wife relinquishes control of her husband. She stops nagging. She is no longer angry and critical. She is full of faith, hope, and love now for her husband. The prayers of her heart come from His word: "Rather let it be the hidden person of the heart, with the incorruptible beauty of a gentle and quiet spirit, which is very precious in the sight of God" (I Pet. 3:4 NKJV). She turns to Jesus each day and prays: "Lord, I usher my husband into Your powerful presence. I renounce trying to change him in my own strength, and instead ask You to take leadership over his life. Speak to him, convict him, transform him from the inside out. Fill him with Your Spirit. Send godly men his way to help him become more like You, Jesus. In Your name I pray. Amen." As a wife faithfully ushers her husband to the Lord like that on a daily basis, she gives space and time for the Spirit to work. He doesn't stand a chance! The Lord transforms him into the kind of spiritual leader he needs to be for her. It didn't happen by her nagging, but rather through the power of the Spirit working through her gentle, quiet vertical stare.

Now the husband begins to encounter Jesus because of his wife's faithful prayers. The Lord speaks to him powerfully: "Husbands, love your wives, just as Christ also loved the church and gave Himself for her" (Eph. 5:25 NKJV). He is convicted to become the loving husband Christ envisioned him to be. And now he begins to pray with all his heart: "Lord, I thank You for the beautiful wife You gave me. Help me to love her the way You love the Church. Jesus, You laid down Your life for the Church. Now help me to lay my life down for my wife. Help me to love her as You do. How do You feel about her today? Feel that through me. What would You like to say to her today? Say it through me. What would You like to do for her today? Do it through me. May she experience Your undying, sacrificial love for her through me this day. In Jesus' name. Amen." And as a wife consistently experiences the love of Jesus expressed to her through her husband on a daily basis, watch how her spirit transforms. It is like water poured on a flower, and she begins to blossom. Can we see how powerful it is when we stay focused on God and not try to change each other in the flesh? That's the power of the vertical stare.

Where is all this heading? What's life like at the tip of the triangle where Jesus, husband, and wife live in wonderful harmony? Well, it sure looks a lot like the Trinity God-Family, doesn't it? We are taking advantage of our access to the perfectly choreographed dance of the Father, Son, and Holy Spirit because that same Spirit dwells in us. Holy Matrimony through the Holy Spirit is such an amazing God thing! This leads us to our second Spiritual discipline of marriage.

The 100-0 Relationship

In marriage Paul says we submit to one another. He goes on to describe the model for that loving submission as Jesus Himself: "Submitting to one another in the fear of God. Wives, submit to your own husbands, as to the Lord. For the husband is head of the wife, as also Christ is head of the church; and He is the Savior of the body. Therefore, just as the church is subject to Christ, so let the wives be to their own husbands in everything. Husbands, love your wives, just as Christ also loved the church and gave Himself for her" (Eph. 5:21-25 NKJV).

Telling women to submit to their husbands won't win you a "people's choice" choice award at the ladies luncheon these days. But what we don't understand is the context of covenant love that forms the foundation for our submission. How did Jesus love the Church? He sacrificed His life for her. If someone was willing to die for you, wouldn't it be real easy to submit to that person? You would probably give your life for that person in return.

Now watch this: When Jesus gave His life for the Church, He didn't say, "I'm going to sacrifice myself a little here, but I want you to meet me half way." No, instead He sacrificed Himself *completely* with no guarantee we would love Him in return. "God demonstrates His love for us in that while we were still sinners, Christ died for us" (Rom. 5:8). Many people think of marriage as a contract. A contract is 50-50: If I put in half, then you better put in the other half, or I'm getting out of this deal. What Jesus is trying to teach us is that marriage is a covenant, not a contract. A covenant is 100-0: I put in 100%, and I expect nothing in return. God's vision for marriage is two people loving one another 100-0. In His wisdom, God knew the destructive power of *expectations*.

A common problem in marriage is that people do not actually marry their spouse; they marry an *expectation* of what they want their spouse to be. When their spouse fails to meet that expectation they get disillusioned and bail on the relationship. We need to be married to our spouses, not our expectations of our spouses. Instead, the Lord wants to take each of us on a wondrous journey of Spiritual Transformation, where over time we learn how to love one another 100-0.

Remember we said that Holy Matrimony is a Spiritual discipline. Of all human relationships the marriage relationship is the most intense of all. So in one sense it is already by nature 100-0. You need to be 100% all in, or it won't work. Divorce is not an option. This is why pre-nuptial agreements are a horrible idea. They are a form of concession from the beginning that we will fail. It's difficult to give your whole heart to someone who's already got one foot out the door. God's way is to be *all in.* Until death do we part. "I love you 100% expecting zero in return."

But we are all still "under construction." Conflict is inevitable because we are two imperfect people trying to be one. The key is to resist the temptation to define our relationship by the temporary conflict we are facing. The heat of the moment will *not* burn us for a lifetime. When our spouse gets upset about something, we're taken aback because we're caught off guard. But look at it this way: you just learned something new about what your spouse is passionate about! Anger could reveal passions. So because we are on course to love 100-0, our marriage is not defined by the momentary setback. It is defined by something far more powerful. We turn our attention to this now.

Commitment

The wedding day is more than just a special ceremony to begin your marriage. On this day husband and wife make vows to one another before God. They usually go something like this: "I, Mike, take you, Mona, to be my wife, to have and to hold from this day forward; for better, for worse; for richer, for poorer; in sickness and in health, till death do we part." We might think those words are ceremonial, but God doesn't. These vows now define your relationship with one another for the rest of your lives. Your relationship is based on this absolute commitment not your temporary circumstances.

For instance, never say, "We had a big fight last night, so I guess he doesn't love me anymore." Instead say, "We made a vow to love each other unto death, so even though things got a little heated last night, we will get through this."

Never define your relationship by the temporary trouble you're in, but by the lifelong love you have sworn.

Love involves emotions, but love is not based on emotions. Feelings do not determine our commitment to one another; instead our commitment determines our feelings. We choose to be together unto death. We have vowed this before God, and God takes it seriously: "If a man makes a vow to the LORD, or swears an oath to bind himself by some agreement, he shall not break his word; he shall do according to all that proceeds out of his mouth" (Num. 30:2 NKJV).

Ultimately, our commitment to one another horizontally is based on the vow we made to God vertically. Therefore, being committed to one another is a function of our obedience to God not how lovable our spouse is at any given moment. Aren't you glad your spouse's commitment to you is not predicated on you being lovable 100% of the time? The Spiritual discipline of commitment invokes the presence of the Lord because we made our vows before Him. We swore to God that we would love one another in sickness, health, rich, poor, better, worse, come what may. Christian husbands and wives are committed to each other out of a sworn obedience to Jesus first, not because their spouse deserves it. That is the nature and power of the Spiritual discipline of commitment.

The Spiritual Discipline of Sex

In conclusion, we need to address the area of sex. Yes, sex is a Spiritual discipline too. Believe it or not, it can usher in the presence of God into our marriage. This one is real easy actually and there's a reason we saved it for last. Every married couple wants an exciting, satisfying sex life. Just look at how much we talk about this on TV, radio, and books. We have sex therapists coming out of the woodwork. The trouble is we focus too much on the sex and not the quality of our connection with one another.

Look at the way God describes the sexual relationship between Adam and Eve. "Adam knew Eve his wife and she conceived" (Gen. 4:1 NKJV). Can we see how knowing, intimacy, and sex are related? The Hebrew word "yada" means "to know, acquire information by experience, observation; have sexual relations; intimacy." The Lord links sex with intimate knowledge about one another. We have first-hand experience of one another that nobody else on the planet shares. That's God's design for a beautiful sex life.

So how do we have an exciting, fulfilling sex life? The presence of the Lord in our relationship is the key from beginning to end. Remember, God designed sex—not Hugh Hefner or the Swedes. If a wife keeps her eyes fixed on God, she will usher her spouse to God and relinquish control over changing him. That makes her incredibly desirable. If a husband has a 100-0 relationship with his wife, he is willing to lay down his life for her like Jesus did for the Church. The wife looks at that and swoons, "My hero!" If a couple bases their love on a sworn commitment to obey God, they will love one another before each has become perfectly lovable. When a husband and wife look at each other and say, "There is no one else in the world for me but you, babe," well you know what's going to happen later on that night. Nothing kills a sex life more than listening to your spouse nag you about all your shortcomings. Nothing kills a sex life more than feeling you don't measure up. Nothing kills a sex life more than realizing that your marriage vows are not being honored. A wonderful sex life is the icing on the cake of a richly meaningful relationship. That's why we saved it for last. *We mistakenly pursue a happy sex life as if it were a goal, when it is actually the by-product of a higher pursuit.*

While walking through a botanical garden one day, I noticed a tree that was beautiful but unusual. I couldn't figure out why exactly until I looked very closely. It was actually *two* trees that had over the years grown into one another. Their trunks had wrapped around each other and their branches so intertwined as to be almost indistinguishable. Separating them would probably mean the death of them. The true purpose of sex is not adventure, exploit, or escapade. Instead it causes you to grow into one another. Your hearts wrap around one another and your souls become intertwined. Your spirits become so intricately united, separating you feels like death.

God's Gift of Marriage

Human beings are *exceptional* among creation because we're the only ones made in the image of God. God, however, is a three-person being, whereas we are single-person beings. The result is we exist with an inbred, profound, existential longing for intimacy that emanates from the deepest recesses of our soul.

Marriage is God's gift to us to fulfill that primal yearning. He designed us to long for this relationship, then takes us on a journey to find that special someone. Our parents could not fulfill this longing. Neither can our brothers, sisters, or friends. A man could never do this for another man, nor a woman for another woman. Certainly not our pets. Luxurious homes and fancy cars won't do it. Husband and wife discover a unique happiness in one another that not even a perfect relationship with God Himself will fulfill. The first time Adam met Eve he was so happy he cried out, "Finally, this is bone of my bone and flesh of my flesh!" When God brings that special someone into your life, that person is His gift to you. Your relationship is so intricate. It has so many dimensions. You will never figure it out by yourself. You need His divine help. And that's the whole point. Marriage is such a God thing!

Discussion Questions

1. What do we mean that marriage is a Spiritual discipline?

2. Discuss what is going on between the horizontal stare and the vertical stare.

3. How does the vertical stare draw couples closer to each other?

4. What is a "100-0" relationship? Why is this discipline so important in connecting you both with God?

5. How do vows made before God form the foundation for the marriage commitment? What does it mean to define your relationship by your vows rather than the current troubles you face?

6. What is the wrong way to approach sex in marriage? How does the proper view of sex bless a marriage relationship?

7. How does the gift of marriage lead us to the gift of God's presence?

8. By faith, what did the Spirit say to you in this chapter? And how will you step out in obedience?

Chapter 12

SPIRITUAL FRIENDS

"Each friend represents a world in us, a world possibly not born until he arrives, and it is only by this meeting that a new world is born."
– Anaïs Nin

When I came to Christ on July 18, 1975, my best friend, Mark Olmos, had just given his life to Christ the day before. And so began the adventures of Mark and Mike. We immediately started reaching out to our high school friends at Radford High by founding the John 14:6 Club. Later we joined the staff of Hawaii Youth For Christ together and led hundreds of kids to Jesus for over a decade. We used to drive around in the same kind of car: 1980 Blue Chevy Chevettes. On the freeway we pretended we were fighter pilots flying in formation. We must've gone to every opening night of every major movie together—Star Wars, Star Trek, Indiana Jones. You name it. Sometimes we camped out overnight to wait in line. We were each other's best man on our wedding days. Even after we were married, when it was "Boy's Night Out," our wives knew exactly what we were up to. I named my firstborn son after him. There was nothing we didn't share with one another. At the center of our friendship was our relationship with Jesus. We always knew it was awesome to be best friends. But looking back, I see how critical it was to have a Spiritual friend like Mark.

As best friends, there were a lot of healthy things Mark and I did that drew us closer to Jesus. And that's what I mean by a "relational discipline." There's a way to live that invites more of God's presence and power into our lives. God initiates. And He is faithful to complete it. That's why true Spiritual friendship is a God thing. I'm not trying to take the fun out of being friends. But if Jesus is not part of your friendships, then it may be a good thing, but it's not a God thing. On the contrary, the presence of God enriches our relationships and makes them more meaningful and satisfying. He is, after all, the eternal, ultimate, loving relationship.

Today my wife, Mona, is the best friend I have in life. By God's design, we are one in so many ways. My children, Mark, Rachael, Caleb and I have a very special friendship dimension to our father-child relationship. I am blessed that my dad, mom, four brothers, and sister are also believers and are among my closest and dearest friends. My staff at the church, the council members, and hundreds of volunteers are more than co-laborers in the mission; they are precious, cherished friends. Mark Olmos and I live in different states now, but will always have that special bond for the rest of our lives.

Larry Crabb and Eugene Peterson collaborated on a book entitled *The Safest Place on Earth*. They talk about a community of friends where we feel safe. I love that. There are a number of legitimately biblical images we have of church— the body of Christ, the army of God, the bride of the Lamb, etc. All of these connote a particular dimension of what the Christian Church is and does. But Crabb and Peterson are reminding us that Christians are family. We call one another brother and sister because we have the same heavenly Father. God knows that every person on earth needs to know that kind of love and acceptance to transform. He knows because He designed us that way. Crabb and Peterson state, "The key to spiritual health is having certain Spiritual relationships in your life."[10] Fellowship is not a place where you are safe *from* people; but a place where you are safe *with* people. Man, this is so important to catch! One of the reasons that ministers commit moral failure is they don't feel safe to talk with anyone about their issues. And it is ironic because it was their leadership that established that culture in their churches.

I was watching the HBO special, "The Trials of Ted Haggard." I love Ted Haggard. I actually met him once and shook his hand at a conference. Being a pastor myself, I observed in amazement as the Lord used him to build New Life Church from nothing to a thriving congregation of over 14,000. He was President of the National Association of Evangelicals. I've heard him speak, read his books, and learned so much from him over the years. I was absolutely horrified when the news broke of his moral failure. I said to myself, "No, God! Not Ted!" A friend of mine who attended New Life told me, "Mike, it feels like a funeral around here, except the guy is still walking around." When Ted went on HBO to tell his story, I wasn't sure if that was going to be a good thing.

---

10   Larry Crabb and Eugene Peterson, *The Safest Place on Earth: Where People Connect and are Forever Changed* (Nashville: Nelson, 1999), 80.

But because I felt connected to him, I wanted to see what he was going through and learn. It was tough to watch. I felt for his wife, Gayle, and their five children. Ted said, *"I'm talking about this now because in the church we won't talk about it."* He tried to talk with someone in church about his struggles, but all this person said was, "Just keep yourself busy with more ministry and you'll be Ok." I felt such an indictment on the Christian church that one of our brothers—our very best—felt he could be more transparent on HBO than in church.

Ted's moral failure became public in November 2006, but obviously he had been struggling in this area long before that—maybe all his life. The next summer it became public that a well-known minister in Hawaii had been in multiple adulterous relationships for decades while he led one of the finest ministries in the islands. This leader was doing amazing ministry and was surrounded by wonderful leaders and yet was able to keep his sin hidden *for decades.* I know because he was my spiritual mentor. It was such a horrific revelation. When he called to tell me, it caught me so completely off-guard I felt I had been sucker-punched in the back of the head. I wept bitterly for him on the phone. And I never heard from him again.

At first I had to fight off cynicism about the transformation that Jesus works in our lives. What do I truly believe happens when a person comes to Christ? I was shaken personally. Hurting emotionally. I couldn't wrap my mind around what just happened. Theologically I was in a haze. First Ted, now my mentor. What's going on? All things for good, right? I was straining to see the good in it.

Three years later, here's what the Lord taught me through this dark valley. I still believe in the regenerative power of being born-again. But the only perfect dimension of this regeneration is spiritual. That is, by sheer grace—and I mean that's all it is—we are brought into a right relationship with God and seated in heavenly places with Christ (Eph. 2:6). The holiness that made this possible had nothing to do with us. It is the righteousness of Christ Jesus imputed or ascribed to us. I knew all this before. But I know it on a whole different level now.

As for us, we all remain broken in our souls. Our spirits are perfect. Our souls are a mess. I know this is true in my own soul. I may not have experienced a public moral failure, but I am aware of my "dark side." I pray I have said nothing to sound in any way arrogant or self-righteous against Ted or my mentor. I am painfully aware of my own glaring issues. And from the looks of things, I am not alone.

Our one hope is that Jesus is with us now. Our spirits are perfectly connected to God by Christ, but our souls need transforming. Our spiritual connection with Jesus can transform our desires, renew our thinking, and heal our emotions. But that is a choice we have to make. We are constantly dealing with the distortions. We see Him as through a dirty, cracked window. We hear Him, but it's a bad connection. Yet He remains faithful to complete what He started in us.

Community does not transform us. Ted was in a Christian community. My mentor and I were in fellowship for decades. Church by itself doesn't change us. Jesus in the Church does. Jesus outside knocking does no one any good. Jesus inside seated at the table as the guest of honor does everyone good. Senior leaders of churches need to step down from their pedestals and allow Jesus to lead. They need to allow Jesus to transform them. They need His transforming power just as much as the congregation does. When it comes to transformation, hierarchies get in the way. Pastors mustn't hide behind their titles. They need to step down from the stage and join the rest of us. Think of a flat structure. No pyramids. There are no mentoring gurus, no Jedi masters. Ted didn't need more fellowship. He needed a Spiritual friend. So did my mentor. So do we all.

So how do we need to *be* with one another in a fellowship like this? This is not like any church we've ever heard of. There are key Spiritual disciplines we practice in relationship *with one another* that invoke the presence and power of the Spirit. This is what we mean by *relational disciplines.* Remember, a relational discipline is a Spiritual discipline practiced in Spiritual fellowship with another whereby we anticipate together the leading, filling, and empowering presence of God.

There are friends, and then there are *Spiritual* friends. Pastors need Spiritual friends as much as the rest of us. There's your bowling buddy, and then there's the person you turn to for prayer in desperate moments. There's the friend you go to the movies with, and then there's the friend you confess your sins to. There's the friend you go to the beach with, and then there's the friend who holds you accountable to God. There's the kind of friend you drop when you no longer get along, and then there's the friend you ask for forgiveness because your friendship means too much to let go. There's the friend you talk about sports with, and then there's the friend you share biblical truths with. Friends are a good thing. Spiritual friends are a God thing.

Sometimes these two kinds of friends are the same person. Sometimes they are not. Obviously, I am not saying that we should not have friends to go to the movies with. But are these the only friends we have? Neither am I suggesting that we all find a pastor to be our Spiritual friend. (He might be the last person you want as a Spiritual friend.) *What I am contending for is a Spiritual transformation in our relationships.* We do not need to be professional counselors. (Although I'm not saying we don't need Christian counselors.) But we are a "priesthood of believers" and capable of more for one another than we think.

The following relational disciplines could make a huge difference in our friendships: mutual acceptance, transparency, feedback, and Spiritual direction.

Mutual Acceptance

Walter Winchell once said, "A true friend is one who walks in when others walk out." If we have a glaring issue or a dark side to our personality, it is natural to keep that hidden for fear of rejection. "If you knew what I was really like, you wouldn't be my friend anymore." So we shut up and keep our glaring issues hidden. But as we've seen, these secret sins have a nasty way of coming out into the open. And when they do, all hell breaks loose. We are heart-broken. We feel betrayed. "How could this happen?" "I thought you were a Christian?" "Some leader you turned out to be!" Lots of pain and suffering.

So what do we do? Typically, we resign from the church. We go someplace where hardly anybody knows us and start over. I'm not saying this is always a bad option, but guess what inevitably happens in this new place? Yup. The same thing happens all over again. More failure, heartbreak, betrayal, pain, and suffering. Why?

Never forget: *"Wherever you go, there you are."*

Wherever we move, our baggage comes with us. We are running to escape, but we cannot escape ourselves. Mutual acceptance is about finding a safe place. You are safe with your Spiritual friends. They know who you are, and they accept you just as you are. You accept them as they are.

The idea is *not tolerance,* but *acceptance.* What's the difference? Tolerance suggests we will be your friend just as you are, and you never have to change.

Mutual acceptance means we accept you as you are, but we love you too much to leave you that way. We will seek the Lord together until Christ is formed in us. Here's how the Lord does acceptance without tolerance: "But God demonstrates His own love toward us, in that while we were still sinners, Christ died for us" (Rom. 5:8 NKJV). Perfect acceptance before perfect acceptability. Did you catch the "while we were yet sinners" part? God didn't wait for us to get our act together first before He decided to love us. Thank God! Because if that were the case, then there was no way He could've loved us. God knows He has to catch His fish first before He can clean them. He did what needed to be done so we could be set free.

So too Spiritual friends practice mutual acceptance because they realize they are mutually broken. We know we need to confess our sins to one another. But that won't happen if we're afraid we'll be rejected by the other. But if we don't confess our sins, we'll never be set free. We need to help one another repent, but we can't do that if we don't know what each of us is repenting from. We need to mutually accept one another *first* before that can happen. Neither of us is the guru. "Bear one another's burdens, and so fulfill the law of Christ" (Gal. 6:2 NKJV). Did you catch that "one another's" part? We are not master and padawan. We are not pastor and parishioner. We do not "shrink" one another. We are not psychoanalyst and patient. We are two beggars sharing the bread. We are Spiritual friends.

Pastors need to come down from our pedestals to be with friends. *The higher the pedestal, the longer the way down.* So you might want to get started. In our defense it is not easy for pastors to know who to share with. The Lord must lead us. My wife is my best friend, but there are certain things I admittedly do not share with her. I have Spiritual friends who are within my congregation, and I feel at liberty to share with them what I do not tell my wife. I have Spiritual friends outside my congregation, and I feel at liberty to share with them what I cannot share with friends in my congregation. By the way, these are not formalized sessions, but there is intentionality. It is Spiritual and very organic—you guessed it, a God thing. Once there is Mutual acceptance in our friendship, the door is open for some other wonderful possibilities.

The Johari Window: Getting to the Truth

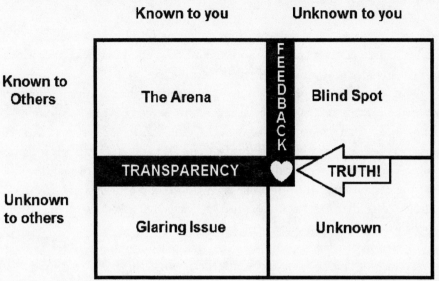

By Joseph Luft & Harry Ingham, 1955

Transparency and Feedback

"Brethren, if a man is overtaken in any trespass, you who are spiritual restore such a one in a spirit of gentleness, considering yourself lest you also be tempted" (Gal. 6:1 NKJV). Who is best equipped to help us with our issues? The bible says "you who are spiritual" must do it. And did you catch that "consider yourself" part? There's that mutual dimension once again.

In 1955 Joseph Luft and Harry Ingham invented a schematic called the "Johari Window" (Joe & Harry, get it?). It creatively illustrates how to arrive at unknown issues in one's life. There are two kinds of issues: "glaring issues" and "blind spots." If an issue is known to you and the other person, then that is called the "Arena" because it's all out there in the open, and we can all deal with it. Now if something is known to you but unknown to others, that is a "glaring issue." What if something is unknown to you but known (sometimes painfully!) to the people around you? That is called a "blind spot."

Here's what I like about this diagram: It shows how Spiritual friends can help us with our "stuff." (Stuff is short for glaring issues and blind spots.) If you have a glaring issue, which is by definition known to you but not to others, then you would need to *self-reveal* that to your friend. This is called "transparency." If you have a blind spot, which by definition is unknown to you but very obvious to others, then you need someone to tell you about it. That's where Spiritual friends come in. This is called "feedback."

As Spiritual friends practice transparency and feedback with one another, they make inroads to the unknown and receive revelation they couldn't have gotten alone. I have an eating disorder called the "Seafood Diet." When I see food, there goes my diet! I've had this problem all my life. In fact, growing up I realize we always had food around. We were a Navy family so my mom would go to the commissary. It seemed like she went every day! We always had food in the car, even if it was just a short trip. So one day I asked my mom. "Why do we always have food around?

I never forgot what she told me. She said that during World War II their town in the Philippines was taken over by the Japanese Imperial Army. And they were put in internment camps. The men were rounded up in the plaza. The women and children were put in the church. She was about 10 years old when this happened. She said they went hungry in the camps. The soldiers didn't feed them enough. So it was like she made a vow to herself: I'm never going through that again as long as I live."

What happened next was awesome. I said, "The war is over now, mom. You never have to worry about going without food ever." It was almost like, "Yes, that's true isn't it." I was transparent with my problem. Then she shared information I had never heard before. And together we arrived at a new revelation. I sensed it was a God moment. Don't get me wrong. We still love to eat! But it's not worry-driven like before.

We are able to bear one another's burdens and fulfill the law of Christ. Spiritual friends tell each other the truth. And the truth brings freedom. It may hurt at first, but it sure feels good long-term. Getting a root canal is not fun, but living with that pain day after day is unbearable. Best to just go after it! Mutual acceptance opens the door to transparency and feedback. Transparency and feedback open the door to Spiritual direction.

Spiritual Direction

Finally, Spiritual friends mutually and humbly approach God for guidance. They involve the Lord every step of the way. He has led them to mutual acceptance, transparency, and feedback. Spiritual direction is the practice of paying attention to and cooperating with the Spirit's direction. Spiritual friends do that by being *anchored to God's word and led by His Spirit*. Spiritual friends are disciples who live by the teachings of Christ and then follow the Spirit of Christ. The Spirit illuminates the word and directs us in transformation vertically and horizontally. The stories and principles of the word lead us to the *Lord Himself*. The word gives us principles on the kind of girl we should marry, but the Spirit gives us confirmation on who that girl is! The word tells us, "Make disciples of all nations." The Spirit tells us precisely which nation, when to go, what to do, and how to do it. Did He not promise us? "I am with you always even to the end of time." These questions require Spiritual friends who help us discern Spiritual direction, i.e. the Spirit's direction.

As a word of encouragement, Spiritual friends can never predict where the pursuit of the Truth will lead. Jack Deere now has two books with titles that begin with the word *surprised*. He is *surprised* by the power of the spirit, and he is *surprised* by the voice of God. As well he should be. A cursory survey of the bible from Genesis to Revelation exposes a *surprising* God who works through various means at times of His choosing: Noah's ark, the burning bush, tablets of stone, a bronze serpent, Balaam's donkey, Joshua's mysterious Angel, the ark of the covenant, Solomon's Temple, Elijah versus the prophets of Baal, Daniel in the lion's den, and the list goes on. The long-awaited Messiah of the Jews dies on a cross and is subsequently resurrected for the salvation of the world. *Surprise!* At Pentecost tongues of flame rest on the heads of each of the disciples filling them with power to make disciples of all nations. *Surprise!* What theologian ancient or modern could have predicted any of these events, much less *how* God intended to bring them about? God things! I'm just saying.

Paul was God's first missionary and church planter to the Gentiles. But although He had general orders to reach Gentiles, He received specific instruction from the Spirit on when to carry out those orders. Take a look at this interesting encounter: "Now when they had gone through Phrygia and the region of Galatia, they were forbidden by the Holy Spirit to preach the word in Asia.

After they had come to Mysia, they tried to go into Bithynia, but the Spirit did not permit them" (Acts 16:6-7 NKJV). Paul is simply carrying out the general orders He received at Antioch to reach the Gentiles for Christ. But now the Holy Spirit is forbidding him to go into certain places. The Lord said, "Make disciples of all nations." Is He contradicting Himself? No. He's just reminding Paul who is the Lord of the Harvest. This is the dynamic of Spiritual direction in action. It is a combination of being "anchored to God's word and led by His Spirit." We need both the *principles* and the *person* of God to lead us.

Spiritual friends know how to do that with one another. Is it a direction from the Spirit? Is it a God thing? I look at it this way: If a person is doing something not directed by God then it is doomed to fail. On the other hand, if a person is called by God, then nothing on earth can stop him. The gates of hell will not prevail against him. Opponents would be well advised, "Do not come against that guy because he is called, and you will find yourself fighting against God!" (My paraphrase of Gamaliel's counsel in Acts 5:39). But if a person's ministry is not a God thing, then it will fail all by itself. No need to oppose him. At New Hope Central Oahu our conviction is to always discern Spiritual direction. We want everything we do to be a God thing not just a good thing. We pray and ask God for confirmation on what He wants us to do. Then we step out in faith knowing that we will be completely invincible as we proceed.

I love the imagery of a midwife. She's the nurse that stands by to help a woman give birth. She did not conceive this baby. She is not giving birth herself. She is there to usher in. So too we cannot conceive anything in the Spirit. That's the Lord's work. The Lord builds the invincible Church. It's His Church. And it's pregnant with possibilities! His laborers are in labor with work in the Spirit. People are being born again. And the Church is a nursery full of God's children who need loving care. Spiritual friends are midwives who faithfully stand by to usher in what the Lord is doing.

I cannot help but wonder what would've happened if our dear brother, Ted Haggard, had a Spiritual friend with whom he could practice mutual acceptance, transparency, feedback, and Spiritual direction. In the HBO special that he made, the interviewer asked a very poignant question: "Ted, do you wish you could go back to being the superstar pastor of a mega-church?" "No," he answered. Because now he is free to truly seek the Lord to heal the brokenness in his soul. He no longer has to hide. While he was on his pedestal, he could not be forthcoming with his personal issues. Now he can seek help. Pastors have a choice of stepping down from their pedestals voluntarily or being knocked off.

The truth is Ted confessed that he struggled with homosexuality his entire adult life. So the whole time he was pastor at New Life he had this secret struggle. The only thing different between pre-2006 and post-2006 is now we all know his glaring issue. But what if he had been in a fellowship that recognized our mutual brokenness and were willing to help him rather than reject him for his struggles? The same Ted Haggard who led New Life to a church of 14,000 was the same Ted who struggled with homosexuality. His heart for Jesus, training leaders, and reaching the lost was the same heart that had this dark side. *Remember, I am in no way condoning his sin or saying he should remain in pastoral leadership.* I am not advocating tolerance of sin; I am contending for us to become fellowships that allow space for precious people like Ted to get help and be set free from their sin. Jesus was crucified so we no longer have to crucify one another.

The Church needs to stop shooting our wounded. If a person is not humble, and is arrogant and prideful about their sin, then we can't help him. But if a person humbles himself and beseeches God to set him free, how should the Church respond? In my view the best place to be transformed should be *in* the Church, before the presence and power of God. Do you think God is surprised by our stuff? He knows everything about us, and His heart is to transform us. He's the only One who can. What if our churches became the safest place on earth? I cannot help but wonder what would've happened if Ted—or my mentor—had some Spiritual friends with whom to practice mutual acceptance, transparency, feedback, and Spiritual direction.

Discussion Questions

1. Have you ever been heartbroken by a moral failure you've seen in Church?

2. What is the difference between a regular friend and a Spiritual friend?

3. How is the Church falling short in being "safe places" for us to transform?

4. What are relational disciplines? And what are they for?

5. Discuss what mutual acceptance is. Why is it not the same as tolerance?

6. How can our Spiritual friends help us with our glaring issues and blind spots? Discuss transparency and feedback.

7. What is Spiritual direction? How can Spiritual friends be midwives of the Spirit's direction?

Chapter 13

COMMUNITY TRANSFORMATION

"The resurrection body of Jesus which at the moment is almost unimaginable
to us in its glory and power, will be the model for our own."
– N.T. Wright

When a person encounters the Lord Jesus, his spirit is transformed forever.
Nothing else in the universe has transforming power like that. As he continues
to encounter Jesus, his soul transforms. So when we talk about community
transformation, we do not mean something different from encountering Jesus.
It's not about educational reform, winning elections, or urban renewal. All of
those things may occur. But they are the fruit not the root. Without God they
are merely good things. We are looking for God things. Community transformation is about cooperating with Jesus on a global scale.

To understand what God is up to in the world, we need to know His end
game. Then God said to Noah, "The end of all flesh has come before Me; for
the earth is filled with violence because of them; and behold, I am about to
destroy them with the earth. Make for yourself an ark of gopher wood" (Gen.
6:13-14 NAS). Noah was told the world, as he knows it, is coming to an end.
So we aren't the first human beings to face "the end of the world." Like Noah
we too are headed for an inevitable consummation. Jesus said, "And just as it
happened in the days of Noah, so it will be also in the days of the Son of Man"
(Lk. 17:26 NAS). The world as we know it will come to an end. A whole
new world will rise. All of history is heading relentlessly and irresistibly in this
direction. There is no stopping it. It will get worse before it gets better. But
Christians don't need to be dismayed.

As my professor at Regent College, R. Paul Stevens, used to say, "The real
issue is not *what the world is coming to*, but *what is coming to the world*."[11]

---

11   R. Paul Stevens, "Work and Heaven: God as Consummator." Marketplace Ministries
     Course Notes, Regent College, Vancouver, B.C., Sep.-Dec. 1997, 66.

Christians need to stop trying to predict when the world is supposed to end. The bible is clear. We don't know. It's not our job to know. Our job is to do everything we can to cooperate with what Jesus is doing as we near the end. So we need to stop predicting and do some serious preparing for the end of the world.

Community transformation is not about christianizing the world. It is about aligning and allying ourselves with the Spirit. Jesus taught us to pray to the Father, "Thy kingdom come, Thy will be done on earth as it is in heaven" (Mt. 6:10). When this prayer becomes the focus of our work and ministry then we're on track for authentic transformation to happen. When we carry out our own campaigns, the results are temporary at best. We're talking about the eternal kingdom of God on earth as it is in heaven.

So God encountered Noah. From that day on, he lived his entire life in preparation for "what was coming to the world." He devoted his life to warning people of what was to come. He became a preacher (2 Pet. 2:5). And then he starts building that ark. Outside of hearing from God, this makes absolutely no sense at all. (Insert scenes from "Evan Almighty" here.) On dry land, without a cloud in the sky, for 120 years he and his family build this huge boat. Total insanity. But as we all know, it worked out. Noah was right. Everyone else drowned. Noah survived the end of the world, and made it into the next life. Amidst the incessant jeering, the laughter, and being booed off stage, he stayed faithful. Can you just imagine his parents telling him, "Noah, when are you going to get a real job?" (Jewish accent) People pretty much ignored the crazy old man on the street corner with the sandwich board that read, "the end is near."

Fireproofing Our Life Work

Sound familiar? It's a picture of Christian ministry in the 21st century. Like Noah we are given details from God that the end of the world as *we* know it is inevitable and likely imminent. So let's ask Noah to teach us how he did it—how to prepare for *our* own apocalypse.

One difference is our consummation will not occur by water but by fire (2 Pet. 3:10-13). Noah had to make sure he used enough pitch for his work. We need a flame retardant for ours. The average person will put in about 88,000 work hours into his career. How do we insure that those hours will not go up in smoke in the end?

How do we fire proof our life work?

To Infinity and Beyond

No, I'm not talking about a work that never ends, but a work with value beyond the end. It's not about having to work all the time, but doing a work that has value for all time. Here's what the Lord says about that:

"Now if any man builds upon the foundation with gold, silver, precious stones, wood, hay, straw, each man's work will become evident; for the day will show it, because it is *to be* revealed with fire; and the fire itself will test the quality of each man's work. If any man's work which he has built upon it remains, he shall receive a reward. If any man's work is burned up, he shall suffer loss; but he himself shall be saved, yet so as through fire" (I Cor. 3:12-15).

God will test every person's work by fire. Everything with eternal value will remain. Everything else will be consumed to ash. So the earth does not blow up like the planet Krypton. Rather, imagine a refining fire that burns away anything not made of eternal material. Wood, hay, and straw are all combustible. But gold, silver, and precious stones are *fireproof.*

Warren Gage wrote a book entitled, *The Gospel of Genesis.* Basically, he states that the end of history can be unlocked in its beginning: "By understanding the historical movement initiated in early Genesis, we may discern the relationship between the beginning and ending of biblical history...the record of postdiluvian history is stylized so as to be essentially a reduplicative chronicle of antediluvian history."[12] If Gage is right and we can know the end from the beginning, then the best way to understand fireproof work is start at the beginning. We need to know who we are, what we do, and where we are going as a human race.

What did God plan for Adam and Eve to *do* on the earth? Before sin entered the world and while they had a perfect relationship with God, Adam and Eve were given work to do: "Be fruitful and multiply, and fill the earth, and subdue it; and rule over the fish of the sea and over the birds of the sky and over every living thing that moves on the earth" (Gen.1:28 NAS). Mankind was to rule the earth and continue the creative process initiated by God. He can do this (as Moltmann states) precisely because he—and he alone—is created in the image of God.[13] This was to be done in cooperation and in relationship with God. In other words, mankind was to be the co-ruler and co-creator of the earth with God. However, all this was nullified by man's sin which resulted

12   Warren A. Gage, *The Gospel of Genesis* (Winona Lake, IN: Carpenter Books, 1984), 9.
13   Jürgen Moltmann, *The Future of Creation* (Philadelphia: Fortress Press, 1979), 127.

in a divorce between man and his God. Man handed the title deed of the earth over to Satan (Gen. 3, Cf. Jn. 12:31) and succumbed to the powers of darkness (Gen. 3, Cf. I Jn. 5:19). Their severed relationship with God rendered Adam and Eve powerless to co-rule and co-create.

This necessitated the arrival of the Second (and Last) Adam, Jesus Christ (I Cor. 15:45). Christ is God incarnate who reconciled man to Himself. His vicarious death and resurrection overcame the power of death and restores relationship between God and believers. This reinstatement of relationship with God through Christ (Jn. 1:12) is key to understanding what work on earth is truly fireproof—work with eternal value.

Watch this: the reunion of God and man through Christ is *itself* a new creation (2 Cor. 5:17) and initiates the renewal of the *rest* of creation. Today the foundation for salvation has been laid in Christ (1Cor.3:11). Do you know what this means? Jesus Christ is the New Ark of the present age! So those who hope in Christ have taken the first step toward the existence that God is bringing—or should I say *returning*—to the world. In the beginning God and mankind were co-rulers and co-creators of the earth. And that's where we're ending, or returning, or beginning again. Well, you know what I mean!

"And when all things are subjected to Him, then the Son Himself also will be subjected to the One who subjected all things to Him, that God may be all in all" (I Cor. 15:28). For our work to be fireproof, it needs to cooperate with that coming reality. We need to be working for eternity.

So where is God taking human history?

Heaven on Earth

With the finished work of Christ, a new administration is dawning upon the world—the monarchy of Jesus Christ upon the earth. As Newbigin writes, "The *news* is that 'the Kingdom of God' is no longer merely a theological phrase. There is now a name and a human face."[14] What the earth has received so far in Christ is the first fruits (I Cor. 15:20-23). But before this is all over, Jesus is going to blow this thing wide open. God's people must align themselves with the pre-ordained destiny of the earth. Alignment is precisely the reason Jesus taught us to pray, "Thy Kingdom come, Thy will be done *on earth* as it is in Heaven" (Mt. 6:10).

---

14 Lesslie Newbigin, *Sign of the Kingdom* (Grand Rapids: Eerdmans Publishing, 1980), 32.

So our New Ark has something to do with Jesus. And He is the key to the new world. But wait a minute. I thought we go to heaven when we die. Why are we praying, "on earth as it is in heaven?" Yes, we will all die some day. But the world of the future is not heaven. It is heaven on earth. It is an existence where heaven and earth are no longer disjoint but fully integrated. As Hoekema states, "For heaven and earth will then no longer be separated, as they are now, but will be one (Rev. 21:1-3)."[15]

In his vision, the Apostle John described the New Jerusalem as "coming down" from heaven to earth. In the Holy City he noted the absence of a temple. Why? Because a temple is no longer required. The majestic presence of Jesus Christ will be everywhere. It's the same reason there's no sun (Rev. 21:23) but everything is still lit up. You don't need a sun if you have the Son. With Christ enthroned in the heart of the Holy City, New Heaven on New Earth become seamless and one. All of creation will be restored to the beauty for which it now groans (Rom.8:19-22), the glory it had before the corruption. But it is not a return to Eden but rather a New Eden. "Drawing heavily on the imagery of Ezekiel (43:1-12; 47:1-12) and Isaiah (65:17-25)", states Stevens, "John envisions for Christians in Revelation 21-22 an even greater hope: a completely renewed creation."[16] Therefore, God is clearly far from through with our world. The fire of the Day of the Lord will be carefully selective, obliterating only the "works of the earth" (2 Pet. 3:10). The "work of the Lord", on the other hand, will endure forever in the Holy City.

And it gets better. On New Earth we will not be disembodied, free-floating apparitions strumming harps on clouds. We will have new, imperishable bodies. What will they look like? They'll be fashioned after the resurrected body of Christ (2 Cor. 5). The resurrected body of Jesus is the prototype for the new human race that will exist on the new earth. As NT Wright states in *Surprised by Hope*, "The resurrection body of Jesus which at the moment is almost unimaginable to us in its glory and power, will be the model for our own."[17] (Cf. Rom. 8:9-11; I John 3:1; I Cor. 15:20) Christ's post-resurrection body,

---

15   Anthony A. Hoekema, *The Bible and the Future* (Grand Rapids: Eerdmans Publishing, 1979), 274.

16   R. Paul Stevens. *End Times: Practical Heavenly Mindedness* (Downers Grove, IL: Inter-Varsity Press, 1994), 32.

17   N. T. Wright, *Surprised by Hope: Rethinking Heaven, the Resurrection, and the Mission of the Church* (New York: Harper-Collins, 2008), 149.

although clearly a physical body capable of eating, touching, and being touched (Jn. 20:17, 27), also had some marvelous, supernatural properties. It could pass through solid objects (Jn. 20:19), as well as vanish from plain sight (Luke 24:31). And if the Transfiguration was somehow a foreshadowing of this new body, then it could also have a gleaming radiance (Luke 9:29). Moreover, Jesus was still somehow identifiable as Jesus, though not always easily as the disciples on the Road to Emmaus will testify. He allowed Thomas a close inspection of the scars on His hands and side. But in His new panoply what were formerly marks of disgrace became badges of God's wondrous grace.

Can you see how incredibly significant our current work on earth needs to be then? Something recognizable from the old world had made it into the new world. Noah spent his entire life building that ark. He was devoted to his family, but he also devoted his family to that work. The face of the earth was swept clean by the worldwide flood. Only Noah, his family, and the animals made into the new world. His life work—building the ark—sure paid off big time. And I mean big time! (His preaching sucked, though. He couldn't get one other person outside his family to get on board? But anyway, how about that ark!) Today we know Jesus is the key to the New Ark we must build. So what is Jesus building? I'm sure you guessed it's the Church. But do you get the sense sometimes that what is happening in church these days has little to do with God's actual plan for the world? Let's ask the Lord to help us see Church in a whole new light. For the Kingdom of Heaven is at hand. That is, He is bringing about what Barnabas in his second century epistle called the "Eighth Day of Creation", *the beginning of another world.*[18]

---

18 R. Paul Stevens, *Disciplines of the Hungry Heart* (Vancouver, BC: Regent Bookstore, 1993), 205.

Discussion Questions

1. What is community transformation? What is it not?

2. How is the story of Noah relevant to us today?

3. Why do we need to "fireproof" our life's work? How do we do that?

4. Describe what is coming to the world and why we are not going to heaven when we die.

Chapter 14

THE 8TH DAY OF CREATION

"Aim at heaven and you get earth thrown in. Aim at earth and you get neither."
— C. S. Lewis

God created the universe in six days and rested on the seventh. Because Jesus has come, we're living in the Eighth Day of Creation right now. God is not done creating. Do you see why doing God things and not just good things is so critical? God is at work, and only God's work will matter in the end. Even good things done in the name of God will be burned away by God's refining fire. God things are fireproof. All our work needs to have that *non-combustible* quality. No wonder Paul urged us with great passion: "Therefore, my dear brothers, stand firm. Let nothing move you. Always give yourselves fully to *the work of the Lord*, because you know that your *labor in the Lord* is not in vain" (I Cor.15:58, italics mine). There is a labor which is not in vain and will stand the test of fire and time. It's totally worth dedicating your whole life to this work. And we are not to budge an inch from accomplishing it. Paul calls it "the work of the Lord"—the God thing.

Gordon Fee is perhaps the world's foremost authority on the work of the Holy Spirit in the epistles of Paul. Here's his comment on what we just read in Corinthians: "It is not absolutely certain what kind of activity Paul had in mind by the phrase 'the work of the Lord.' Minimally, it may refer more broadly to whatever one does *as a Christian*, both toward outsiders and fellow believers; but along with the next word, 'labor,' Paul frequently uses it to refer to the actual ministry of the gospel."[19]

So what should we be doing in the Eighth Day? The ministry of the gospel.

Soul winning. And I want to underscore how huge that is later. But it is more than that. It's not just *what* we do, but *how* we do it. The work of the Spirit must have the unmistakable mark of the Spirit on that work. The world can

---

19   Gordon D. Fee, *The First Epistle to the Corinthians* (Grand Rapids: Eerdmans Publishing, 1987), 808.

sniff out a phony pretty quickly. On the other hand, if our work is graced by the character of Jesus, then the world senses His presence and hears His voice. This is why Mother Teresa's ministry has had such a powerful impact on even the most diehard unbelievers.

Prof. Stevens once again sheds light on this:

"In some way beyond our understanding even the contributions we have made to life in this world, if done in faith, hope and love (I Cor. 13:13: I Thess. 1:3) will outlast the world, and may even have a place in the new earth, while many so-called Christian activities may go up in smoke on the Day and be burned with the hay and stubble (I Cor. 3:10-15)."[20]

Here Stevens alludes to how Paul commends the Thessalonians not for "loving their work" (which is often the highest accolade we can give to work in a secular society), but "instead, he affirmed them for being people whose "labor was *prompted by love*" (I Thess. 1:3 italics mine), a much deeper thing."[21] Often we hear people say, "I love my work." That's fine, but the greater question is, "Did love motivate my work?" Moreover, the Thessalonians are remembered before God for work "produced by faith" and "inspired by hope" in our Lord Jesus Christ.

Therefore, in the Eighth Day of Creation, we must do the work of the Lord and we must do it God's way. But we must also *work in light of Christ's return.* Stevens quotes C. S. Lewis: "The Christians who did the most for the present world were just those who thought most about the next...It is since Christians have largely ceased to think of the other world that they have become so ineffective in this. Aim at Heaven and you will get Earth thrown in; aim at Earth and you will get neither."[22]

The new world will be ushered in at the personal return of the Lord Jesus Christ. Christians are not Jehovah's Witnesses. We will not bring about the Kingdom of God apart from the direct intervention of the personal return of Jesus Christ to the earth. His return is what every believer longs for (Rev. 22:20) and mysteriously, we can even hasten Jesus' return (2 Pet. 3:11-12). As C. S. Lewis reminds us, it is when believers have their eyes fixed on the soon coming King, that they make the greatest impact for the Kingdom coming soon. The

---

20 Stevens. "Work and Heaven: God as Consummator," 68.

21 Stevens, *Disciplines of the Hungry Heart*, 18.

22 Stevens, "Work and Heaven: God as Consummator," 66.

reason for this is that a believer whose mind is fixed on the Return of Christ is not so tethered to the mundane concerns of this world. He is not planning to stick around! He realizes that compared with eternity, this life is the length of one breath and as brief as a heartbeat. So his work might be *in* this world but it is not *of* this world. It is *for* the next world and *of* the Lord. Believers must always work in light of the Second Coming.

That said, we cannot allow ourselves to become "so heavenly minded that we are no earthly good." During the early 1970's abortionists managed to legalize abortion in Hawaii and opened a floodgate to the nation which eventually led to the landmark case of Roe v. Wade. Since then an average of one million babies per year have been aborted in the greatest holocaust ever inflicted on humankind. (Do the math. That's 1 million per year since 1973.) During World War II, the Nazis slaughtered six million Jews. Stalin slaughtered twenty million Russians. The abortion holocaust dwarfs both of those combined. So where was the Church in 1970 when all this took place? Most of us were waiting for the rapture. The Second Coming of Christ should motivate us to dream passionately for the world, not send us adrift on a hyper-spiritual daydream. Because we know Jesus is coming soon, we become very engaged in business, education, and government.

There is, after all, something of our nationhood that makes it into the Holy City. "And the nations shall walk by its light, and the kings of the earth shall bring their glory into it...and they shall bring the glory and the honor of the nations into it" (Rev. 21:24-26). In some way beyond our imagination, the people of God contribute to the building of the New Jerusalem. "In some sense our environment is going to Heaven. So is our culture, our government, our crafts, and our work," states Stevens.[23] But sadly, too many believers see their life work as having no connection to the coming Kingdom. It is imperative for believers to set their hearts again toward building the Holy City.

The New Ark is the Church

How is Christ bringing about His Kingdom on the earth? Here's His answer: "And I also say to you that you are Peter, and upon this rock I will build My Church; and the gates of Hades shall not overpower it" (Mt. 16:18). Did you catch the co-creating and co-ruling between Jesus and Peter? Just like

---

23 Stevens. *Disciplines of the Hungry Heart*, 31.

Genesis! Jesus builds the Church, but He's also using the Church (Peter) as the means to build it. The Church is the end, but it's also the means. God's people are co-workers with God in building His Kingdom on the earth. But we also cooperate with what He's building in us. We are both the builders and the building. When we catch that we're in the Eighth Day.

So as we approach the end, God and His people are had at work building the New Ark—the Church of Jesus Christ. This is His vehicle of salvation of the present age. The true Church will carry us through into the new world. And every believer must discern which part of the ship he is to work on.

To do this God thing with Jesus, we need to understand the difference between an occupation and a vocation. An occupation is your job that occupies much of your work week. Vocation comes from the Latin word voce, or voice. A vocation is what we do when we hear the voice of God. We do our occupation to make money. But our vocation is what we are called to do. Noah's occupation was farming, but his vocation was preacher and ark builder. Paul's occupation was tent maker, but his vocation was apostle and church planter. Peter went from fisherman to fisher of men. Jesus went from carpenter to Messiah. For some there is a sense of "dropping your nets and following Him." We leave our occupation and devote our lives to our vocation. But that is not the case for everyone.

For the latter, the difficult question is how to integrate *vocation* with *occupation*. I was discussing this issue with a brother in Christ who, for his doctorate, was working on discovering a cure for Toxic Shock Syndrome (TSS). After a fascinating discussion on some of his findings, I said, "Ryan, your work has great eternal value. Think of all the ramifications of a Christian discovering the cure for TSS!" To which he added, "Yes, but it is not only the ministry potential which would give it value, but the entire experience surrounding the work: my work ethic, my relationships with co-researchers, my attitudes toward the whole project." Ryan got it! Because the Kingdom of God is in his heart, his work life is infused with Kingdom values. When we realize that "the Kingdom of God is at hand", our whole *work experience* is transformed. Our work becomes more than just a job. We become concerned for the personal growth and career advancement of our co-workers. We might demonstrate new zeal for the success of the company. The tone of our voice might express more patience and understanding when things don't go right. We might remember the birthdays and anniversaries of our co-workers. And very significantly, we develop *a deep burden for the personal salvation of everyone at work.* We pray for them and look for opportunities to share. The key is that our actions are prompted by love, produced by faith, and inspired by hope in our Lord Jesus Christ. Ryan is well on his way to successfully integrating *vocation* and *occupation.*

Later that night, I pondered how our existence on New Earth will be without pain, suffering, or death (Rev. 21:4). Even the very purpose of Ryan's work—finding a cure for TSS—reflects the heart of Jesus. He is building the Holy City. He is working in the Eighth Day.

Newbigin summarizes it this way: "We can commit ourselves without reserve to all the secular work our shared humanity requires of us, knowing that nothing we do in itself is good enough to form part of that city's building, knowing that everything–from our most secret prayers to our most public political acts–is part of that sin-stained human nature that must go down into the valley of death and judgment, and yet knowing that as we offer it up to the Father in the name of Christ and in the power of the Spirit, it is safe with him and–purged in fire–it will find its place in the holy city at the end."[24]

The story of Noah holds the key for understanding community transformation. By God's grace Noah was given the "plan of salvation," then he "worked out" his salvation. Because he was in tune with God's purposes, he knew his life vocation, and carefully sealed his labors with the pitch of faith, hope, and love. In the eyes of the world Noah's vocation was an object of derision and scorn, but in the eyes of God it was his vessel to a new world. Today Jesus tells us He is building a New Ark—the Church. And He invites us to come aboard an amazing journey—one that will take us safely into the new world.

Our Great Co-Mission with Jesus

So what's our focus? When Jesus gave us the Great Commission He said, "Make disciples of all nations, and I am with you always to the end of time." Authentic community transformation happens only as the nations become genuine followers of Christ. It does not happen by educational reform. Our goal is not to make everyone politically conservative. Society will not change because we insist on hanging the Ten Commandments in our courtrooms or putting Nativity scenes at city hall. Passing laws banning Gay marriage does not sud-

---

24 Newbigin. *Honest Religion for Secular Man,* 136.

denly make them heterosexual. I know Christians get really worked up about this, but we need to keep it all in perspective. We are not here to *Christianize* everyone. We are here to make everyone *Christian*. When we Christianize we are trying to make society look Christian from the outside in. Becoming a Christian happens from the inside out.

Now let me balance that off. In America we have the right to vote. We need to exercise that right powerfully as Christians and vote for righteous leaders. It is an important part of the transformation of our communities. For example, Gay marriage and abortion violate God's will. When it comes to voting it is not about right versus left but right versus wrong. Our first criteria is not Republican versus Democrat or conservative versus liberal, but rather righteous versus unrighteous. The State Motto of Hawaii is "Ua mau ke ea o ka aina i ka pono." "The life of the land is perpetuated in righteousness." That was first penned by Kamehameha III during those early missionary years as he had given his heart to Christ. As we look at the state of the union today, that has never been truer.

Let me add that the way Christians express themselves has massive impact. Not everyone who is homosexual is a Gay activist. To homosexuals who are struggling with their sexual identity like everyone else, our approach should be *compassion that leads them to clarity*. To Gay activists who are trying to redefine marriage and family, our response should be *clarity born of compassion*.

So Christians are engaged in every facet of society. But we have one, clarion mission—*evangelism*. If we really want to see our communities transform, then focus like a laser on this one thing—the *new birth*. It's got to be a God thing. As you already know, once a person encounters Jesus, it's all over. They will never be the same again. I love this quote from John Piper in his book, *Finally Alive*:

> "So if your heartache is for your own personal change, or for change in your marriage, or change in your prodigal children, or in your church, or in the systemic structures of injustice, or in the political system, or in the hostilities among nations, or in the human degradation of the environment, or in the raunchiness of our entertainment culture, or in the miseries of the poor, or in the callous opulence of the rich, or in the inequities of educational opportunity, or in arrogant attitudes of ethnocentrism, or in a hundred areas of human need caused by some form of human greed—if

your heart aches for any of these, then you should care supremely about the new birth."[25]

Midwife the new birth in people's lives. Let's ask the Lord how this happens on a community-wide scale. The reality of an "open heaven" is profoundly intriguing. Scripture says, "He saw the heavens opening" (Mk. 1:10 NAS). How many of us have been praying for revival? How many of us have been praying *for years* for revival? Me too. And what I am about to say should not be construed as a word against praying for revival. Story goes that Charles Finney, the great revivalist, was about to preach. Just before speaking the organizers of the rally gathered around him. Just then one of the guys said, "We're so glad you are here because we have been praying for revival for two years! May we pray for you?" Jokingly, Finney said, "No, thank you. You've been praying for revival for two years, and God doesn't hear your prayers!" He was being funny, but maybe Finney understood something. Sometimes we need to stop praying for revival and start reviving people!

There are times when it is not God's will for us to pray but to obey. We have been teaching some classic Spiritual disciplines that the Church has used for thousands of years to draw near to the presence of God. First and foremost we seek His face. But once we have encountered the *presence* of God, we catch the *heart* of God. And He came to seek and to save lost people. Spiritual disciplines—solitude, silence, sabbath, etc.—are not ends in themselves. We must not come to a place where we become satisfied with merely doing disciplines. "Well, I did my devotions for today. Glad that's over with!" And we shut our bibles and move on to the next thing. Their primary purpose is the Face of God, but once we're there, be ready to obey what God tells us in His presence. The Lord told Joshua, "Rise up! Why is it that you have fallen on your face?" (Josh. 7:10, 13 NAS) *Joshua was praying when he should've been obeying.* The Lord brought Joshua into His Presence, and then sent Him out to conquer the Promised Land. We reach a moment when it's time to stop praying and start conquering!

When Jesus was baptized in the Jordan River, He saw an open heaven. That's when the Spirit rested on His shoulder like a dove. And He performed

---

25 John Piper, *Finally Alive: What Happens When We Are Born Again* (Minneapolis, MN: Desiring God Foundation, 2009), 191-192.

extraordinary works. At the end of His ministry He prophesied about His disciples, "Greater works than these will he do" (Jn. 14:12 NAS). He meant for His baptism in the Spirit to be the prototype for ours. Statements like these are exciting, but they're also disturbing. I don't believe my church has come anywhere near the "greater works" Jesus is prophesying here. So I tense up when I read that. (In Hawaii we say, "I stay pinching." Don't ask.) But I want to get there. I don't want to find some theological loophole that excuses us from being the Church Jesus envisioned. Jesus does not say, "Do greater works." It's more of a prediction: "Greater works will he do." So what do you do when Jesus prophesies a reality that you're not fully experiencing yet? Here it is:

We should allow God to define our experience, not redefine His word to match our experience.

We don't need to make anything happen. Allow Jesus to build this in us. Just don't miss any opportunities He puts before you. Before He ascended into heaven He said, "But you shall receive power when the Holy Spirit has come upon you; and you shall be My witnesses both in Jerusalem, and in all Judea and Samaria, and even to the remotest part of the earth" (Acts 1:8 NAS). Jesus' baptism in the Holy Spirit was the prototype for Pentecost. But lest you conclude that this is only a contention for signs and wonders (as crucial as that is), keep going!

At Pentecost Peter and the Apostles were baptized in the Holy Spirit and received the same capacity as Jesus to transform the world. It was clear from Peter's sermon on that day that he realized that everything Jesus prophesied had come true. Peter declared that this was the fulfillment of what the Prophet Joel said centuries earlier, "And it shall be in the last days, God says, that I will pour forth of My Spirit upon all mankind; and your sons and your daughters shall prophesy, and your young men shall see visions, and your old men shall dream dreams" (Acts 2:17 NAS; cf. Joel 2:28).

The New Covenant, specifically Paul, introduces us to a new term for the new person we become when we are filled with His Spirit—*pneumatika*, spirit people (1 Cor. 3:1; Gal. 6:1 NKJV). As we are transformed from glory to glory we become people of the Spirit—*Pneumatika*.

When Jesus shows up, you get open heaven. When you get open heaven, people are filled with His Spirit. When you get people on fire with His Spirit, then other people come to Christ. Through Spiritual disciplines we live in a God-soaked world the way Jesus did. As we are baptized in the Spirit like Jesus, we take on not only His character but His supernatural ministry. We have both Christ-like character and Christ-like ministry. Believers are *pneumatika*. Jesus' vision is of a Church endowed with His own supernatural presence performing greater works than even His own earthly ministry. I always have to scratch my head as I humble myself before John 14:12. But, hey, it's a God thing! Of course it's over my head. It's Jesus Himself once again at work! Only now the Church has become the body through whom Jesus Himself *continues* to do His *greater* work. Gordon Fee states, "Above everything else, as fulfillment of the new covenant, the Spirit marked the return of the lost presence of God."[26] Community transformation happens as believers are Spiritually transformed into—here it is—*hosts of God's presence and power on the earth.*

We began our journey by saying that Spiritual transformation happens from glory to glory, degree by degree (2 Cor. 3:18). The first step remains our supreme desire. God brought us into a relationship with Jesus. Now we long for greater intimacy with God. But where is Jesus? What's He up to? Well, He's spanning the globe turning people into His followers! He said, "As you transform the nations into My disciples, I am always right there beside you." *If you're looking for Jesus, you'll find Him in the harvest field.* Jesus didn't send us away on a mission. He's doing the mission with us! This is our Great Co-Mission with Jesus.

What is coming to the world? "The kingdoms of this world have become the kingdoms of our Lord and of His Christ and He will reign forever and ever" (Rev. 11:15 NKJV)! Here are a couple of powerful examples of community transformation.

The Good Ol' Days

On April 4, 1820, a small band of American missionaries from New England landed on the shores of Hawaii. A few years earlier a young Native Hawaiian named Henry Opukaha`ia came to Christ at Yale College and became impassioned by God to return home to Hawaii and share his newfound faith with his people. Unfortunately, he became ill with Typhus Fever and died at the age of 26. From his deathbed he pleaded with his fellow divinity students to take the Gospel of the Kingdom back to his people. Hiram Bingham and

---

26 Gordon D. Fee, *Paul, the Spirit, and the People of God* (Peabody, MA: Hendrickson Publishers, 1996), 10.

his team answered the call and landed in Kailua-Kona on the Big Island on April 4, 1820.

Over the next 50 years more and more missionaries would arrive, transforming Hawaii from a heathen place to the Kingdom of God. Hiram Bingham became a trusted counselor to the royal family, advising them wisely on dealings with foreigners. Other missionaries helped the business economy, established the education system, and reformed Hawaiian family life. The missionaries brought a printing press with them on their maiden voyage to print bibles. When they realized the Hawaiians had only an oral tradition, the Christians developed an alphabet and taught them to read and write. They were engaged in every facet of society, but they never took their eyes off the ball. They helped the nation of Hawaii become disciples of Jesus. They were engaged in authentic community transformation.

By 1870 possibly as high as 90% of the Kingdom of Hawaii had come to Christ, making it one of the most successful missionary endeavors in the history of the Church. So successful in fact, the American Board of Commissions on Foreign Missions (ABCFM), declared the Hawaii mission "closed" on its 50-year Jubilee Celebration. By that time the Hawaiians were evangelizing other island nations, including the cannibals of Marquesas. The Kingdom of Hawaii had been transformed into the Kingdom of God on Earth.

Here's another great illustration of powerful community transformation. Sister Aimee Semple McPherson was the founder of the Foursquare Church and a powerful hostess of God's Presence—*pneumatikos*. Her Spirit-empowered ministry at Angelus Temple had given Los Angeles a vivid taste of community transformation. Heaven had come to earth and people were being saved, the blind could see, the lame could walk, and captives were being set free. Describing her approach to ministry Sister Aimee said,

"We do not have an evangelistic ministry. We preach Jesus Christ as Savior. We do not have a healing ministry. We proclaim Jesus Christ as healer. We do not teach the baptism of the Holy Spirit. We profess Jesus as the baptizer in the Holy Spirit. We do not have a ministry for social change. We believe Jesus is the King of heaven and earth."

Ministry is not first about church any more than church is first about ministry. Our focus is not first on salvations, healings, baptisms, leadership, discipleship, children, youth, seniors, the poor, justice, politics, America, or even transformation. The focus must never be taken off the person of the Lord Jesus Christ. Excellent church leaders will approach ministry with His leadership on their sleeves. With Him now squarely in the fore view, transformation is understood correctly as the on-going, daily invasion of the kingdom of heaven onto the earth. It is the by-product of praying daily, "Thy kingdom come, Thy will be done on earth as it is in heaven."

Jesus on Jesus

After Jesus was resurrected, He met up with two of the disciples on the road to Emmaus. In that account we read, "Then beginning with Moses and with all the prophets, He explained to them the things concerning Himself in all the Scriptures" (Lk. 24:27 NAS). Imagine that. Jesus takes time out to speak in detail to just two guys on how the Old Testament pointed to Him. That's one bible commentary I wish I had! Jesus on Jesus. Maybe like me, you don't lead a big ministry. You feel like, "Why would Jesus reveal Himself to someone like me? I'm nothing special." So you buy all these books by experts on ministry, go to every conference with the latest speakers, and spend thousands of dollars on seminary. Been there, done that, got the t-shirt. And I am not saying you shouldn't do all that. But would you at least be as insistent that Jesus be with you? Every discipline outlined in *God Things* is there to help us embrace His personal touch on our lives. He will reveal Himself to you too just like He did with those two guys on the road to Emmaus.

Through Eternal Eyes

He doesn't send us out on a mission. He invites us on a co-mission with Him. Jesus' words to us in the Great Commission are amazing not only for *what* He said, but *when* He said them. He spoke them after being resurrected. So they are the words of a formerly dead person. Have you ever said to yourself, *"If I only knew back then what I know now."*

When I was in first grade, I had a crush on a girl named Mary Jo. But back then you weren't supposed to like girls. They had coodies. They were gross. So even though I liked her, I never told her how I felt. What did I know? I was six.

Fast forward to middle school. In 7th grade, it became ok to like girls. I can't remember exactly which of the guys broke rank first, but it seemed liked all the cool "mature" guys had girlfriends. Mary Jo, *if I only knew back then what I know now.* Life sure is different when you're twelve. And so began my "Filipino playboy" years, and jumping from relationship to relationship.

Fast forward again. Now I'm 25 years old. It's our wedding day. The Filipino playboy thing has definitely lost its appeal. In fact, it turned out to be one of the most disappointing and empty philosophies I ever believed in. And with my bride now standing here by my side at the altar before the Lord, I wish I could do that part of my life completely over. *If I only knew back then what I know now.*

And so my life went on. At every major milestone, I found myself looking back on my life and saying, *"If only I knew back then what I know now!"* At 35 it was compound interest and real estate. At 45, it was home equity. What will it be at 65, 75, and 95?

As a pastor, I have had the unique experience of sitting with several people at their deathbed. They are normally surrounded by family. And if they are conscious and can speak, they wonder about God. In all my years of ministry, never once have I heard someone in his last moments say, "If I only spent a few more hours working overtime at the job, my life would be fulfilled," or, "If only I had bought that third BMW." No, their thoughts turn to family...and to God. Some look back with sadness on their deathbeds and say, *"If I only knew back then what I know now."*

But let's take this one step further. What if you died? What if you could depart this life and enter the next life? What if you could have a perspective on this life from *beyond life?* Such a life would be divinely inspired, for you would be looking at mortality *through eternal eyes.* It would be the ultimate experience of *if only I knew back then what I know now.*

Mt. 28 is after Jesus has risen from the dead. So these are the words of a formerly dead guy. He could have said, "Hey Peter, remember all that stuff I said about doing my Father's will, accomplishing His work? Forget it. I was wrong. There's nothing back there. When I died I saw everything and there's nothing after you die!" Well, that's not what He said.

Instead He comes back from the dead and says *with all the authority in the universe,* "Make disciples of all nations, baptize them, and teach them to obey Me. It is all that's going to a matter in the end. I've seen the next life, and I've come back to tell you. Trust me, I know."

At the end of your life, you will pass into eternity just like Jesus did. What will you find? You will discover a spiritual community Jesus calls His Kingdom, and it is made up of His followers He calls His disciples. And so if in this life you devoted yourself to being His disciple and helping other people become His disciples, you will *not* find yourself in the next life saying, *"If only I knew back then what I know now."*

President John F. Kennedy once said, "Let us go forth to lead the land we love, asking His blessing and His help, but knowing that here on earth, God's work must truly be our own." Kennedy's spiritual life is a mystery, but that was well said.

In conclusion, community transformation is this massive God thing that's been going full-steam ahead since Jesus came. Maybe the end is near, maybe it's not. But one thing's for sure, the end is *next*. Christians need a perspective of fireproofing our life work like Noah waterproofed his. We do that by working toward the relentless heaven-on-earth reality that is bursting forth on the scene before us. For we are living in God's Eighth Day of Creation where He is building a New Ark—the Church of Jesus Christ. Jesus is building the Church, but the Church is also co-builder with Jesus. We are on a co-mission with Him. He has returned from the dead to tell us He has seen the new world. And with all the authority in the universe He says, "Look for me on the harvest fields making disciples of all nations. It's the only thing that will matter in the end."

Discussion Questions

1. What is the "Eighth Day of Creation?" And how do we cooperate with what God is creating?

2. What is the New Ark God is building today? How is He building it? Through what means?

GOD THINGS

3. What is our co-mission with Jesus? By faith what is God saying to you about the mission of the Church?

4. Explain what this means: "If I only knew back then what I know now."

5. In light of what you now know, how is the Lord calling you to obedience?

150

EPILOGUE

The waters have receded now. The ark has run aground on what Noah will later realize is the top of Mount Ararat. The azure sky is clear and glorious, and there is a chill in the air on this high peak. Noah and his family step forth from the great bow of their faithful vessel. He turns and places his hand on its gopher-wood hull one more time. No words, just overwhelming gratitude. For a moment he remembers the lifetime of labor they spent building it...and the pain. But only for a moment. His wife puts a warm cloak on the shoulders of her husband. "You were right this time," she says, as Noah turns and embraces her. As he opens his eyes, his expression blossoms to utter amazement as he gazes for the first time on the grandeur of the new world before him. The valley below him is a lush green, the ocean a deep blue. His animals roam freely. Just then a dove captures his attention as it flies skyward, and that's when he sees it. The rainbow of the Lord. Noah and his family fall to their knees and worship El Yeshua, the God who saved them. Jesus.

Final Thoughts

After 30 years of ministry, you get tired of playing church. And you hunger for the real thing. You see the church's unseemly underbelly—the consumerism, hypocrisy, bureaucracy, sectarianism, narcissism, religiosity, harlotry, duplicity...well, you get the idea. And you want nothing to do with that. It makes you want to puke. In fact, I think Jesus actually did once in that passage that says, "I spit you out of my mouth" (Rev. 3:16). The Greek word "emeo" could be translated as vomit, spew, upchuck, or hurl.

Simultaneously, you see amazing transformation. My mother-in-law, Joyce, was a lifelong Buddhist and came to Christ at 81 years of age. Another guy named Gilbert (totally unsaved) was on his deathbed. All I said to him was, "Gilbert, it looks like you might be seeing Jesus soon." And with his family and friends standing around him starts saying, "That's right. And I accept Jesus into my heart as my Lord and Savior. I turn away from my sin and ask His forgiveness. I believe in Him with all my heart, etc." I mean, Gilbert went on like that for a full minute non-stop! It was the easiest time I ever had trying to lead somebody to Christ. I'll never forget it. Then there's this boy in my church who suffered from a rare blood disease with no known cure and was miraculously healed. One day our church gave a $45,000 love offering to help build a school for horrifically abused orphans in Uganda. It built a whole dormitory! There are several couples whose marriages were on the verge of divorce who did a full 180, and today they've become some of the best volunteers you've ever seen. I saw an exhausted, sleep-deprived, mother of four become an outstanding, full-time pastor. I watched my firstborn son become a full-time pastor. Seriously, I could go on and on. The list is endless. It is as endless as the list of unseemly stuff.

What was the one thing that made all the difference between these two lists? Well, you know the answer—the God thing! So a few years ago, I decided I wanted nothing to do with that other church and just be totally focused on *the* Church. I stopped doing "ministry" and just focused on Jesus. I realized that all my attempts to pump people up for Jesus weren't helping anyway. They eventually ran out of gas, then ran to another church. What they needed was their own encounter. Once activated, there would be no stopping them.

So I prayed, "Lord, would You help me grow in intimacy with You today." Nothing weird. At church, staff meetings, *every* meeting, I would just acknowledge His presence to lead us. It's not an "opening prayer." It's a genuine invocation or invitation for Jesus to show up. I would pray, "Lord, you are the head of the Church, not me. We invite Your guidance as our Chief Shepherd. Without You, we're sunk anyway. We want none of our own plans to succeed. We only want to do what You are doing, build what You are building. We want to be who You want us to be—the receptacles of Your presence on the earth."

At our Christian college we invite Jesus to teach class. It's the exact opposite of secular colleges where you're not even allowed to say the name of Jesus. At New Hope Christian College, we *insist* on His presence. We still have our liturgy, programs, sermons, and lesson plans (because the Spirit also plans ahead). But we're highly sensitized to His real-time promptings. And then we would proceed with our session. But we're also waiting to see what happens. Without fail, there is that moment when you become consciously aware of His presence. Of course He's been there all along. But sometimes He's like the guy who's been sitting there silent throughout the meeting and then decides to speak up. And when He does, it is truly life transforming. We have promise after promise that He would be with us to the end of the age, where two or more are gathered, personally building the Church. So we're just taking Jesus at His word.

Sometimes it feels like being the true Church is such a fragile, brittle thing. With one subtle turn in our hearts, we instantly degenerate into some lower form. Church becomes about something else with but the slightest whisper. And it's because these other things seem so good. As C. S. Lewis said, "Brass is more mistaken for gold than clay is." We start off worshiping Jesus, but then slip into worshiping worship without even realizing. We want to evangelize the world for Jesus, then end up as "evangelists" who forget about Jesus. Healing ministries become more about the healing than the Healer. We deform instead of transform. Church ceases to be about God because of 1,001 good things.

There are good things, and then there are God things. We can burn ourselves out doing 1,001 good things. Worse yet, we can spend a whole lifetime doing good things, only to have Jesus tell us in the end, "Get away from Me, I never knew you" (Mt. 7:23). Or, we can wait for the God thing and grow deeper and deeper in love with Jesus. Heaven is not a place, it's a Person. Heaven is a Who before it is a where. If this book helped you get a little further down that road, then I consider that a God thing.

APPENDIX

DISSERTATION NOTES

INTRODUCTION

Hypothesis

A course on Spiritual Transformation will enhance the development of community trans-formers at New Hope Christian College in Honolulu, Hawaii.

Background and Significance

This research project began with the concern that the pastor of New Hope Central Oahu had only a vision for building his own church plant congregation rather than the kingdom vision of community transformation. What would it take to break this pastor out of the narrow vision of "church growth" to the kingdom vision of discipling nations? How could he expand his present job description of working within the borders of the four walls of his own congregation to a *borderless* job description of reaching his city for Christ? How could he be re-trained to see every person in his community as a part of his congregation rather than just the crowd he sees on Sunday morning? As if the demands of developing his own internal church staff team were not difficult enough, how could he now find time to co-labor with other senior pastors in his city for community transformation? Would they even be interested? And when he solved those issues, how could he then become a transformer of nations? So this research journey began with trying to understand the biblical, theological, and applicational challenges of being a "community transformation church."

Then, in the third year of the Doctor of Ministry program (August 2007), an unexpected tragedy took place. A spiritual mentor, whom this researcher held in the highest esteem, informed the researcher of multiple, clandestine, adulterous affairs he had engaged in for decades during the time of their ministry together. It was heartbreaking news of unimaginable proportions. There was absolutely no hint of impropriety during the years they had been together, and so the researcher was completely blind-sided by this revelation. This spiritual father had established an ultra-conservative counter-culture in the fellowship that was respected as exemplary among the Christian ministries of that day. News of high-profile Christian leaders experiencing moral failure is always gut-wrenching, but this one was deeply personal. It had a profound impact on the researcher and adjusted the emphasis of this professional project. The phrase "glaring issue" was born.

Believing that the timing of these events had to be orchestrated by the Holy Spirit, the researcher now began to explore the devastating effects of moral failures on a congregation and its astounding impact on the outcomes of community transformation. How can a senior pastor retain his vision for community transformation when he must simultaneously confront "glaring issues" of sin in his own soul? At one point the researcher asked himself, "This is a fine question but is it completely separate from the question of developing community transformation churches?" That is precisely when breakthrough occurred! "What then is the transformation to which one is called if there is no essential, qualitative difference between Christians and non-Christians, let alone Christian *senior pastors?*" the researcher pondered. It was a compelling moment; perhaps even a divine one. An adjustment to the current professional project was no longer optional; it had become an imperative.

The Transformation Scale or "T-Scale" is a simple graphic or visual aid illustrating how both the vertical, y-axis of nexus intimacy with God and the horizontal x-axis of kingdom influence in the community are essential to the Spiritual transformation process of community transformers. Heaven and earth must first converge within the Christian leader before the world can be transformed.

Definitions of Terms
Community Transformation
The inevitable, irresistible establishment of the kingdom of Christ on earth as it is in heaven through the agency of the prevailing Church filled with the eschatological Spirit. Community transformation has to do with the coming of that kingdom both as future, prophetic destiny *and* current, eschatological reality.

Community Transformer
A Christian who has adopted the call and vision of community transformation, lives in nexus intimacy with the Trinity, has developed perichoretic identity, and cooperates with like-minded Christian leaders perpetuating uranogaic influence.

Spiritual Transformation
The process of learning to dwell in nexus intimacy with God as Father, Son, and Holy Spirit, resulting in the formation of perichoretic identity (Abba's child) and every spiritual implication of that reality: growing freedom from glaring issues (strongholds), embracing virtuous character, adopting a Christian worldview, and ministering in Spirit-empowerment in increasing measure from glory to glory.

Nexus Intimacy
Specifically, nexus means "connection point": onto-relational dwelling within the Trinity—God's empowering, manifest presence; whereas the Holy Spirit is the third person of the Trinity, and whereas the Holy Spirit fills a person, therefore the person exists in the unspeakably joyful reality of perichoretic union with God, becoming the locus of His presence on the earth. Intimacy suggests "knowledge" or revelational access to the mind, purposes, and nature of God. Thus, onto-relational becomes onto-revelational. In "Diagram A" it is the Y-axis of vertical intimate union with God.

Perichoretic Identity
Identity formation is the abandonment of the "orphan spirit" in favor of full adoption as a child of the Father. The phrase "perichoretic identity" is used to link identity formation with onto-relational connection with the Trinity. Identity is the Y-X intersection of "who I am" and "what I do." Implication? Because a child of the Father knows what the Father is doing and thinking, their ministry is about God-things not solely good-things.

Uranogaic Influence
Influence is the ushering in of the kingdom of heaven (οὐρανός/uranos) onto the earth (γῆ / gai) (Matt. 6:10) through a child of God who has become

a community transformer. "Uranogaic influence" is contending for all that exists in heaven—total submission to the sovereignty of Christ, worship in His manifest presence, virtuous character, freedom from sin, absence of sickness, deliverance from evil, etc.—to exist on the earth. In "Diagram A" it is the X-axis of horizontal ministry with people as by-product of the Y-axis of vertical intimacy with God.

Glaring Issue

A stronghold or issue of sin in the life of a minister so *glaringly self-obvious* that if left unresolved, could result in the end of his/her ministry; a sin issue which could be a gateway to a potentially career-ending disaster.

Trinity

God's self-revelation in the holy scripture as three persons—the Father, Son, and Holy Spirit—each being fully God, yet existing as one God not three separate gods; formulated by the Council of Constantinople (381 AD) and articulated in the Athanasian Creed. In His very essence God reveals that He is relational.

Perichoresis

Verna Harrison states that perichoresis is a transliteration from the Greek which means "interpenetration," first used in a theological context by Gregory Nazianzus (329-389 AD) to describe the interaction of the persons of the Trinity with one another and with God's children in transfigured creation.[27] Perichoresis: "peri" means "around" as in "perimeter" or "periscope;" "choresis" is the root of "choreography." Hence, a Christian's identity comes from "dancing around" with God.

Pneumatika

The Spirit people or spiritual ones; the true Church as believers filled with the Holy Spirit, hosting His presence to the earth, bringing kingdom reality and transforming communities, cities, and nations.

---

27 Verna Harrison, "Perichoresis in her Greek Fathers, from St. Vladimir's Theological Quarterly (Vol. 35, No. 1, 1991), 54.

Transformation Scale (t-Scale)

A simple graph or visual aid intended to remind community transformers of the importance of progressing along both the vertical y-axis of nexus intimacy with God and the horizontal x-axis of community transformation. Its similarity to the cross is intentional.

CHAPTER ONE

BIBLICAL-THEOLOGICAL BASE

Comprehending God's Heart for Transformation

The concern of this project is the development of a practical model for Spiritual transformation that produces effective community transformers at New Hope Christian College in Honolulu, Hawaii. This focus, however, is a single cord with multiple strands. What are the key biblical-theological issues relevant to the formation of a community transformer? As postulated they would need to confront issues affecting both nexus intimacy along the vertical y-axis and community transformation along the horizontal x-axis. What follows is a review of biblical-theological issues that are considered critical to the formation of an effective community transformer:

1. Understand the ultimate outcome of Spiritual transformation as nexus intimacy with the triune God: Father, Son, and Holy Spirit.

2. Learn how nexus intimacy forms onto-relational, perichoretic identity, leading to uranogaic influence which defines and advances true, biblical community transformation.

3. Understand the biblical view of one's sexual identity.

4. Comprehend the biblical purpose of Spiritual disciplines as "clearing a pathway for the seeking Father" toward immersion theology versus moralism, neo-gnosticism, or sectarianism.

5. Discern the negative, deleterious effects of "ministry" on the human soul.

6. Identify strongholds or glaring issues and how the Spiritual transformation process brings freedom.

7. Learn how Spiritual disciplines empower Christians to *choose* "no" (askesis) to sin and "yes" (aisthesis) to obedience.

8. Awareness of some of the classical Spiritual disciplines of the Christian faith: (1) solitude and silence, (2) prayer and fasting, (3) celibacy, (4) stewardship (or frugality) and secrecy, (5) service and submission, (6) sabbath, (7) study and meditation, (8) bible journaling, (9) worship and celebration, and (10) fellowship or Spiritual community.

9. Characterize community transformers as pneumatika: synthesizing the practices of resurrection, pentecost, and hosting His presence toward a new heaven and new earth.
10. Utilize the "Transformation Scale" (T-Scale) as a paradigm for progress along both the vertical y-axis of nexus intimacy with God and the horizontal x-axis of community transformation.

The Outcome of Spiritual Transformation

Teaching Outcome: Convey the ultimate outcome of Spiritual transformation as nexus intimacy with the triune God: Father, Son, and Holy Spirit.

What is wrong with the world? And what are Christians to do about what is wrong with the world? The answers to these questions are founded in teleology, i.e. the study of design and purpose. And teleology is rooted in theology. For human beings the fundamental implication of God as Trinity is His onto-relational nature as basis for both intimacy with Him and fellowship with others. God does not simply desire a personal relationship with human beings; He is relational in essence. Human beings are made in the image of God and are therefore likewise predisposed to be intensely relational. The result is an ontological yearning for God and others which powerfully manifests itself not from mere emotional need (or neediness) but from the fundamental core definition of what it means to be human. Human beings were created by a divine being who used His own onto-relational design as the blueprint for their creation. Therefore, while humans "suffer" from an ontological yearning for God and others, God Himself "suffers" the same ontological yearning for His children. Far from being a deficiency on God's part, this "suffering" originates from the way God be's[1] and serves as a kind of Master plan for comprehending theology, cosmology, anthropology—basically everything! This project refers to this concept as the "Ultimate Theory of Everything" (UTE).

God is one God *and* He exists as three persons—Father, Son, and Holy Spirit—relating to one another perfectly and eternally. This unique interpersonal, intrapersonal, interpenetrating relationship is described as perichoresis. Perhaps its first clear articulation was in the Athanasian Creed (4th century):

---

1   Wess Pinkham's description on the perichoretic inter/intra-relationship of the Trinity as heard in lectures to students in the Doctor of Ministry program at The King's Seminary, Van Nuys, CA, 2004-2006.

"The Father is God, the Son is God, and the Holy Spirit is God, and yet there are not three Gods but one God." As the Holy Spirit dwells within a believer he/she is given access to the perichoresis of the Trinity. James B. Torrance comments on the importance of the Trinity:

"At the center of the New Testament stands not our religious experience, not our faith or repentance or decision, however important these are, but a unique relationship...between Jesus and the Father...By His Spirit He draws men and women to participate both in His life of worship and communion with the Father and in His mission from the Father to the world."[2]

As Thomas F. Torrance summarizes, "One Being, Three Persons; Three Persons, One Being; Trinity in Unity and Unity in Trinity."[3] The implications for human relationship with God are enormous while the potentiality for humans in relationship with other humans is staggering.

Grenz weighs in on the Ultimate Theory of Everything: "Foundational to our entire world view is our testimony that we have come to know the only true God. We understand ourselves, our experience, and even the world itself from the perspective of our acknowledgment of the God who chooses to be known by his creatures."[4] Zizioulas contends for the Church universal to heed the implications of the UTE:

"The Church is not simply an institution. She is a 'mode of existence,' *a way of being.* The mystery of the Church, even in its institutional dimension, is deeply bound to the being of man, the being of the world and to the very being of God...Orthodoxy concerning the being of God is not a luxury for the Church and for man: it is an existential necessity."[5]

---

2   James B. Torrance, *Worship, Community and the Triune God of Grace* (Downers Grove, IL: Inter-Varsity Press, 1996), 30-31.

3   Thomas F. Torrance, *The Christian Doctrine of God: One Being Three Persons* (Edinburgh, Scotland and New York, NY: T & T Clark LTD, 1996), 112, 136, & 168.

4   Stanley J. Grenz, *Theology for the Community of God* (Grand Rapids: Eerdmans, 1994), 29.

5   John D. Zizioulas, *Being as Communion: Studies in Personhood and he Church* (Crestwood, NY: St. Vladimir's Seminary Press, 1997), 15.

As Zizioulas highlights, it is God's *way-of-being* that establishes the foundation for the Church's *way-of-being*, indeed, what the world's *way-of-being* ought to be.

What is wrong with the world? And what are Christians to do about what is wrong with the world? It is all about connections versus disconnections. The *telos* of humans is to *be* in connection with God. When sin disconnects humans from God, there is a rupture in the human spirit and the human soul, affecting the human's physical reality. Martin Buber, best known for reviving Hasidic Judaism, refers to this as the "severed" life in contrast with the intensely relational, deeply personal life of "I and Thou (God)."[6] The consequences of this rupture are tragically comprehensive. Disconnection ruptures a human's spiritual *being-in-the-presence* of God. What follows is the rupturing of the human's *being*, fracturing one's identity and clouding one's sense of purpose. A severed life means that all human existence will now be lived in egocentricity. The world and all human relationships suffer the abuse of persons whose primary obsession is self.

The Gospel of Jesus Christ is God's rescue plan for a severed world. Golgotha was the ultimate expression of God's ontological yearning, healing the rupture between Himself, His human beings, and His creation. Calgary perfectly satisfies the justice requirements of a holy God as evidenced by the empty tomb. Faith in Christ establishes and assures relationship with God in heaven for all eternity, but beyond this, human *way-of-being* on earth is also being redeemed. Spiritual connection is restored as Christ ushers human beings *beyond the veil* and back into the fellowship of the Trinity. The Person of the Holy Spirit inhabits a person, transforming personhood—identity and purpose. A transforming person may now cooperate with God in transforming the world. Transforming lives transform lives. Just as the consequences of disconnection were tragically comprehensive, so too are the blessings of connection likewise comprehensive. Spiritual transformation then is a kind of journey back to Eden; back to a *way-of-being* when God, humans, and the world lived in harmonious connectivity (nexus) and loving community (intimacy) with one another. Obviously, there is

---

6   Martin Buber, *I and Thou* (New York, NY: Simon & Schuster, 1996), 56-57, 93. While the father of modern Hasidic Judaism casts a clear of vision of what should take place, it is Christianity—specifically, Pentecostal Spirituality—which provides God's answer: the Holy Spirit indwelling the Church.

no going back to Eden; but it is always helpful to look back to Eden inasmuch as such an exercise provides a clear vision forward to a *way-of-being* intended by God. As Zizioulas points out, comprehending God's *way-of-being* is indeed an existential necessity to understanding what is wrong with the world and what Christians can do about it. Existential necessity leads to experiential reality. Spiritual transformation perpetuates community transformation.

Here is the mission statement of New Hope Central Oahu, the researcher's pastorate: "The purpose of New Hope Central Oahu is to connect people with God and equip them to be fruitful followers of Christ." In terms of transformation connection with God is seen as the Ultimate Theory of Everything. The motto of the State of Hawaii is "the life of the land is perpetuated in righteousness." In Hawaiian it is written, "ua mau ke ea o ka aina i ka pono." It is a not-so-subtle declaration by the state's founding fathers of their belief that God's righteousness was absolutely indispensable to the prosperity of Hawaii's people. The reference to the land was also purposeful and consistent with the Hebrew notion of the land being blessed as well as that of other native peoples. Connection with God solves what is wrong with the world.

The following, therefore, are not the *ultimate* outcomes of Spiritual transformation: personal character development, godliness, holiness, ministry proficiency, a better life, better relationships, happiness, self-improvement, spiritual power, or spiritual maturity. Indeed, spiritual transformation is not the ultimate outcome of Spiritual transformation! It is not an end in itself, but rather a means to a much higher end. The ultimate outcome of Spiritual transformation is nexus intimacy with the triune God.

Spiritual transformation is understood as *Spirit*-ual transformation. It is not spirituality as understood by New Agers, psychics, or Oprah. It is a personal encounter with Jesus Christ, the Holy *Spirit*, in on-going relationship with the Father.

Peterson defines Spirituality:
Living with the conviction that everything that God reveals in Jesus can be lived in and through the Holy Spirit, but only in and through the Holy Spirit. Spirituality is always primarily the work of the Holy Spirit. It is never learning a truth about God and then applying it to our lives. It is never learning how to do something right and then putting it into practice. Spirituality

is the discipline of insisting that there is no such thing as mere doctrine or mere ethics. It all can be, must be, lived by and through the Spirit.[7]

Living in the reality of the manifest presence of God is called the *nexus*. Nexus intimacy is the conviction that such an experience is not only possible, but God Himself initiates such encounters. It is the conviction of the reality of Jesus' statement, "...I will build My church and the gates of Hades shall not prevail against it" (Matt. 16:18 NKJV). This is not seen as simply historical rhetoric but current reality—Jesus continues to build His Church today. It is as He promised and prophesied to His apostolic disciple-makers: "I am with you always even to the end of the age" (Matt. 28:20 NKJV).

This is not an attempt to undermine or supplant the importance of knowing and studying the Scripture. Rather, this teaching contends for the heart of the Christian Gospel—a truly personal, interactive relationship with God.

Bockmuehl points out that the understanding that "God guides from within" is consistent with the bible and church history. David states, "I will hear what God the Lord will speak. For He will speak peace to His people and to His saints..." (Ps. 85:8 NKJV). Bockmuehl says,

> Perhaps closer to the original Hebrew, the Greek Septuagint and the Latin Vulgate translate, 'I will listen to what God speaks in me.' The same process of inner revelation is referred to in Psalm 51:6, which the Revised Standard Version translates, 'Behold, thou desirest truth in the inward being; therefore teach me wisdom in my secret heart.'[8]

How was Jesus able to do the amazing things He did in His earthly ministry? The standard Evangelical response is, "He was 100 percent man and 100 percent God; therefore, He could die on a cross like a human and perform miracles like God." What does that exactly mean? Jesus was most certainly human in every respect. He grew hungry. He grew thirsty. He grew weary. He grew sleepy. He grew! God does not *grow* from an infant to an adult. Yet He was able to walk on water, multiply bread, raise the dead, and Himself come back from

---

7   Eugene Peterson, *Christ Plays in Ten Thousand Places* (Grand Rapids: Eerdmans, 2005), 13. This is God's answer to the dilemma articulated by Buber.

8   Klaus Bockmuehl, *Listening to the God Who Speaks.* Colorado Springs: (Helmers & Howard, 1990), 37.

the dead. Did He toggle back and before between His two natures? The Apostle Paul sheds some light on the nature of Christ: "who, although He existed in the form of God, did not regard equality with God a thing to be grasped, but emptied Himself, taking the form of a bond-servant, *and* being made in the likeness of men" (Phil. 2:6, 7 NAS). The Greek word *kenosis* means to empty or divest oneself of stature or power. This passage uses the incarnation as a model for humility. That is, just as God humbled Himself to become human, so human beings ought to humble themselves. Jesus was not a superhuman; He was merely human. There was no retention of omniscience, omnipotence, or omnipresence on Jesus' part. All that was gone when He became human.

Catholic theology, in an attempt to reconcile the obvious contradictions of having both a divine and human nature, goes to some lengths to describe the nuances of two-nature existence. For example, Catholics hold that "God's all-preserving power inhabiting the body of Jesus did not allow any corruption; it all prevented disease or the beginning of corruption."[9] But He "freely subjected" Himself to fatigue, hunger, injury, etc. The Catholic doctrine of *communicato idiomatum*[10] upholds that Jesus was 100% divine and 100% human, and that the properties of divinity can be ascribed to the man Christ and the properties of the man Christ can be predicated to the Living Word Christ.

The kenosis passage supports the view of Jesus freely setting aside his "equality with God" and fully embracing the human state.

So how was Jesus able to do all the miraculous things He did? The same way humans do it today—the empowering presence of the Holy Spirit. Jesus was in effect the ultimate, Spirit-filled human. As is the case for all humans, Jesus' only recourse as a human was to follow the promptings of His heavenly Father: "...the Son can do nothing of Himself, but what He sees the Father do; for whatever He does, the Son also does in like manner" (John 5:19; cf. 5:30; 8:26, 28; 12:49, 50 NKJV). Jesus, according to Bockmuehl, was the "Great Listener."[11] Spiritual transformation does not make one superhuman, but rather *fully* human.

9   New Advent Encyclopedia, http://www.newadvent.org/cathen/08617a.htm.
10 Ibid. Conservative Protestant doctrine likewise affirms that Jesus was 100% God and 100% man, i.e., one person with two natures. The minority Pentecostal view of the kenosis does not dispute this view, but rather anticipates the advent of the ministry of the Holy Spirit at Pentecost.
11 Ibid., 48.

Germane to the current discussion, listening to the speaking God in the inward person is a result of nexus intimacy. Listening in this context is synonymous with obedience. Listening to God has a non-negotiable dimension to it. If one hears a good idea from a preacher, then one has the option to say, "That was a nice idea, but it is not compulsory for me to obey it." If one hears the voice of God, however, there is no choice but to obey.

The great need in the Church today is for leaders who have the capacity by reason of their intimate relationship with God to discern His voice. The ultimate outcome of Spiritual transformation is to usher believers into nexus intimacy with God so they can do precisely that. Bockmuehl quotes Frank Buchman, "When man listens, God speaks. When man obeys, God acts…We are not out to tell God. We are out to let God tell us…The lesson the world most needs is the art of listening to God."[12]

Intimacy, Identity, and Influence

Teaching Outcome: Demonstrate how nexus intimacy forms onto-relational, perichoretic identity, leading to uranogaic influence which advances true biblical community transformation.

Once *intimacy* with God is established it forms the *identity* of the individual which leads to effective *influence* in the world. This is a central focus of this project: *Transforming lives transform lives.*

It must not be overlooked that nexus intimacy with the heavenly Father (Hebrew *Abba*) transforms a person, as Manning says, into "Abba's child."[13] "But as many as received Him, to them He gave the right to become children of God, to those who believe in His name" (John 1:12 NKJV). At the beginning of his gospel, the Apostle John establishes a major theme of his message—full adoption in the family of God through Christ. Later he quotes Jesus as saying, "I will not leave you as orphans…" (John 14:18 NKJV) in anticipation of the ministry of the Holy Spirit. Through the indwelling Spirit an orphan spirit is replaced by a spirit of adoption. This is the significance of the phrase "perichoretic identity." Through the baptism of the Holy Spirit the believer is given access into the relationship between the Father and the Son. Hence, salvation

---

12 Ibid., 8.

13 Brennan Manning, *Abba's Child: The Cry of the Heart for Intimate Belonging* (Colorado Springs: NavPress), 2002.

is seen as far more than the avoidance of hell and going to heaven. It is the highest and most powerful possible affirmation for any human being. One of the greatest puzzles of humanity—"Who am I?—is profoundly answered by the triune God.

The result is a transformed life who transforms the lives of others. Identity can also be understood as the intersection of "who I am" and "what I do," the former informing the latter. The formation of perichoretic identity involves the process of *becoming* children of God (heaven, y-axis) then *doing* the will of God (earth, x-axis). This is the kingdom of heaven transforming the earth. The nature of true Christian ministry in the world is uranogaic influence.

Before continuing with the train of thought, it should be noted that considerable distortion of a minister's identity may have occurred. This distortion is a direct consequence of sin. This sin may either consist of sins committed *by* the minister or *against* the minister. Both produce distortion. Dr. Leah Coulter has done considerable work in the field of defining "sinners" in contrast with the "sinned-against."[14] Sinners require repentance; the sinned-against require rescue. The gospel of the kingdom has to do with both. Forgiveness and reconciliation might need to take place between the minister and people from his past. If the minister has sinned against another, he needs to repent and seek forgiveness from the victim. If the minister has been sinned against, he needs to confront the sinner, forgive, and, when possible, be reconciled. If this does not occur then the distortion of his true identity may persist. Unforgiveness may be the root cause behind issues of anger, fear, stress, or anxiety. Often the sinned-against will replay the offense again and again, as if to hold the sinner on trial for his sin. Coulter points out, however, that this is a kind of "court proceeding" where the victim is anguished over the injustice. Repentance and forgiveness is the pathway to freedom. In cases where a face to face meeting with the sinner is no longer possible (due to the death of the person) or not safe, Coulter teaches the sinned-against to "adjourn" their lower court proceedings and appeal to the Supreme Court of Heaven for justice. This is a profession of faith in a just God—the Supreme Judge—who will deliver a fair and appropriate sentence either in this lifetime or the next. Hence, the formation of identity involves a process of both casting off distortions and embracing the truth.

---

14   Leah K. Coulter, *Rediscovering the Power of Repentance and Forgiveness, Finding Healing and Justice for Reconcilable and Irreconcilable Wrongs.* Atlanta, GA: Ampelōn Publishing, 2006.

Uranogaic influence is the result of nexus intimacy forming perichoretic identity. Heaven transforms the earth through a transformed life. The community of believers regains its identity as the body of Christ. The Spirit of God which abandoned the earth at the Fall in Genesis returns to the earth at the Pentecost in Acts. Where the first Adam failed, the second Adam—Jesus Christ—succeeds. But where on earth is God? Now by reason of the indwelling Spirit, the Church becomes the locus of God's presence on the earth, transforming the world into the Kingdom of God. This is the immense significance of Pentecost. Uranogaic influence was at the heart of Christ's calling of the Apostle Paul: "I will deliver you from the Jewish people, as well as from the Gentiles, to whom I now send you, to open their eyes, in order to turn them from darkness to light, and from the power of Satan to God, that they may receive forgiveness of sins and an inheritance among those who are sanctified by faith in Me" (Acts 26:17-18 NKJV). Uranogaic influence is what naturally follows when a human being's very identity has been transformed through perichoresis as one is immersed in nexus intimacy with the trinity.

Community transformation is the conversion of the world such that it reflects the kingdom of heaven. Its full consummation will occur at the Second Coming of Jesus Christ, but it begins now. Community transformation is neither a Christian utopia nor a christianized society. It is not the establishment of a Christian theocracy. Community transformation is kingdom reality forming human reality, and the Church's uranogaic influence defines and achieves community transformation. It defines community transformation in that it is driven by the triune God Himself at work through the Church establishing the immediate priority, determining the strategy, and executing the plan for transformation. The Church's uranogaic influence achieves community transformation in that it is the only conduit through which God's transformative power spreads across the earth.

The Sexual Dimension of Identity

Teaching Outcome: Comment on the biblical view of one's sexual identity as a critical issue of a pastor's spiritual formation.

Hayford identifies sexual sin as "worse than others."[15] It is regrettably an all too common disqualifier of many Christian ministers. One possible approach

---

15 Jack W. Hayford, *Fatal Attractions: Why Sex Sins Are Worse Than Others* (Ventura, CA: Regal, 2004), 12.

is to not overly emphasize the "thou-shalt-nots" of sexual sin, but rather the Spiritual formation of sexual identity. "Thou shalt not covet thy neighbor's wife." "Thou shalt not commit adultery." "Thou shalt not look upon a woman to lust for her." Although the biblical negatives are clear, it is obviously important to remind believers, Christian leaders, and oneself of them. The relativistic milieu of the present culture creates a powerful undercurrent causing the unanchored soul to drift very easily. Hayford does a splendid job of this in *The Anatomy of Seduction*, where he emphasizes prayer to strengthen one's heart in the Spirit to remain faithful. A good summary of his approach is seen in his "four liberating keys: repentance, renunciation, recitation, and release."[16] Ted Roberts likewise prefers the direct approach as he states in his book, *Pure Desire:* "The first reason people remain in sexual bondage is that they *refuse to follow directions.*"[17] Roberts warns against the assumption that people cannot change their actions until they first change their feelings. Many mistakenly see the sequence of transformation like this: changed feelings lead to changed thinking which leads to changed behavior. But the practical reality for those caught in a sexual addiction is exactly the reverse: changed behavior leads to changed thinking which leads to changed feelings. What is greatly appreciated is Roberts' insistence on dealing with these matters in the context of marriage and family. He involved his wife, Diane, in the writing of his book so that she could comment on "his realities and her realities." For the woman dealing with the revelation that her husband is a sexual addict she says, "It is important that wives understand the addictive cycle, because the first tendency a woman has is to try to control her husband so he will stop his behavior. But the more she tries to control, the more he is thrown into the addictive cycle of acting in (holding down the addiction) and then acting out (reverting back to his old habits).[18] The idea of involving the family system in the freedom process is hugely significant. Gordon MacDonald ironically wrote a book entitled *Ordering Your Private World* and then fell into sexual sin. After all the headlines he was asked about what he had learned through his ordeal. His answer had to do with accountability, community, and friendship—the need for someone to look him straight in the eye and ask him

16   Jack W. Hayford, *The Anatomy of Seduction: Defending Your Heart for God* (Ventura, CA: Regal, 2004), 102-109.

17   Ted Roberts, *Pure Desire* (Ventura, CA: Regal, 1999), 107.

18   Ibid., 256.

how he is *really* doing. The biblical "thou-shalt-nots" are critical to the equation of the Spiritual formation of sexual identity, but focusing on it negatively is only half the answer.

Sexual identity is derived from Genesis and the account of the creation of Adam and Eve. Mankind is created in the image of God—imago Dei. Men and women both reflect the imago Dei. Since God is three persons in one, then the wedding together of a man and woman unified in holy matrimony also reflects the imago Dei. God is intensely relational to the core of His essence; His children made in His image are no different.

At each phase of creation, God declares the creation as "good" (Gen. 1:4, 10, 12, 18, 21, 25). After man was created in His image, God looked upon all of creation and declared that it was "very good" (Gen. 1:31). However, within His perfect creation, there is one thing that was "not good." "...It is not good for the man to be alone; I will make him a helper suitable for him" (Gen. 2:18 NAS). Adam is in a perfect relationship with God yet it is "not good" that he is without a wife. Adam is a single person created in the image of a Triune God. Adam, like His Creator, is intrinsically and essentially relational. The onto-relational nature of Adam, however, creates aloneness not characteristic of God who is three persons in perpetual relationship with one another. Adam is a deeply relational being, but he is alone. God's remedy is to create ex nihilo a helper suitable—Eve. Richard Foster, in his book, *Money, Sex, and Power,* talks about how the man and the woman were "naked and not ashamed," extolling the beauty of human sexuality as reflecting the image of God. Foster contends that sexuality was never to be divorced from Spirituality, and that God's purposes are fulfilled not only in the marriage season but also through singleness. This understanding of Genesis accounts for the naturally powerful attraction that men and women have for one another while at the same time affirms the divine design for one man and one woman living in holy matrimony.

Joe Dallas is President of Exodus International, a ministry which ministers lovingly to those being set free from homosexuality. He contends boldly and with great compassion the biblical position:

"'If people want to accept homosexuality as normal, that is there option, but they do against the indisputable teaching of the bible,' says Doctors Glenn Wood and John Dietrich in *The AIDS Epidemic: Balancing Compassion* *and Justice…*Homosexuality is *never* mentioned in Scripture in anything but negative terms…and there is nothing in the entire bible offering any commendation of or instruction for homosexual relationships."[19]

In it he addresses the significance of the father and son relationship for the transference and integration of male gender identity and the formation of biblical masculinity. His warning is that this transference is not automatic and can be interrupted.

Sexual identity is not just a homosexual issue, however. Heterosexuals likewise have their identity issues. The key ones are monogamy and chastity. In his book *Marriage Spirituality*, Paul Stevens discusses ten disciplines for couples who love God. They include Prayer: sharing a special intimacy; Conversation: listening to the heart; Sabbath: playing heaven together; Retreat: sharing solitude; Study: hearing God speak together; Service: full partnership in ministry; Sexual Fasting: the discipline nobody wants; Obedience: doing God's will together; Confession: the surgery of forgiveness; and Mutual Submission: reversing the curse. The intentionality of the disciplines as a pathway to reflecting the intensely relational dimension of imago Dei is the strength of this approach. Monogamy, chastity, and intimacy are the by-products of husband and wife loving one another in the presence of God.

The season of singleness that every person must endure is divine preparation for monogamy. Jesus establishes the standard for purity in the Sermon on the Mount: "But I say to you that whoever looks at a woman to lust for her has already committed adultery with her in his heart" (Matt. 5:28 NKJV). Paul affirms this, "For this is the will of God, your sanctification: that you should abstain from sexual immorality" (I Thess. 4:3 NKJV). The season of singleness is an opportunity *from* the Lord to prepare the spirit, soul, and body for a marriage that reflects kingdom values and is a positive transformational influence on the earth. Four key areas must first be developed before courtship can begin: Spiritual intimacy with Christ, horizontal ministry calling, completion of educational goals, and a career choice which provides enough income for the family. The help of a spiritual mentor or Christian parents in the development of these areas would be strongly recommended before courtship begins.

19 Joe Dallas, *Desires in Conflict: Answering the Struggle for Sexual Identity* (Eugene, OR: Harvest House, 1991), 282.

The Spiritual transformation of sexual identity occurs by embracing in obedience the biblical negatives—"thou-shalt-nots"—and the positive reality that men and women, both single and married, reflect the image of God to world. There seems to be inadequate formation of the sexual identity of Christian leaders resulting in a number of sexually-related glaring issues. This is a key problem requiring serious attention in the formation of effective community transformers. In his book, *Ordering Your Private World*, Gordon MacDonald quotes Thomas Kelly, "We are trying to be several selves at once, without all our selves being organized by a single, mastering Life within us…Life is meant to be lived from a Center, a divine Center. Each one of us can live such a life of amazing power and peace and serenity, of integration and confidence and simplified multiplicity, on one condition—that is, *if we really want to.*"[20]

The Purpose of Spiritual Disciplines as Immersion Theology

Teaching Outcome: Convey the biblical purpose of Spiritual disciplines as "clearing a pathway for the seeking Father" versus moralism, neo-gnosticism, or sectarianism.

Here now is the life verse of this researcher: "More than that, I count all things to be loss in view of the surpassing value of knowing Christ Jesus my Lord, for whom I have suffered the loss of all things, and count them but rubbish so that I may gain Christ" (Phil. 3:8 NAS). Consistent with Paul's heart, the purpose of Spiritual disciplines is to become more intensely hungry for Jesus. The objective is not moralism which is the creation of a life so good one no longer needs God. Neither is it neo-gnosticism which is the creation of a spiritual elite with a special knowledge of how to gain access to God. Commoners need not apply. And it is certainly not sectarianism which is the creation of a divided body of Christ around favorite doctrines.

The result of the correct practice of Spiritual disciplines is a Church which rightly reflects the image of God by reason of counting all as rubbish except for knowing Him, and then is empowered to bear witness of Him to the world. It does not permanently isolate the Church from the world in order to preserve itself, its values, and culture. Instead, it burdens the Church with compassion for the world with the burden of Christ's compassion for the world. Jim Scott, Chief Operations Officer of the Foursquare NCO quotes Dr. Ralph Winter,

20 Gordon MacDonald, *Ordering Your Private World* (Nashville, TN: Nelson, 2003), 273.

"Until the future of the world is more important than the future of the church, the church has no future."[21] It is the vision of Isaiah: "...Holy, holy, holy is the LORD of hosts; the whole earth is full of His glory" (Isa. 6:3 NKJV).

That said, Spiritual disciplines baptize a believer in God's holy presence. Jesus said, "He who believes and is baptized will be saved" (Mark 16:16 NKJV). The value of Spiritual disciplines is best understood in light of immersion theology. The Greek word rendered "baptized" (βαπτίζω / baptizo) is significantly precise in this context. Boice offers this profound insight germane to the current discussion:

> "The clearest example that shows the meaning of baptizo is a text from the Greek poet and physician Nicander, who lived about 200 B.C. It is a recipe for making pickles and is helpful because it uses two words both translated baptism. Nicander says that in order to make a pickle, the vegetable should first be 'dipped' (bapto) into boiling water and then 'immersed' (baptizo) in the vinegar solution. Both verbs concern the baptizing of vegetables in a solution, but the first is temporary while the second produces a permanent change."[22]

Pickled vegetables (such as Korean Kim Chee) can be overwhelming in aroma. This happens because the vegetable is first overwhelmed not just by a dipping (bapto) process but by a full immersion (baptizo) process. This is identified as "immersion theology"—the long-term, on-going immersing of believers in the presence of the Lord. The living water of the Holy Spirit washes the mind and transforms a life through constant abiding in His presence. Now the purpose of Spiritual disciplines becomes clear. Mere temporary dipping in the Trinity will not do. A criticism of much of Christian experience is its emphasis on event-experiences versus abiding in His presence. Being baptized as ceremonial dipping (bapto) in church is only meaningful if it is representative of an on-going *baptizo* in relational connection with the Trinity. Periodic, intermittent exposure to God's presence in church services or bible studies should lead to moment-by-moment walking with God throughout the day. Only full immersion through Spiritual disciplines will overwhelm the believer, bringing

---

21   Jim Scott, Teaching Session, Foursquare Regional Conference, Hilo, HI: Nov. 6, 2008.
22   James Montgomery Boice, *Bible Study Magazine*, May 1989.

permanent transformation. Once overwhelmed he/she then in turn overwhelms the world. Transformed lives transform lives.

How Ministry Can Harm the Soul

Teaching Outcome: Reveal the negative, deleterious effects of "ministry" on the human soul.

FASICLD (Francis A. Schaeffer Institute of Church Leadership Development) reports some startling statistics on the ministry experiences and spiritual condition of American pastors. Krejcir writes it has been compiling this data for over eighteen years and the results are supported by findings in similar studies. 1,050 pastors were surveyed at two pastor's conferences in Orange County and Pasadena, and a much larger sampling was involved in a Fuller Institute study in the late 1980's. Here is a sampling of findings reported by Krejcir in his article, "Statistic on Pastors."[23]

- 70% of pastors are so stressed out that they regularly consider leaving the ministry.
- 35% of pastors actually do leave, most after only five years.
- 100% of the 1,050 pastors surveyed had a close associate who had left the ministry due to burnout, church conflict, or moral failure.
- 77% felt they did not have a good marriage.
- 72% studied the bible only to prepare for a sermon (leaving 28% who are doing their devotions).
- 38% said they were divorced or currently in the process of getting divorced.
- 30% said they had either been in an ongoing affair or one-time sexual encounter with a parishioner.

Studies by Barna, Focus on the Family, and Fuller Seminary yield similar findings. It is clear that a fundamental shift in ministry approach must take place for pastors to survive the pressures of ministry. By contrast Jesus describes the positive benefit of doing ministry: "...My food is to do the will of Him who sent Me, and to finish His work" (Jn. 4:34 NKJV). For Jesus ministry had

---

23   Richard J. Krejcir, "Statistic on Pastors." www.churchleadership.org. Francis A. Schaeffer Institute of Church Leadership Development (research from 1989 – 2006), c. 2007.

the effect of nourishing His soul. He felt energized afterward, not unlike after a good meal when one has been hungry. So why then are pastors reporting that ministry has the opposite effect on their soul?

The answer is fairly clear and straightforward. Jesus never said, "My food is to do ministry." Instead, Jesus said, "My food is to do the will of Him who sent Me." Implication? It is possible to do work under the guise of "ministry" which in the final analysis is not actually the will of God! Ministry is good, but ministry is not God. Pastors must stop doing "ministry" and start doing the will of God. Then they will discover that serving God in church is a positive experience and a blessing to the pastor's soul, family, and church.

When does ministry cease being the will of God? Each pastor must evaluate his/her own experience, but here is some stimulus for thought:

1. A ministry schedule which does not allow for a weekly Sabbath Day may not be within the will of God.
2. If the marriage relationship between pastor and spouse has soured but continues to be neglected in favor of ministry.
3. If the pastor's children are not spiritually doing well and this continues condition unabated in favor of more church ministry.
4. Acting like God's slave and not His child may not be the will of God.

Freedom from Strongholds

Teaching Outcome: Define strongholds and how the Spiritual transformation process brings freedom.

A "Glaring Issue" is a stronghold or glaringly self-obvious issue of sin in the life of a minister which, if left unresolved, could result in the end of the ministry; a sin issue which could be a gateway into a potentially career-ending disaster. Its correlate is a "Blind Spot" which is not obvious to the minister but conspicuous to those around him.

The moral failure of any pastor has a deleterious effect on ministry; the moral failure of a senior pastor has a devastating effect. This researcher went through the unsavory experience of witnessing his spiritual mentor go through just such a moral failure. This involved no one with whom the researcher is currently ministering but rather took place in a previous ministry setting. The following are some observations on that experience.

The mentor's extra-marital affairs transpired over a span of more than sixteen years. There were multiple extra-marital affairs that involved several of the single women in the ministry, some occurring simultaneously. No one had any clue that these affairs were taking place, apparently not even his wife. The strong controlling influence of this individual coupled with his adulterous lifestyle created a "perfect storm," carefully keeping the glaring issue perfectly hidden. None of the women came forward until years after the affairs had ended.

While these trysts were taking place, the ministry grew tremendously under this individual's leadership gifting. Thousands of people were reached for Christ. Over 100 volunteer staff were trained and mobilized. There was an exceptional full-time staff team of a half-dozen gifted individuals. By any standard of measure this individual led one of the finest Christian ministries in the nation.

One of the greatest puzzles is how the head of the ministry could be engaged in such blatant, disqualifying sin, yet the ministry was so amazingly fruitful and blessed. The fact remains that the same person who was involved in these extra-marital affairs was also the same individual who *simultaneously* led the ministry to such great heights. This can only be attributed to the grace and long-suffering of God—grace for the leader in hopes that he would transform and grace for the thousands who came to Christ through such an imperfect vessel. It is difficult to imagine that the ministry could have been as successful without this person's spiritual gifts. The thousands who came to the Lord seemed to have been genuinely converted.

In retrospect it must be concluded that the Spirit was patiently working in this pastor's life, bringing conviction each time he sinned, urging him to repent during the course of his infidelities—however unsuccessfully. Simultaneously, the Spirit was merciful and gracious to the thousands of teens who came to Christ during the ministry tenure of this pastor. There is apparently no connection between a pastor's "worthiness" to be blessed and the fruitfulness of his ministry. Experience suggests that gifts of the Spirit can operate quite effectively and powerfully resulting in real conversion and genuine Spiritual transformation while at the same time there are glaring dysfunctions privately in the fruit of the Spirit. In the case of this mentor there was an eventual earthly "judgment day" which exposed his duplicity, but it occurred at a time when his ministry season was over and the damage was as minimal as could be. Interestingly, when the news broke of his immorality in August 2007, he had apparently not been in any adulterous relationships for seven years. So for seven years he had been living morally repentant and faithful to his wife. What was the point of exposing his sin then at that moment? Was it to emphasize "we will reap what we sow?" Or was it a work of darkness—a demonic attack? It would not be farfetched to conclude that both of those were probably in play.

The Christian Church must find a different way to deal with the glaring issues in the lives of its leaders. There is no question that freedom and deliverance must be sought. However, perhaps in some ways the expectation that pastors be perfect contributes to the problem rather than solve anything. This is not at all intended to communicate that there should not be the standard biblical qualifications for elders of the Church. But if a pastor secretly begins to fall from those standards, the milieu in the fellowship is likely not conducive to him revealing that to anyone. (This would be a cultural milieu the minister himself would have helped create.) He must sin in silence and in secret in order to protect the ministry from being discredited. Moreover, if the ministry is fruitful, what about all those others who still need to accept Christ? In the case of the researcher's mentor the very culture of "strong accountability" appeared to play out in favor of deception and façade. Because of the strong teaching on accountability no one would have suspected that the teacher himself was duplicitous.

Glaring issues thrive in religious environments where strong human accountability is taught and listening to the personal voice of the Spirit is either de-emphasized or out of fear is altogether neglected. Freedom from strongholds occurs when the pneumatika humbly invite the Spirit to accomplish His work of conviction, healing, and deliverance. "For whom the Son sets free is free indeed." Paul teaches the fundamental pathway to Spiritual transformation: "But we all, with unveiled face, beholding as in a mirror the glory of the Lord, are being transformed into the same image from glory to glory, just as by the Spirit of the Lord" (2 Cor. 3:18 NKJV).

In order to be set free pastors must enter into the vertical y-axis of unveiled encountering of the Spirit, granting them access to the fellowship of the Trinity. It entails a process of "beholding the glory of the Lord" which transforms the pastor "into the same image." Understanding that this is a process rather than a one-time event is critical for patience. Transformation occurs from glory to glory or degree by degree. The acknowledgment of the need for glory-to-glory transformation is also critical. It is no surprise that the researcher's mentor was able to lead the ministry to tremendous heights of success while simultaneously experiencing moral failure in secret. It is not an all-or-nothing proposition. He was not as bad as he could be, and he was not as good as he should be. When one beholds the glory of the Lord with unveiled face there is the inevitable hearing of the Spirit's voice. This links transformation with obedience. "Good ideas" on how to live a holy life are optional; the voice of the Lord is non-negotiable and must be obeyed. Remaining in a state of unveiled beholding of the face of God increases one's capacity to discern His voice. Spiritual transformation is the conviction that only face to face encountering of God (the vertical Y-axis) can truly change a pastor's soul.

This project examines the critical need for Christian leaders to deal with glaring issues because they are glaring. And it is more than likely that the Spirit Himself has revealed these issues to the minister. Ignoring them could prove spiritually, personally, and publicly disastrous. What about non-glaring issues? Certainly, all ministers have "blind spots"—issues that are in plain view to others but invisible to the minister. There could also be issues known neither to the minister nor to those around him. What about those?

McIntosh and Rima in their book, *Overcoming the Dark Side of Leadership: The Paradox of Personal Dysfunction*, provide excellent, critical insights into the personal dysfunctions of leaders in the hope of understanding, discovering, and redeeming the "dark side." They do not see the dark side as necessarily demonic or sinister requiring spiritual deliverance, but rather a "dysfunction" or brokenness within the person. McIntosh and Rima suggest that initially there is a "basic need" which is not being satisfactorily met, causing a "traumatic experience" and a feeling of failure.[24] This causes a sense of "existential debt" which the person attempts to pay through unhealthy behaviors during adult years. The interplay of basic need, traumatic experience, and existential debt results in the development of the "dark side." Think of the dark side as a kind of overcompensation or over-reaching caused by the need-trauma-debt experience. In this paradigm the dysfunction is not something to be freed from but rather mitigated so it is not allowed to destroy the life and ministry of a leader.

---

24 McIntosh, Gary L. and Rima, Samuel D. *Overcoming the Dark Side of Leadership: The Paradox of Personal Dysfunction* (Grand Rapids: Baker Books, 1997), 60-61.

Interestingly, the authors contend that the dark side may also be used to accomplish positive results. Canadian Rob Angel felt he was an academic failure because of a spelling test at Washington State for which he was unprepared. He later became the creator of Pictionary, a game of pictures not words, and made millions. McIntosh and Rima contend for a five-step process to overcome and redeem the dark side: (1) acknowledge the dark side, (2) examine the past, (3) resist destructive expectations imposed by others, (4) practice progressive self-knowledge, and (5) understand identity in Christ.[25]

Askesis and Aisthesis

Teaching Outcome: Communicate how Spiritual disciplines enable Christians to *choose* "no" (askesis) to sin and "yes" (aisthesis) to obedience.

First, it should be reiterated that the practice of Spiritual disciplines is not a self-help approach to Spiritual formation, but an insistence on the Holy Spirit's presence and power to transform. Specifically, it is the conviction that Spirit-filled life empowers the believer to choose the will of God. As creatures made in the image of God, human beings are never without the capacity to make a decision. On the cross Jesus chose to remain obedient to the will of His Father despite the most severe negative circumstances. On the other hand, Adam and Eve chose to sin against God despite the most positive circumstances. Humanly speaking Jesus would have been perfectly justified to turn His back on the will of the Father under the torturous duress of the cross, but He chose to obey. Adam and Eve had no sinful nature to contend with and the most idyllic of circumstances, yet they chose to disobey. The contrast of Jesus' obedience on Calvary versus Adam and Eve's disobedience in the Garden underscores the significance of choice.

Askesis disciplines spiritually enable the choosing of "no" to disobedience. Aisthesis disciplines spiritually enable the choosing of "yes" to obedience. Askesis is demonstrated in Jesus' crucifixion. Aisthesis is demonstrated in His resurrection. Askesis has to do with debris removal from one's old life; aisthesis, the formation or building up of a new one. Askesis is John the Baptist exclaiming, "Repent!" Aisthesis is John the Apostle exclaiming, "Behold!"

Spiritual disciplines typically have both an ascetic and aesthetic characteristic to them. For example, fasting is saying "no" to food in order to say "yes"

---

25 Ibid.

to prayer. Sabbath is saying "no" to work and saying "yes" to rest. Secrecy is saying "no" to public acclaim in order to say "yes" to the Father's reward.

Christian leaders must not simply "try" to be obedient; they must "train" to be. Spiritual disciplines are an invitation to the Holy Spirit to enable a leader to do just that. They help clear a pathway (askesis) for the Father to the form the spirit (aisthesis).

Classic Spiritual Disciplines

Teaching Outcome: Refresh awareness of some of the classical Spiritual disciplines of the Christian faith: (1) solitude and silence, (2) prayer and fasting, (3) celibacy, (4) stewardship (or frugality) and secrecy, (5) service and submission, (6) sabbath, (7) study and meditation, (8) bible journaling, (9) worship and celebration, and (10) fellowship or Spiritual community. Some of the disciplines of Spiritual community include accountability, confession, and forgiveness. These are not intended as means to self-improvement but as ways to clear a pathway for the seeking Father.

The purpose of Spiritual disciplines is not merely to grasp but to be grasped. Brennan Manning quotes Gregory of Nyssa, "Concepts create idols. Only wonder understands anything."[26] Manning quotes German theologian Karl Rahner: "Some things are understood not by grasping but by allowing oneself to be grasped."[27] Spiritual disciplines are not a human effort to acquire God (which of course is impossible), but instead to express a human's willingness to God to be acquired.

Solitude is the practice of being by oneself yet not alone. "Now in the morning, having risen a long while before daylight, He went out and departed to a solitary place; and there He prayed" (Mark 1:35 NKJV). It is a remarkable fact that Jesus Himself would find it essential to regularly meet with His heavenly Father, yet many pastors do not. Solitude opens the door to silence. Silence is refraining from speaking so that the Spirit might redeem one's speech.

Prayer is the practice of listening for the voice of the Lord and making the appropriate response. Jesus logically links prayer with fasting. Fasting is abstaining from any time-consuming activity in order to tune in to God.

---

26 Brennan Manning, *The Relentless Tenderness of Jesus* (Grand Rapids: Fleming H. Revell, 2004), 12.
27 Ibid.

Celibacy is abstaining from sex for the purpose of prayer and fasting (I Cor. 7:5). It is a reminder that sex is a gift rather than an entitlement, and that abstaining from sex for a season does not cause death. Celibacy provides an opportunity to again reflect on the divine design of the human body and the proper purpose and function of sex.

Stewardship (or frugality) is the Spirit-led use of one's resources in order to be free from greed. It cultivates a generous and sacrificial heart. It is a reminder of the true Source of all resources. Jesus links secrecy with charitable giving (Matt. 6:3-4), prayer (Matt. 6:6), and fasting (Matt. 6:18). Secrecy diminishes the craving for human approval in order to be free from man-pleasing. Then it augments the desire for God's approval.

Service and submission cultivate the formation of servant leaders. The heart of true leadership is servanthood, not glory, rank, or power. Beware of a leader who delegates duties but has not himself learned submission to authority. Service involves the celebration of work and the joy of productivity. Submission is the flexing of tremendous spiritual power in order to yield to God or another person.

Sabbath means to rest from labor to enter the peace of Christ. Sabbath-breaking was one of the key infractions behind Israel being cast into exile.

Study and meditation are companion disciplines that cultivate a fear of the Lord and a sense of awe in the human mind. McCullough observes,

> Visit a Church on Sunday morning—almost any will do—and you will likely find a congregation comfortably relating to a deity who fits nicely within precise doctrinal positions, or who lends almighty support to social crusades, or who conforms to individual spiritual experiences. But you will not likely find much awe or sense of mystery. The only sweaty palms will be those of the preacher unsure whether the sermon will go over; the only shaking knees will be those of the soloist about to sing the offertory.[28]

Meditation is patient contemplation on the oracles of God.

Bible journaling is attentiveness to the written word in order to access the living Word.

Worship is on-going existence in the manifest presence in spirit and truth.

---

28 Donald McCullough, *The Trivialization of God* (Colorado Springs: NavPress, 1995), 13.

Celebration is the capacity to focus on the absolute goodness of God regardless of the circumstances.

Fellowship or Spiritual community is living in Christian love with Spirit-filled friends who co-exist in the company of the Trinity. Fellowship may require the disciplines of accountability, confession, and forgiveness.

Community Transformers

Teaching Outcome: Characterize community transformers as pneumatika: synthesizing the practices of resurrection, pentecost, and hosting His presence toward uranogaic influence.

In a recent interview with "Christianity Today," Jack Hayford said he sometimes receives mental impressions from the Spirit so strong he feels he could almost say, "The Lord told me, and I quote."[29] He continues, "I'm not glib about that. The Lord and I don't have an ongoing conversation. We *do* have an ongoing relationship."[30] According to Hayford, this daily, attentive, childlike relationship with God is at the heart of Pentecostal theology, and he hopes every Christian might experience it. Hayford is a "Spirit person"— πνευματικος / pneumatikos (pl. πνευματικα / pneumatika), and he is a modern-day community transformer. Community transformers enjoy on-going nexus intimacy with the Trinity and are consequently forming perichoretic identity, leading to uranogaic influence. The practice of Spirit-ual disciplines facilitates Spirit-ual transformation into a community transformer. Paul describes it this way, "But a natural man does not accept the things of the Spirit of God, for they are foolishness to him; and he cannot understand them, because they are spiritually appraised. But he who is spiritual (pneumatikos) appraises all things, yet he himself is appraised by no one" (I Cor. 2:14-15 NASB). Paul forcefully contends for this spiritual dimension: "And I, brethren, could not speak to you as to spiritual men, but as to men of flesh, as to infants in Christ" (I Cor. 3:1, NAS). Who is a mature person in Christ? This passage asserts: pneumatikos, a spiritual person.

Jesus was the ultimate pneumatikos. Christ was "Exhibit A" for how pneumatika operate on the earth. He demonstrated a wondrous, unhindered relationship with His heavenly Father, unimpeded by sin. Everything He saw the Father

---

29 Tim Stafford, "The Pentecostal Gold Standard," *Christianity Today*, July 2005, 27.
30 Ibid.

do, He did. Whatever the Father told Him to say, He said. He did nothing unless He discerned the Father doing it first. At the Incarnation the eternal God became a human being and emptied himself of omnipresence, omniscience, and omnipotence. Some have referenced Paul's statement to the Philippians as the biblical basis: "Have this attitude in yourselves which was also in Christ Jesus, who, although He existed in the form of God, did not regard equality with God a thing to be grasped, but emptied Himself (κένωσεν), taking the form of a bond-servant, and being made in the likeness of men" (Phil. 2:5-7 NAS). Because the Greek κένωσεν comes from the root "kenosis," it is sometimes alluded to as the kenosis passage. This project understands the ambivalence of referencing the kenosis passage as biblical basis for Christological nature since it could be a reference to His emptying Himself of divine stature (equality with God) rather than divine attributes. The context might be commenting more on "have this attitude" (Christian humility) rather than the nature of Christ. On the other hand, it could be making the case that Christ's emptying Himself of divine attributes (likeness of men) was the manner in which He emptied Himself of divine stature and provides the supreme example for Christian humility. That said, the kenosis passage may not even be essential to demonstrate the full humanity of Christ's nature. By reason of Him being born human, He was by nature no longer omnipresent, omniscient, or omnipotent.

Why is the exact nature of Christ important to establish? If God as Jesus Christ retained any of His divine attributes while becoming human, then that would logically and easily explain the supernatural dimension of His ministry. If He did not (which is the leaning of this project) then there must be an alternate explanation. Jesus was not without advantages—His sinlessness, for example, was a huge one. Other than that, however, He was exactly like any other human being. So from where did He desires His divine enablement? At the outset of His earthly ministry, Jesus' baptism in the Holy Spirit in the Jordan River was more than mere identification with humanity. It was the establishment of a critical precedence on how every human must be empowered for both holiness and enablement. Just as Jesus was pneumatikos, so too Christians are pneumatika—a spiritual people.

The opposite of a spiritual person is a "natural" person (ψυχικς/psuchikos). This refers not only to the physical being but to behavior influenced by the world or fallen human nature (I Cor. 15:44, 46; James 3:15; Jude 19).

Jesus came in the form of flesh but He lived according to the Spirit. Christians are physical beings, but have the capacity to live as spiritual ones. C. S. Lewis describes human beings as "amphibians" by reason of their ability to exist in two worlds. This leaves open the frightening possibility that ministry can be performed in the natural. *Psuchikos* or *Pneumatikos*? Christians must decide which it will be.

The Apostle Paul had to make this choice in his letter to the Corinthians: "And my speech and my preaching were not with persuasive words of human wisdom, but in demonstration of the Spirit (pneuma) and of power, that your faith should not be in the wisdom of men but in the power of God" (I Cor. 2:4-5 NKJV). TDNT suggests that the pneuma of this passage might be the spirit within each person. This is an interesting ambiguity. Is it a demonstration of the spirit of Paul or the Holy Spirit? Better yet, could it be a combination of both—the spirit of Paul empowered by the Spirit of Christ, the two so closely entwined they cannot be distinguished? This is corroborated by Paul's statement, "...We have the mind of Christ" (I Cor. 2:16).

Eloquence, oratory, and persuasive speech, are outstanding communication skills. But is this what Paul is opposing? The issue for Paul does not appear to be *delivery* but spiritual *content*. Paul contends for something he calls "the demonstration of the Spirit and power." That way the faith of his hearers does not rest on human wisdom, but on the power of God. Therefore, the choice is between the "wisdom of men" and the "power of God." Wisdom of men: σοφία ανθρώπων: sophia anthropon. Power of God: δυνάμει θεου˄: dunamei theo. Certainly Paul's "demonstration of the Spirit and power" would not exclude signs and miraculous wonders. But recall that Jesus says that it is possible to perform signs and wonders and not know Jesus. "Many will say to Me on that day, 'Lord, Lord, did we not prophesy in Your name, and in Your name cast out demons, and in Your name perform many miracles?' "And then I will declare to them, 'I never knew you; DEPART FROM ME, YOU WHO PRACTICE LAWLESSNESS'" (Matt. 7:22-23 NAS). So it would appear that true Holy Spirit power is not only about miraculous signs and wonders. Instead, the "demonstration of the Spirit and of power" has to do with Spiritual transformation. Paul makes this contention: "So then neither the one who plants nor the one who waters is anything, but God who causes the growth" (I Cor. 3:7). Because Spiritual growth is something only God can do, Spiritual transformation is clear evidence of His presence. Signs and wonders can be performed without God's help. But Spiritual transformation is *never* the work of flesh. Conversion from unbeliever to believer is only possible by the anointing of God. "No one can come to Me, unless the Father who sent Me draws him; and I will raise him up on the last day" (John 6:44). Being transformed from a disobedient person to an obedient one is only accomplished by the power of God. Only God can cause Spiritual transformation. Therefore, the "demonstration of the Spirit and of power" is the transformation of a person's life from ungodliness to godliness. It is the formation of Christian character. It is the drawing of a soul into a more intimate relationship with God. The performing of signs and wonders can be suspect. That is, there can always be a question as to where the power came from, for the devil can duplicate some of God's signs. Intimacy with God, however, can never be suspect. The devil cannot duplicate that. So any drawing near that takes place in one's life can only occur by the "demonstration of the Spirit and of power." Nexus intimacy is the purest manifestation of the power of the Spirit. When people are turning from their wicked ways and becoming obedient, that can never be attributed to the devil. Hungering for God is never the devil's work. Hungering for power, however, could be attributed to the natural or darkness. Passion for God is the hallmark sign of the pneumatika.

Does this mean that the Lord prefers the spiritual world to the physical one? In addition to the Incarnation, two other events indicate God's steadfast commitment to the earth: the resurrection and the pentecost. The resurrection of Jesus Christ is God's stamp of approval on the physical world: "Now as they said these things, Jesus Himself stood in the midst of them, and said to them, 'Peace to you.' But they were terrified and frightened, and supposed they had seen a spirit. And He said to them, "Why are you troubled? And why do doubts arise in your hearts? Behold My hands and My feet, that it is I Myself. Handle Me and see, for a spirit does not have flesh and bones as you see I have" (Luke 24:36-39 NKJV). Jesus then requests food and eats fish in front of them, something a spirit would not do. Jesus does not return as a spirit or ghost (NIV), but bodily comes back from the dead. It is a stern warning against a neo-gnostic spirituality and wondrous affirmation of the physical world He created. Ghosts do not eat. When Jesus returned from the dead He was no ghost. Jesus' return to the physical world demonstrates God's ultimate affirmation for the earth He created.

Beyond the inauguration of the Christian Church, the Pentecost event is the return of the presence of the LORD fused with believing mankind who had been lost in the Garden of Eden. In the beginning Adam and Eve were created in the image of God and enjoyed uninhibited, unveiled access to His presence. At the Fall there was a dimension of God's presence leaving the earth. At Pentecost, however, His presence returns. Redeemed humanity (the Church) becomes the locus of God's presence on the earth. The historical reality of sin complicates this new union with God, and it is by no means complete. However, the fulfillment of Joel's prophecy (Joel 2:28) is a kind of return to Eden which bodes well for the earth. The Pentecost is yet more evidence of God's eschatological designs for earthly existence. Just as Adam and Eve were the image of God and re-presented Him on the earth, so now redeemed human beings filled with His Spirit (pneumatika) once again become the locus of God's presence on the earth. Jesus prophesied, "But you shall receive power when the Holy Spirit has come upon you; and you shall be witnesses to Me in Jerusalem, and in all Judea and Samaria, and to the end of the earth" (Acts 1:8 NKJV). Then again, "...Lo, I am with you always, even to the end of the age" (Matt. 28:20 NKJV).

The true nature of Christian ministry has little to do with human attempts to Christianize society and everything to do with what the Spirit of Jesus is accomplishing through redeemed humanity to establish the Kingdom of Heaven on the earth. Heaven meets earth through the pneumatika, the Spirit-filled Church. This is what is meant by "Uranogaic Influence." It is what happens when the Church prays, "Your Kingdom come, your will be done on earth as it is in heaven" (Matt. 6:10 NKJV). The Church filled with the Spirit is the Manifest Presence of heaven's God transforming the earth.

Christians are privileged to host the presence of the Lord on the earth. How does heaven transform the earth? Through the pneumatika His presence and power is experienced. "I am the vine, you are the branches. He who abides in Me, and I in him, bears much fruit; for without Me you can do nothing" (John 15:5 NKJV). Earth is linked to heaven through these Spirit-ual ones. Instead of yet another "witnessing seminar," the Church must examine the vitality of its connections with the Vine. Sin matters because of its corrosive influence on that vitality. Glaring issues are the starting points for repentance. The fact that they are glaring is the work of the Spirit highlighting this issue. This project explores "Uranogaic Influence" as the mission of the Church rather than training ministers on "how to grow a church."

Both the vertical y-axis of nexus intimacy with God and the horizontal x-axis of marketplace ministry are essential to the Spiritual formation of community transformers. The biblical-theological foundation here has to do with navigating through both the Great Commandment (Matt. 22:37-40; cf. Mark 12:29-31; Luke 10:27; Deut. 6:4-5) and the Great Commission (Matt. 28:19-20)—the vertical y-axis of responding to God and the horizontal x-axis of ministering to people. It should be immediately pointed out that no such dichotomy exists in the mind of God, for the Great Commandment includes loving God and loving people. Loving God and loving people are a seamless concept in the heart of God. It is the ministers of God who have difficulty holding the two together while navigating through in the realities and complexities of life and ministry.

In terms of the vertical dimension of loving God, Hayford's contention for what has already been set forth in Scripture is extremely helpful: "Spirit-born, Spirit-filled, and Spirit-formed."[31] Vertically, the believer is transformed from glory to glory: from one who has gained entry into a relationship with God through salvation in Christ, to one empowered by the Spirit in new dimensions of worship and prayer, to one formed by the Spirit to Christ-likeness by His lordship. This encounter with Jesus Christ both as initiation and as on-going relationship must be retained as the central focus. Nothing can happen without new birth in Christ. As John Piper states in his book, *Finally Alive:*

"So if your heartache is for your own personal change, or for change in your marriage, or change in your prodigal children, or in your church, or in the systemic structures of injustice, or in the political system, or in the hostilities among nations, or in the human degradation of the environment, or in the raunchiness of our entertainment culture, or in the miseries of the poor, or in the callous opulence of the rich, or in the inequities of educational opportunity, or in arrogant attitudes of ethnocentrism, or in a hundred areas of human need caused by some form of human greed—if

31 Jack Hayford, *Living the Spirit Formed Life: Growing in the 10 Principles of Spirit-Filled Discipleship* (Ventura, CA: Regal, 2001), 8-9.

your heart aches for any of these, then you should care supremely about the new birth."[32]

The cultivation of a heart that *chooses* "yes" (aisthesis) to the will of God and "no" (askesis) to disobedience emerges as a vital process to understand. Obviously, this does not encompass all of what it means to be intimate with God, but it does address a critical problem among Christian leaders facing the realities of their own Spiritual formation (or lack of it). Doubtless there are innumerable issues that every Christian must grow in, so where does one start? A "glaring issue" could be the Spirit's way of highlighting a moral problem area that must addressed. It is glaring in the sense that it is obvious to the believer. It may not be known to anyone else, but it is a very obvious issue to the Christian. Another possibility is that it is known to everyone else, but not to the Christian. Either way it is glaring. The utilization of Spiritual disciplines is a way of slowing down a leader, resting and causing him or her to reflect on their spiritual condition. It is a serious invitation to the Holy Spirit to speak into the life of leaders in order that they may respond obediently. The goal is to put "distance" between them and incidents of sin. At first, it may be useful to track "Days Without Incident" (DWI) much like an addict. Ultimately, the objective is not to focus on the sin, but to be grasped by the presence of the Lord in their lives. Rather than facing their sin and backing into God, imagine reaching toward God and distancing themselves from sin.

In terms of the horizontal dimension of loving people, the following guidelines could be helpful in discerning Spiritual direction for transformation along the x-axis. The structure was inspired by similar approaches such as the Engle's Scale by James Engle:

0.   Christian: A clear decision was made to believe in Jesus Christ as Lord and Savior, resulting in being born-again. Along the horizontal scale this is classified as "zero" since it represents a special moment of decision for relationship with Christ rather than a decision to ministry.

I.   Discipler or Minister: Demonstrates a clear commitment to minister for Christ, including evangelism, fellowship, bible teaching, and Christian service.

---

32   John Piper, *Finally Alive* (Minneapolis: Desiring God, 2009), 191-192.

2. Leader: Committed to leading a team of Christians whom one has selected to equip to ministry.

3. Overseer: Oversees and equips leaders, resourcing them to fruitfulness in Christian ministry.

4. Champion: All of the above, but has also cultivated a deep passion birthed in the Spirit—a specific "cause"—such as Hudson Taylor's passion for China or Mother Teresa's passion for the poorest of the poor in India. A "Champion of a Cause" might spend a lifetime accomplishing this goal.

5. Hero: Committed to community transformation through all the above and is dedicated to the core values of nexus intimacy, perichoretic identity, and uranogaic influence. A hero has devoted his talents and resources to "saving the world" by facilitating its transformation from darkness to Light.

The Transformation Scale, or "T-Scale," is proposed as a simple visual aid to remind ministers of the importance of navigating both the vertical y-axis of responding to God and the horizontal x-axis of serving people. It is also intended to be a reminder that "y" informs "x." That is, Spiritual direction first comes from the Lord; ministers then proceed to serve others, not the reverse. This is of vital importance in true community transformation. Christians are servants of God on behalf of the people, not servants of the people on behalf of God. Before proceeding, the early Church first watched for evidence of God's leading: "...They chose Stephen, a man full of faith and of the Holy Spirit...Now Stephen, a man full of God's grace and power, did great wonders and miraculous signs among the people" (Acts 6:5, 8 NIV). In the process of choosing Stephen as a leader, the Church first saw evidence of God's hand on Stephen's life along the y-axis and then selected Him for ministry along the x-axis. This has always been the biblical template: "...The God of glory appeared to our father Abraham while he was still in Mesopotamia..." (Acts 7:2 NIV). Abraham did not decide to become the forefather of nations (x-axis); he was responding to the God of glory who appeared to him (y-axis). Once again "y" precedes "x." Joseph's rise to rulership in Egypt was likewise a "God thing." "...But God was with him and rescued him from all his troubles. He gave Joseph wisdom and enabled him to gain the goodwill of Pharaoh King of Egypt; so he made him ruler over Egypt and all his palace" (Acts 7:9b-10 NIV). God's empowering presence precedes Joseph's ascension to power in the palace. Moses' remarkable achievements in setting the Hebrews free from Egypt came from the Lord: "Moses…heard the Lord's voice" (Acts 7:31 NIV). Therefore, the value of the T-Scale is its insistence that the "y" encounter leads to the "x" experience.

Before concluding this chapter some commentary should be made on the biblical-theological basis for cities as the target for transformation. Silvoso, in his book *Transformation* states, "The Gospels record two incidents when Jesus wept, once for a friend, and another time for a city. His tears show how deeply He loves individuals *and* cities."[33] Silvoso makes a compelling case that cities are significant to God because His intent is to disciple nations. "Make disciples of all nations," has been interpreted and applied to mean the discipleship of individuals when God intended it for (ethnos), a race, nation, or large people group identifiable by a culture or geography. Jack Dennison, in his book, *City Reaching*, contends that in the first century it was generally understood that there was one church per city. This was true for Jerusalem, Antioch, Rome and everywhere else Christianity spread. Dennison quotes New Testament scholar and theologian Rex Koivisto:

"In the New Testament, there are three fundamental dimensions of the church: the believers who frequently gather as a house church; the believers who periodically gather as a local (city) church; and the entire community of believers in Christ who do not have opportunity to gather all at one time, but of which each believer is a part."[34]

Dennison believes that the various congregations within a city today are equivalent to the house churches of the first century.

Ted Haggard and Jack W. Hayford co-authored *Loving Your City into the Kingdom* where they discuss 21st century strategies for reaching cities for Christ. It contains short essays from a variety of outstanding Christian leaders such as

33   Ed Silvoso, *Transformation: Change the Marketplace and You Change the World* (Ventura, CA: Regal, 2007), 170.
34   Jack Dennison, *City Reaching: On the Road to Community Transformation* (Pasadena, CA: William Carey Library, 1999), 44

Bill Bright, Tony Evans, Ed Silvoso, George Otis Jr., and Jack Dennison on how to pray, plan, and go in unity to reach cities for Jesus. The key word there is "unity." The starting point? Hayford offers this advice, "A genuinely dynamic prayer fellowship would not only require mutual trust as a beginning point, but it would also multiply prayer."[35] Hayford recommends first gathering the senior pastors—the shepherds—of a city for prayer.

Conclusion

There is little doubt that Christ's goal for the Twelve was to lead them on a Spiritual journey along *both* the y and x-axis. The problem among some Christian churches today is they tend to over-emphasize one in favor of the other. The pressure to grow a church gives rise to an inordinate amount of messages on "each one reach one" or "discovering your spiritual gifts" to serve the body. Worse yet "serving Christ" might be the sole paradigm informing the congregation of the characteristics of healthy spirituality. Such a church has swung widely to the x-axis and will likely leave its congregants with a variety of spiritual and emotional issues that will go unresolved. On the other hand, a fellowship might swing widely to the y-axis and focus completely on personal or interpersonal issues. This is typically characterized by an inordinate amount of messages on "being set free," "emotional health," or "help for your marriage and family."

Obviously, a church needs both, but "balance" might not necessarily be the answer. Eugene Peterson offers the paradigm of "rhythm" over "balance."[36] Like a musical piece, it is immediately detectable to most people whether a song is being sung too fast, too slow, or off beat. In the same way, during the course of its life, it may feel as if a church is moving too rapidly, too slowly, or off beat, and an adjustment needs to be made. The Lord has put Himself in charge of building His Church. Pastors need to discern if He wants to spend a season dealing with deliverance matters and growing deeper in the Spirit or if it is a season to plant a new ministry or new work. Spiritual direction in this case might have more to do with "rhythm" rather than "balance."

---

35   Ted Haggard and Jack W. Hayford, *Loving Your City into the Kingdom* (Ventura, CA: Regal, 1997), 199.

36   Peter Santucci, "In Sync: Interview with Eugene Peterson," The Life@Work Journal, Vol. 3, No. 6, 50.

The goal is never the establishment of a Christian organization or a Christianized society, but a devotion to mentoring others to become full citizens of Christ's Kingdom. For Jesus this meant transformation from glory to glory along both the x and y axis. As Riggle says, "Never use people to get the ministry done; instead use the ministry to get the people done."[37] The result is not that the people become super human, but fully human. It was God's desire from the beginning to fill human beings with His Spirit so that they reflect His image on the earth. They experience full adoption into His Kingdom and family. The outcome is the world around them becomes transformed. The land is profoundly impacted as the Spirit takes them from Spirit-born to Spirit-formed and from "zero to hero."

In the foreword to Larry Crabb's monumental work, *The Safest Place on Earth*, Eugene Peterson states, "Most of us assume that having decided to follow Jesus as our Lord and Savior we will find ourselves in a spiritual community of like-minded friends, a family of brothers and sisters, enjoying one another's companionship on our way to glory. More often than not we are disappointed."[38] This chapter attempted to review the biblical-theological underpinnings of the learning outcomes of the Spiritual Transformation course which hopes to train pastors who will lead fellowships that will not disappoint. The next chapter will review some of the key literature of Spiritual formation particularly as it relates to the development of community transformers.

---

37 Steven Riggle, "Christian Leadership." Lecture: Van Nuys, CA: The King's Seminary, 2005.
38 Larry Crabb, *The Safest Place on Earth* (Nashville, TN: Thomas Nelson, 1999), vii.

CHAPTER TWO

REVIEW OF RELATED LITERATURE

Transformation

This research is concerned with one dominant biblical theme—transformation—which can be studied along two dimensions: spiritual (inward) and community (outward). This chapter is interested in reviewing literature related to spiritual and community transformation and especially the relationship between the two. As reminder this research hypothesizes that a course on Spiritual transformation taught at New Hope Christian College will enhance the development of community transformers. These community transformers will presumably serve as ministers within the church or in cooperation with a local church in order to transform the marketplace. And that is precisely the problem that Eugene Peterson addresses in the foreword of *Safest Place on Earth.* The Church's mission is to provide answers to the dysfunctions of the world, but all too often appears inept at dealing with its own. The old adage, "the cure is worst than the disease" sadly comes to mind. This researcher's Doctor of Ministry journey took place from 2004-2009. During that time Ted Haggard's secret sin was exposed (November 2006) followed by his own self-disclosure on Oprah and HBO. Then in August 2007 this researcher learned of the secret sin of a long-time mentor and friend. Then in March 2008 a member of his pastoral staff had to resign due to moral indiscretions. In December 2008 another long-time, personal friend and fellow senior pastor finalized his divorce from his wife of 28 years. It was as if the Spirit Himself was fueling the urgency of this doctoral project in a deeply personal way. It became clear that God would not allow this literature review to be written in a vacuum devoid of personal investment. Although this is a research project which must have a dimension of tombstone objectivity in its approach, the stakes for the church, for ministers, and for this researcher could not be higher. This literature review will first explore thoughts both current and time-honored on Spiritual formation; then examine writings on approaches to ministry, i.e., community transformation.

Transformation: Spiritual (Vertical)

Beloved Catholic theologian Henri Nouwen perhaps phrased it best when he described ministers as "wounded healers."[39] The juxtaposition of the importance of engaging in a ministry of healing while simultaneously being oneself in need of healing is a profound insight worthy of the deepest meditation. Equally significant is his provocative assertion, "In our woundedness, we can become a source of life for others."[40] This has immediate ramifications for how the church views itself and its ministry to the world (which would be more appropriate in the next section). The literature on inward, spiritual transformation explores (1) the church's true need (or ultimate reason) for Spiritual formation, (2) ways of rightly thinking about (or approaching) Spiritual formation, and (3) Spiritual disciplines as a pathway to Spiritual formation.

Wounded healers are in need of healing for themselves. No serious author of Christian doctrine or godly living would disagree. But why exactly does the believer need Spiritual formation? Is it only for the sake of healing? Is it merely to save the church from embarrassment? Is it for ministry effectiveness? Personal piety? Emotional freedom? Is a spiritually formed life the reason for Spiritual formation? Most books on Spiritual formation focus on the personal benefits of living a transformed life. Ortberg entices the reader that Spiritual formation will result in the "life you've always wanted."[41] He continues by saying in effect that a Spiritually formed life is every wife's dream for her husband and every child's dream for a parent. Ortberg's book, with his engaging stories and humorous anecdotes, is perhaps the most delightful and accessible book one might read on the topic of practicing Spiritual disciplines. This is one reason it has been one of the main textbooks of the Spiritual Transformation course for the past decade. But while its treatment of the disciplines is excellent, it falls just shy of clearly stating the ultimate reason for Spiritual transformation.

Hayford's opening statement in the prologue of his masterpiece, *Living the Spirit Formed Life* states, "This is an invitation to adventure. You hold in your hands a handbook designed to help serious Christians find fulfillment in life and

---

39 Henri J. M. Nouwen, *The Wounded Healer: Ministry in Contemporary Society* (New York: Doubleday, 1972), cover.

40 Ibid.

41 John Ortberg, *The Life You've Always Wanted: Spiritual Disciplines for Ordinary People* (Grand Rapids: Zondervan, 1997).

maturity under Christ's lordship by linking their souls to timeless practices and principles set forth in scripture and proven valid."[42] His treatment of the classical disciplines is far and away the most superior for the disciple intent on being Spirit-filled. It warrants revisiting in the section on Spiritual disciplines in this literature review. Yet again, the ultimate reason for Spiritual transformation in his book is not front and center, but found in profound quotes of classical writers in the margins (or, as Hayford himself seems to admit, in other books he has written—such as *Manifest Presence*).

Dallas Willard's thesis in *The Spirit of the Disciplines*, widely regarded as one of the best books ever written on the subject of Spiritual formation along with Richard Foster's *Celebration of Discipline*, is "we *can* become like Christ by doing one thing—by following him in the overall style of life he chose for himself... We can, through faith and grace, become like Christ by practicing the types of activities he engaged in, by arranging our whole lives around the activities he himself practiced in order to remain constantly at home in the fellowship of his Father."[43] Willard goes on to speak about an *"ongoing spiritual presence* that is at the same time a *psychological reality"*[44] guiding believers into consistent engagement with the realities of God's Kingdom on a daily basis. Willard's forthrightness about the ultimate reason for Spiritual formation as "constantly remaining at home in the fellowship of the Father" is greatly appreciated and wonderfully refreshing. Is it that other authors do not believe that intimacy with God is the ultimate reason for Spiritual formation? Of course not. The conversation on Spiritual formation has been going on for centuries and it is more likely that authors are assuming that readers already know this obvious truth. The concern here is that this is such a critical point in understanding the true need for Spiritual formation that it should not be assumed that students, especially new disciples, know this. The more immediate needs—emotional freedom, deliverance from addictions, a more holy life, greater ministry effectiveness—tend to be so prominent and pressing, they more often than not quickly usurp the centrality of Jesus as the ultimate reason for Spiritual formation.

---

42 Jack Hayford, *Living the Spirit Formed Life* (Ventura, CA: Regal, 2001), 7.

43 Dallas Willard, *The Spirit of the Disciplines: Understanding How God Changes Lives* (New York: HarperCollins, 1988), ix.

44 Ibid, xi.

GOD THINGS

Richard Foster like Dallas Willard is equally careful not to assume that ministers already understand that intimacy with God is central to Spiritual formation. Ten years before Willard's book he writes, "The primary requirement is a longing after God."[45] For the past 30 years Foster has been regarded as the father of the modern Spiritual formation movement. *Celebration of Discipline* is largely responsible for touching off renewed interest in spiritual maturity through the practice of the classical disciplines. Foster also founded a ministry called Renovaré[46] which continues to advocate and resource believers around the world to become like Jesus through the pursuit of God's presence.

The true or final need for Spiritual formation must be stated clearly from the outset lest Christians are led astray by moralism or legalism. Any statement that supplants Jesus with some well-meaning need such as, "I want to experience Spiritual formation so I can be emotionally set free" ultimately ends in failure. Human beings cannot fix themselves by their own power or discipline. The heart of Spiritual discipline is that it is indeed "Spirit-ual" discipline, and encounter with the Holy Spirit. It is not about spirituality or mystical experiences, but knowing who God truly is and being filled with His empowering presence. It is the conviction, as Peterson points out, that life in Christ can only be experienced in, through, and by the Holy Spirit. Only Jesus can transform a life. Therefore, the supreme contemplation of Spiritual formation must never be anything but the experience of God's presence—at home in the fellowship of the Father.

It would seem that in order to capture the clearest intention for Spiritual formation, the further back one goes in the historical literature the better it gets. Next to the bible, it has been said that the best-selling book of all time is *Imitation of Christ* by Thomas a Kempis. The 14th century German mystic and priest is impeccably bold, leaving no possibility of misconstruing his understanding of Spiritual formation:

> Above all things and in all things, my soul, rest always in the Lord, for He is the eternal resting place of the saints. Grant, O most sweet and loving Jesus, that I may repose in You above every creature—above health and beauty; above honor and glory; above power and dignity; above knowledge

---

45 Richard Foster, *Celebration of Discipline: The Pathway to Spiritual Growth* (San Francisco: Harper & Row, 1978), 2.
46 Thomas a Kempis, *Imitation of Christ* (Chicago: Lumen Books, 1954), 90.

198

and cleverness; above riches and above praise and fame; above sweetness and consolation; above hope and promise; above merit and desire; above all gifts and favors that You can give me; above all the joy and exultation that the mind can experience; and finally, above the Angels and Archangels and all the heavenly host; above all things visible and invisible; and may I seek my resting place in You above everything that is not You, my God.[47]

Thank you, Thomas a Kempis, for revealing in no uncertain terms the true need and ultimate reason for Spiritual transformation.

The journey of Spiritual formation is like the initial drive on the golf course: one needs to keep his head down, eye on the ball, and concentrate on proper swing form in order to hit it straight down the fairway. The temptation to look up and down the fairway is irresistible, for one is eager to know the result. However, the very act of checking for results causes the ball to hook or slice. In the same way the true need of ministers is to keep their eye on Jesus, not on all the benefits and blessings down the fairway. For the very act of looking for blessing could take the focus off the Blesser. But if ministers can remain focused on God—the true need of their spiritual lives—then genuine Spiritual formation occurs.

Nouwen's identification of ministers as wounded healers is not only an accurate assessment, it is tremendously effective in a subversive sort of way. It acknowledges the minister's personal need for transformation while at the same time provides inspiration and motivation to the minister to go through the healing process. What motivation? It will make him/her a more effective minister. Nouwen writes, "Whether he tries to enter into a dislocated world, relate to a convulsive generation, or speak to a dying man, his service will not be perceived as authentic unless it comes from a heart wounded by the suffering about which he speaks."[48] Nouwen's approach to transformation turns a liability into an asset, a potentially shameful embarrassment into an opportunity to connect with the shamed and embarrassed.

The literature review on the nature of the true need for Spiritual formation reveals a conversation where the ultimate reason seemed clearer the further back

47 Henri J. M. Nouwen, *The Wounded Healer: Ministry in Contemporary Society* (New York: Doubleday, 1972), xvi.
48 R. Paul Stevens quotes C. S. Lewis, *Disciplines of the Hungry Heart: Christian Living Seven Days a Week* (Vancouver, BC: Regent Bookstore, 1993), ix.

in history one goes. Recapturing and restating that clear focus is critical since no serious Christian author on Spiritual formation believes human beings can change themselves, and every author denounces legalism. Ministers who take their eyes off Jesus because of over-eagerness for the benefits of Spiritual formation need to remember the words of C. S. Lewis: "I believe in Christianity as I believe that the Sun has risen, not only because I see it but because by it I see everything else."[49]

The question now is, "What are some ways of thinking about or approaching Spiritual formation so as to avoid the common pitfalls?" In a conversation with Wess Pinkham, esteemed Dean of the Doctor of Ministry Program at The King's University, he asked this researcher a provocative question: "Is loving God an ultimate objective or a by-product of being loved by God?" It is a poignant question and one that introduces this next thread beautifully. The phrase "ultimate objective" could connote that intimacy with God is something which could be made into an objective. This of course is ludicrous. The obvious intent is merely to establish intimacy with God as the central *reason* for Spiritual formation above the potential benefits and blessings. This is a critical corrective for human beings whose natural propensity is toward legalism, gnosticism, sectarianism, individualism and self-sufficiency. Admittedly the capacity for being misconstrued exists. So the question remains, "How then does intimacy with God happen?" Pinkham's suggestion that intimacy is a by-product of being loved by God is the answer.

Brennan Manning quotes German theologian Karl Rahner: "Some things are understood not by grasping but by allowing oneself to be grasped."[50] The phrase "Spiritual transformation" suggests that the human soul needs forming so that it once again has the capacity to "grasp" the love of God. And as will be discussed later, the Spiritual disciplines are not a human effort to acquire God (which is humanly impossible), but instead to express a human's willingness to God to be acquired. As Rahner suggests, the love of God can be grasped; indeed, it is what human beings were designed to do. Willard reminds believers that bodily expression in worship is to be encouraged for the body is designed by God to be the temple where worship happens. Rahner is quick to point out, however, that there is a journey to go on in order to cultivate the grasping

---

49   Ibid.

50   Eugene Peterson, *Christ Plays in 10,000 Places: The 1998 J. J. Thiessen Lectures* (Winnipeg, Manitoba: Christian Press, 1999), 11.

ability. It is the Spirit of God who does the initial grasping so as to transform the human soul into one who can once again receive, retain—grasp—the loving presence of God. God is the first Lover. His love transforms souls into His children with the capacity to love Him back.

Peterson attributes G. K. Chesterton with saying that there are two kinds of people in the world: "When trees are waving wildly in the wind, one group of people thinks it is the wind that moves the trees; the other group thinks the motion of the trees creates the wind."[51] For most of human history people believed the former, that the wind moves the trees. In the modern age, however, the new way of thinking is that only what is visible is real. This comes against the conventional wisdom which for generations rightly believed that it was the invisible which energized the visible.

If being grasped rather than grasping is the answer, and intimacy is indeed a by-product of being loved by God, then what is the right approach to Spiritual formation? Peterson lists three critical pitfalls: "Gnosticism dishonors the Father;"[52] "moralism dishonors the Son;"[53] and "sectarianism dishonors the Spirit."[54] Peterson defines modern gnosticism as the creation of an elitist class of hyper-spiritualists within the church who alone share the secret to God. They shun the physical life as beneath their dignity; the incarnation, the thought that God would interact with unwashed humans; the crucifixion, that God so loved the physical world. It is better to remain aloof and detached in religiosity. Gnosticism dishonors the Father for He is the Creator of heaven and earth. Moralism is the cobbling together of a life so good it no longer needs God. "Morals" and "morality" are good things which breathe life, but moralism is a lethal legalism that kills—a humanly constructed existence which dishonors the Son because it says, "Thank you for dying on the cross for me, but it really wasn't necessary." Finally, sectarianism is often disguised as community, but is actually an excuse for not hanging out with certain kinds of people "we don't approve of." Sectarianism constructs religious clubs rather than redemptive communities. "Sects are termites in the Father's House."[55] It dishonors the

---

51 Ibid., 33.
52 Ibid., 47.
53 Ibid., 64.
54 Ibid., 64.
55 Brennan Manning, *The Relentless Tenderness of Jesus* (Grand Rapids: Fleming H. Revell, 2004), 12.

Spirit whose heart is to unify all God's children as one just as the Spirit is one with the Father and the Son. By dishonoring the Trinity through gnosticism, moralism, and sectarianism the true love of God is distorted in the fellowship.

Brennan Manning quotes Gregory of Nyssa, "Concepts create idols. Only wonder understands anything."[56] The connection between knowledge and hubris is well known. Yet it seems the modern church is obsessed with acquiring more knowledge as a means to God. Nyssa warns that human knowledge or concepts create idols. These are more preferable and more controllable than the living God who is a consuming fire. If the fear of the Lord is the beginning of true knowledge and wisdom, then there is a "knowing" associated with the veneration of God. When the presence of God becomes manifest, fear, awe, and wonder are standard responses. The person becomes aware of Who is truly in control of the universe and worthy of the deepest worship and highest praise. In that moment that the believer is overcome by awestruck wonder he has gained a knowledge far beyond mortal ken. His life has been grasped by God.

Such a pursuit requires a total transformation of heart desires. "There is none who seeks for God" (Rom. 3:11). As Foster writes, the typical person is consumed by money, sex, and power. John Piper, in his book, *The Pleasures of God*, recalls a day he decided to re-read *The Life of God in the Soul of Man* by the Rev. Henry Scougal. Scougal wrote this masterpiece at the age of 27 shortly before his death by Tuberculosis on June 13, 1678. He attended the University of Aberdeen in Scotland when he was 15, then was appointed instructor of philosophy at 19. He was a pastor at 23 then was called back to King's College to teach divinity at 24. In short he was a spiritual prodigy. Scougal writes, "The worth and excellency of a soul is to be measured by the object of its love."[57] Piper meditated on this statement for three months and then wrote *The Pleasures of God* where he applies this idea to God's soul. Turns out God has the capacity to experience pleasure! He delights in His creation, people, His Son, justice, obedience and a host of other things which comprise His Kingdom. What occurs in the Spiritual formation process is the complete overhaul of one's life as "the life of God fills the soul of man." The desires of the world decrease as hunger for God increases. The pleasures of God become the pleasures of the believer. There is a sense of weariness, even disgust, with worldly pleasures and

---

56 Henry Scougal, *The Life of God in the Soul of Man* (Harrisonburg, VA: Sprinkle, 2005), 62.
57 Ibid., 71-72.

selfishness, replaced by taking pleasure in God. Scougal continues, "Never doth a soul know what solid joy and substantial pleasure is, till once, being weary of itself, it renounce all propriety, give itself up unto the Author of its being, and feel itself become a hallowed and devoted thing, and can say, from an inward sense and feeling: 'My beloved is mine.'"[58]

The literature suggests that the right approach to Spiritual formation has to do with becoming a person with the capacity to experience God's love. Being intimate with God is not a human effort attainable by secret insider knowledge (gnosticism), self-righteousness (moralism), or joining a religious club (sectarianism). It is an inward transformation that occurs because the presence of the living, loving God who is an uncontrollable, consuming fire has overwhelmed the individual in such a way that the life of God now fills his soul. In that moment he drops to his knees in worship grasping a knowledge of God attained not by his capabilities or worthiness (because he has neither) but by sheer revelation. Grasped by God he now understands with a knowing born of wonder not effort. This was Adam and Eve talking to God in the Garden, Noah looking at the sky, barefoot Moses staring at a burning bush that did not burn, Daniel un-eaten in a den of lions, Balaam talking to his donkey, Jonah praying inside a fish, Paul blinded on the road to Damascus, Peter contemplating improbable friendships on his rooftop, John on Patmos, Brother Lawrence worshiping in tears as he does the dishes, Charles Finney doing devotions in the woods, Madame Guyon praying the Our Father in the Bastille, Abraham Lincoln at Gettysburg, Thomas Merton at the Abbey of Gethsemani, Father Damien at the leper colony on Molokai, and billions of other saints who simply allowed themselves to be grasped by God's love.

Finally, what does the literature say about Spiritual disciplines in relation to inward transformation? There are a variety of lists of disciplines recommended by various authors. Foster[59] suggests there are twelve classical disciplines: the inward disciplines of meditation, prayer, fasting, and study; the outward disciplines of simplicity, solitude, submission, and service; and the corporate disciplines of confession, worship, guidance, and celebration. This list has the

---

58 Richard J. Foster, *Celebration of Discipline: the Path to Spiritual Growth* (San Francisco: Harper & Row, 1978).

59 John Ortberg, *The Life You've Always Wanted: Spiritual Disciplines for Ordinary People* (Grand Rapids: Zondervan, 1997).

greatest appreciation for the historical efficacy of the disciplines. Ortberg[60] lists ten: celebration, slowing, servanthood, confession, Spiritual guidance, secrecy, scriptural reflection, suffering, and prayer. This list is designed to combat the issues of modern man, equipping believers to change as they face the challenges of contemporary society. Hayford[61] suggests ten: committing to hear God's voice, living in the power of baptism, celebrating the lord's table, walking in the spirit of forgiveness, feeding on the Word of God, maintaining integrity of heart, abiding in the fullness of the Spirit, living a life of submission, practicing solitude, and living as a worshiper. These disciplines are geared toward the formation of pneumatika.

The literature is unanimous in teaching that to be like Christ one needs to live like Christ. The Spiritual disciplines are essentially exercises which provide a means by which that happens. They clear a pathway in one's life for the seeking Father to speak, guide, command, bless, prune, disciple, convict, heal, deliver, commission and bring about the glory of His image in His children. Jesus said, "I am the Way, the Truth, and the Life" (Jn. 14:6). As Peterson states in his book, *The Jesus Way*, "The Jesus way wedded to the Jesus truth brings about the Jesus life."[62]

Every author warns against any legalistic effort in the practice of the disciplines. But the disciplined life requires obedience. Does this not involve effort? Why would this not be considered legalism? The answer may lie in Greek grammar. English verbs are typically either active ("I throw the ball.") or passive ("I am being thrown."). Greek grammar, however, has something called a "middle voice."[63] It appears as a passive verb, but is translated active. In this case two wills are in operation, neither excludes the other, neither cancels out the other, and each respects the other. Prayer, for example, is a middle voice verb. Christians pray but it is the Lord who may be compelling them to pray. Marriage, sex, and worship are likewise middle voice experiences. God initiates creation, redemption, grace, transformation, etc. Man responds. God's vision is that the

60 Jack Hayford, *Living the Spirit Formed Life: Growing in the 10 Principles of Spirit-Filled Discipleship* (Ventura, CA: Regal, 2001).
61 Eugene H. Peterson, *The Jesus Way: a Conversation on the Way that Jesus is the Way* (Grand Rapids: Eerdmans, 2007), 4.
62 Eugene H. Peterson, *The Contemplative Pastor* (Grand Rapids: Eerdmans, 1989), 102-105.
63 Klaus Bochmuehl, *Listening to the God Who Speaks: Reflections on God's Guidance from Scripture and the Lives of God's People* (Colorado Springs, CO: Helmers & Howard, 1990), 37.

Church and He live in consonant unity. It is not legalism to respond to grace and truth. That is called obedience. Legalism is an attempt to win God's love. Obedience flows from a soul already secure in God's love. The most effective ministry of all happens out of middle voice. Spiritual disciplines are a means to middle voice living.

Middle voice living requires hearing the Other voice. The deepest longing of the transformed soul is to be connected with God and engaged in communication with God. The minister begins to hear the voice of God. The entire bible is the record of God speaking to mankind. He has never ceased speaking to the Church. Klaus Bockmuehl's last words to humanity (before dying of cancer) are contained in his classic book, *Listening to the God Who Speaks.* In it he contends for listening for the voice of God in scripture, in human history, and through an "inner inspiration"[64] (Ps. 85:8; 51:6; 32:8). He describes Jesus as the "Great Listener"[65] ever attentive to the Father's leadings and an exemplar for all believers. In his book, *Experiencing Jesus,* John Wijngaards shares an encounter he had as a young missionary in India when a Hindu college student suddenly asked him, "Have you experienced God?"[66] Hearsay is one thing; but it is first-hand experience of Jesus that the bible promises. Even unbelievers see this! The Church has not always supported this belief. Dr. Charles Caldwell Ryrie is a noted cessationist who does not support this view. Jeanne Guyon was arrested and her prayer instructional book, *Experiencing the Depths of Jesus Christ,* was burned in the streets of 17th century France for teaching this. On bible reading, Guyon writes,

> Of course, there is a kind of reading the scripture for scholarship and for study—but not here. That studious kind of reading will not help you when it comes to matters that are *divine!* To receive any deep, inward profit from the scripture, you must read as I have described. Plunge into the very depths of the words you read until revelation, like a sweet aroma, breaks out upon you.

Guyon's use of the word *revelation* is problematic for some in the Church. Cessationists believe that the canon of scripture is complete; therefore, no

---

64 Ibid., 48.
65 John Wijngaards, *Experiencing Jesus* (Notre Dame, IN: Ave Maria Press, 1981), 9.
66 Jeanne Guyon, *Experiencing the Depths of Jesus Christ* (Sargent, GA: Christian Books, 1975), 8.

further revelation from God is possible. Continuationists are not contending for adding to or amending Scripture but rather Spiritual direction. Cessationists would argue that the principles of Scripture provide Spiritual direction. Continuationists would agree, but also contend for guidance coming out of a personal relationship with the Spirit of Jesus, not principles alone. Continuationists would argue that hearing God's voice is not only possible, it should be normative for those who claim to have a relationship with God.

To summarize this section a literature review on some of the leading writers of inward transformation reveals that the earlier writings on the true need or ultimate reason for Spiritual formation—intimacy with God—seem clearer than more recent writings. It could simply be the case that the later authors are building on truth already well-established by their predecessors. That is, they may see their writings as adding to a conversational thread begun centuries earlier. The obvious drawback is that new readers may be unaware of these earlier contributions. So it is always best to state the obvious: the true need for Spiritual formation is to encounter Jesus. It is not a better life, emotional healing, ministry effectiveness, or any other secondary blessing. To gain an audience with God, however, is not humanly possible. So the right approach to Spiritual formation is to intentionally make oneself available to God. Because He is God He cannot be grasped, but believers can allow themselves to be grasped by Him in awestruck wonder. Intimacy is a by-product of being loved by God. (A better life, emotional healing, and a more effective ministry are by-products of intimacy.) God initiates; His children respond. Spiritual disciplines are the Jesus way, which when wedded to Jesus truth, results in the Jesus life (Jn. 14:6). Jesus was the Great Listener who remained in real-time communication with the Father. His Spirit now abides in the Church, making real-time communication with the Father a continuing reality.

Spiritual formation is needed for wounded healers in need of healing. Thomas Merton was a Cistercian Trappist monk from the Abbey of Gethsemani, the most stringent, ascetic order in the Catholic Church. He summarizes the journey of Spiritual transformation:

> What has to be healed in us is our true nature, made in the likeness of God. What we have to learn is love. The healing and the learning are the same thing, for at the very core of our essence we are constituted in God's likeness by our freedom...and before He will give us His love, God must cleanse our

souls of the lies that are in them. And the most effective way of detaching us from ourselves is to make us detest ourselves as we have made ourselves by sin...That is the meaning of the contemplative life.[67]

Transformation: Community (Horizontal)

Contemplatives, however, do not fit the profile of the high-powered senior pastor of a modern-day super church in America. Sometimes a mega-church is run by a supremely gifted, charismatic leader who operates more like a CEO of a business than a good shepherd. Wounded healer would most certainly not apply. But after Jimmy Swaggart, Marvin Gorman, Jim Bakker, Gordon MacDonald, Frank Tillapaugh, Ted Haggard, and a host of others, the Church began to once again take interest in Spiritual formation.

Up to now the literature review on transformation has focused on the inward Spiritual formation of an individual Christian—a single life. But how does this translate into "life together?" What does the prevailing literature say about how a community of those being transformed helps the surrounding community be transformed? What has been the approach to wed individual Spiritual formation with community-wide transformation? Has there been one?

In an interview on Spiritual transformation in Leadership Magazine, Dallas Willard stated,

Spiritual formation isn't new; it's only been lost for awhile. It was lost because of the Modernist-Fundamentalist controversy. The liberal end of the church focused on social action. The conservative church became fixated on correct belief as the key to heaven when you die—that became their gospel. Both sides lost the notion of life transformation.[68]

Neither social action nor doctrinal accuracy by themselves leads to Spiritual formation. So how have Christian communities organized themselves for spiritual maturity?

On an average weekend both Willow Creek Community Church in South Barrington, IL and Saddleback Church in Lake Forest, CA each have almost

---

67 Thomas Merton, *The Seven Storey Mountain* (Orlando: Trustees of the Merton Legacy Trust, 1976), 372.

68 Marshall Shelley, Editor. "Leadership" Vol. XXVI, No. 3, "The Apprentices" (Carol Stream, IL: *Christianity Today*, Summer 2005), 20.

20,000 people in attendance. (Their attendance could double on Easter.) Pastor Rick Warren of Saddleback is regarded by many as "America's Pastor," while Pastor Bill Hybels of Willow likewise has interviewed US presidents and had national—even international—impact. They are regarded by many as two of the most successful churches in America. How do they approach discipleship? Both have capitalized on dominant biblical principles to guide their congregations. They describe a fundamental pathway which distills the totality of God's word into actionable steps accessible for brand new believers. Hybels was one of the first to articulate these as the "Five Gs: Grace, Growth, Group, Gifts, and Good Stewardship."[69] Hybels comments,

> We call this description of participating membership the Five Gs—five specific qualities that describe a Christian...who's progressing toward full devotion to Jesus. The Five Gs aren't a finish line or a rigid checklist to be achieved through legalistic efforts. They're more like a baseline of maturity that indicates a person has appropriated God's grace and is cooperating as the Holy Spirit conforms him or her, over time, into the image of Christ.[70]

Warren began Saddleback Church five years later after completing a Doctor of Ministry degree on the Purpose-Driven Church at Fuller Theological Seminary. Instead of Five Gs he has Five Ms: Membership, Maturity, Ministry, Missions, and Magnification. These Ms are magnificently embossed into the thick Plexiglas walls of the Saddleback sanctuary foyer to remind every person of their purpose. Warren's strategy is to again make the pathway to maturity clear and accessible to every person who comes to Christ in his church. He is intentionally taking them from the outside *community* to sitting amongst the *crowd* in church to eventually becoming an official member of the *congregation* where they become *committed* to Christ and serve as part of the ministry *core* (Five Cs). "Successful ministry," states Warren, "is building the church on the purposes of God in the power of the Holy Spirit and expecting the results from God."[71] Wayne Cordeiro, leader of the New Hope movement in Hawaii uses Five Es:

69 Lynne and Bill Hybels, *Rediscovering Church: The Story and Vision of Willow Creek Community Church* (Grand Rapids: Zondervan, 1995), 198-200.
70 Ibid., 198.
71 Rick Warren, *The Purpose Driven Church: Growth Without Compromising Your Message & Mission* (Grand Rapids: Zondervan, 1995), 397.

Evangelism, Edification, Equipping, Extension, and Exultation. Whether there are Five Gs, Ms, Cs, or Es the intention is clear: Make certain the pathway to spiritual growth is clear to novice believers in the church. But is it accomplishing Spiritual formation?

A 2004 survey of his own congregation revealed that after more than 30 years of ministry at Willow, Hybels' church was not doing as well as expected in terms of spiritual growth. A highly sophisticated and meticulous self-diagnosis of the congregation is found in *Reveal: Where Are You?* The news was not all bad: 50% of the congregation reported they were spiritually healthy and "loved God more than anything else." (How many would say they were secure in God's love for them?) But 25% of the people at Willow Creek reported they were "stalled in their spiritual growth or dissatisfied with the church—and many of them were considering leaving."[72]

It is important to note that the methodology of organizing one's church to make the pathway clear for novices in the faith has proven effective for thousands of believers. But what needs improvement? The Willow team is still praying through their findings (and recovering emotionally), but here is the direction they are headed: (1) They want to adjust their messages to the congregation so they no longer communicate, "We know what you need, and we can meet those needs for you." (2) They want to move the congregation from dependence (spiritual parenting) to interdependence through spiritual coaching. (3) They want to somehow expand church services to meet the needs of those further along the spiritual continuum. Their research indicates that their weekend services are an important element in the early stages of spiritual growth but become less and less valuable to seasoned Christians.[73]

Feeding Yourself

Wayne Cordeiro avoids Willow's dilemma of a dependent congregation by attempting to establish a different culture at New Hope. In his book *Divine Mentor* Cordeiro states, "For the past ten years, we have intentionally built a culture that includes a self-feeding program for each individual, beginning with our staff." The Spiritual discipline of choice is bible journaling. Pastors around the world have asked him to share the secret behind the potency of his preaching

72 Greg L. Hawkins, Cally Parkinson, et al, *Reveal: Where Are You?* (South Barrington, IL: Hawkins, Parkinson, & Arnson, 2007), 4.
73 Ibid., 64-66.

ministry. Cordeiro attributes it to what the Lord speaks to him through his bible journaling discipline. By raising up self-feeding leaders, New Hope Oahu and her daughter churches on the island of Oahu now average over 15,000 in attendance on any given weekend and have planted nearly 100 churches world-wide. It is inspiring, revelatory, and affirming to hear a bona fide community transformer such as Cordeiro point to his daily encounters with the Lord through the discipline of bible journaling as the reason for such Spiritual vitality. *Divine Mentor* has sent many Christians back to their bibles with renewed vigor. It is a compelling piece, not only contending for how to read the bible, but how to hear the real-time voice of God in timeless scripture. Cordeiro's contention is that believers can be daily mentored by God Himself through the authors of the books of the bible. It is a deeply satisfying vision for where every pastor could take his congregation—the diligent, daily encounter of the Lord in scripture. Cordeiro's "friendship" with Jeremiah, David, and other characters of the bible is a fresh approach to hearing God's voice in the word of God. This project bases its understanding of the bible journaling discipline on the journaling discipline of Cordeiro established in the New Hope culture. It may be Cordeiro's most significant contribution to the Church at large rivaling *Doing Church as Team*. Cordeiro is a prime example of y-axis personal intimacy with Jesus through the practice of Spiritual disciplines resulting in x-axis community transformation. He is postured to listen to the leadings of the Spirit by reason of His vital connection with the Divine Mentor, and this results in powerful transformation of lives around him. Cordeiro is a transforming life transforming lives.

Cordeiro's earlier writing, *Doing Church As Team (DCAT)*[74] DCAT is a monumental work, responsible for a significant paradigm shift in the local church. It is a rebuttal to the model of hiring pastors to do the ministry and instead compellingly advocates for the mobilization of the entire body of Christ. *DCAT* focuses more on the divine design of believers as providing Spiritual clues as to how one should serve in Church. Interestingly, this has facilitated community transformation as thousands of volunteers are mobilized to serve Christ both within the church and in the community. Cordeiro personally ministers in many venues outside of his pulpit, speaking in business and political arenas. He has met with Hawaii State Governor Linda Lingle on a number of key occasions and mentored born-again Lieutenant Governor James Duke Aiona in

---

74 Wayne Cordeiro, *Doing Church As Team.* Ventura, CA: Regal, 2004.

bible journaling. Moreover, New Hope Oahu's "Spirit of Aloha" projects have blessed the homeless, the families of prison inmates, the troops overseas, and countless others. It seems that the fundamental model of "following the Spirit" rather than "church growth" naturally leads a church toward uranogaic influence. At the heart of Doing Church As Team is staying focused on the work and presence of the Holy Spirit in a believer's life rather than on "volunteer mobilization."

At Saddleback Rick Warren takes his members through a series of classes and small groups which teach them how to self-feed from the word of God. He then wants to turn every member into a minister by helping them discover their SHAPE (spiritual gifts, heart, abilities, personality, and experiences).[75] Through his strategy Warren has influenced thousands of leaders and impacted many countries across the world including North Korea.

In *Transformation*[76] Silvoso re-works the "Five Pivotal Paradigms" of marketplace ministry to cast a vision for transformation. His organization, "Harvest Evangelism," is the brains behind the "International Transformation Network" (formerly known as the "Apostolic Transformation Network). Silvoso seriously takes Jesus' call to "make disciples of all nations," and maintains a vision of "nation Transformation."

The five pivotal paradigms are:
1. The Great Commission is about discipling nations, not just people.
2. The marketplace (the heart of the nation) has already been redeemed by Jesus and now needs to be reclaimed by His followers.
3. Labor is the premier expression of worship on Earth, and every believer is a minister.
4. Our primary call is not to build the Church but to take the kingdom of God where the kingdom of darkness is still entrenched in order for Jesus to build His Church.
5. The premier social indicator that transformation has taken place is the elimination of *systemic* poverty.

---

75 Rick Warren, *The Purpose Driven Church: Growth Without Compromising Your Message & Mission* (Grand Rapids: Zondervan, 1995), 369.

76 Ed. Silvoso, ed. *Transformation: Change the Marketplace and You Change the World.* Ventura, CA: Regal, 2007.

Silvoso makes an excellent observation in saying the Church has applied the Great Commission to the discipleship of individuals above the transformation of nations. In 2006 this researcher was privileged to observe Silvoso's ministry in his home country of Argentina. The Church is clearly transforming some key cities there, including Buenos Aires. Olmos Prison, which was once a high-security prison for the worst inmates, has been supernaturally transformed into a Church. Prisoners serve as pastors and worship leaders, and regular bible classes carry out on-going discipleship. The fruit of community transformation in Argentina is nothing short of astounding.

Jack Hayford led Church on the Way to a congregation of over 15,000 in Van Nuys, CA. In *Living the Spirit-Formed Life* Hayford expands on the ten principles of Spirit-filled discipleship necessary for the formation of a vital relationship with God and equally excellent for the making of disciples.[77] On Sunday rather than a seeker-sensitive approach, Hayford's weekend services could be characterized as Spirit-sensitive. He places an extremely high value on singing in worship, making the exultation of God the main event, deflecting attention away from the charismatic leader. The focus of Hayford's Sunday service is the Manifest Presence[78] of God. It is this encounter with God at some point during the service which is his primary hope and aspiration for the Spiritual formation of his congregation. Since the Church is the body for the Spirit of Christ on the earth, Hayford's strategy is the manifestation of the Spirit through the Church (or in whatever way He deems) to bring about Spiritual formation in the people. He remains to this day perhaps the strongest advocate for the spiritual gift of tongues (indeed, all the spiritual gifts) as a powerful resource for prayer, worship, and connection with the Spirit. A person filled with the Spirit will display the fruit of the Spirit and minister powerfully through spiritual gifts resulting in Spirit-empowered witnessing and discipleship.

Another strong advocate for seeking the detectable presence of God for Spiritual transformation is Bill Johnson, fifth-generation senior pastor of Bethel Church in Redding, CA. His book, *Face to Face with God*, presents the clearest case

---

77 Jack W. Hayford, *Living the Spirit Formed Life: Growing in the 10 Principles of Spirit-Filled Discipleship* (Ventura, CA: Regal, 2001).

78 Jack W. Hayford, *Manifest Presence: Expecting a Visitation of God's Grace through Worship* (Grand Rapids: Chosen Books, 2005).

yet for what Johnson calls "the ultimate quest"[79]—experiencing the presence of God. Johnson's approach is to empower members not just for supernatural experiences in church but to regularly go out into the marketplace where they pray "heaven-on-earth" for the unchurched of their city. Testimonies of miraculous healings abound as a "Jesus Culture" is established in Redding. There have been so many occurrences of healing from cancer that Johnson's goal is to make Redding a "cancer-free zone." Significantly, however, Bethel Church would not characterize itself as a "miracle" church, but rather a fellowship that hosts His presence. Johnson and Bethel Church are exceptional expressions of community transformers who are ministering heaven superimposed upon the earth.

When the researcher visited Bethel Church in the summer of 2008 to attend the "Worship and Revival Culture Conference," there was an obvious "anti-religious" spirit in favor of pursuit of the real-time presence of God. There was a strong worship discipline, with a contemporary-alternative style led by homegrown ministers. A commitment to authentic worship typically characterizes ministries in pursuit of His presence. With regard to teaching, Johnson blithely jests that he actually only has one sermon—pursuing the face of God—and it is 500 hours long!

Hybels in Chicago, Warren and Hayford in Los Angeles, Silvoso in Argentina, Cordeiro in Honolulu, and Johnson in Redding each have their approach to Spiritual formation in a church setting. Each has found a workable paradigm to turn spiritual novices into effective ministers. All are consummate examples of community transformers, each led of the Lord in nuanced ways to reach their cities for Christ. Each is insistent on vital Spirituality in their congregations which welcomes the Manifest Presence of God resulting in heaven transforming earth. Willow's direction from a dependent congregation (spiritual parenting) to interdependence (spiritual coaching) is reminiscent of Sjogren's and Robison's book, *Cat and Dog Theology*[80]. In it he explains that a dog says to his master, "You feed me, bathe me, and shelter me; you must be God." A cat says, "You feed me, bathe me, and shelter me; I must be God." With regard to Willow's third point, "extend the impact of the weekend service to *meet the needs* of those who are farther along the journey," they should refer back to point one.

---

79 Bill Johnson, *Face to Face with God* (Lake Mary, FL: Charisma House, 2007).

80 Bob Sjogren and Gerald Robison, *Cat and Dog Theology: Rethinking Our Relationship with Our Master* (Colorado, CO: Authentic Publishing, 2005).

It would seem they still need to break out of the spiritual parenting mode of thinking! Their second directive—spiritual coaching—has great merit. This is a classical methodology introduced by Jesus Christ Himself.

Mentoring

The Masterplan of Evangelism[81] has been regarded by many as the fundamental manual on discipleship since it was published in 1963. Robert E. Coleman, distinguished Professor of Discipleship and Evangelism and considered by many to be the elder statesman of discipleship strategy, outlines eight basic principles of personal discipleship based upon observations from Jesus' ministry. It is the essential treatise on the Master's plan of evangelism through geometric disciple making rather than solely a mass evangelistic approach. The eight principles are selection, association, consecration, impartation, demonstration, delegation, supervision, and reproduction. One potential drawback to Coleman's approach is that it could be read as a human effort of reproducing discipleship—purely a methodology—rather than a cooperative work with the Holy Spirit. This would be no fault of the author, but since dependence on the Spirit is not specifically emphasized; it must be assumed that readers are already dependent on the Spirit—a potentially dangerous assumption. For the first twenty years of this researcher's ministry, he did not understand the Spirit's leading in disciple making. In an attempt to clearly teach a method, writings such as Coleman's could inadvertently be construed as a formulaic approach to Spiritual formation rather than following the real-time directives of the Spirit of Jesus who promises to build His Church. Again, this would be no fault of the author who clearly teaches an organic approach. Coleman is clear that Jesus' method was people not programs. With regard to x-axis community transformation, however, Coleman's *Master Plan of Evangelism* remains one of the most influential and effective paradigms ever written.

What Willow has discovered is actually a rediscovery of the reproductive discipleship vision of Jesus: make disciples who make disciples who make disciples. It is life on life, face to face, intensely personal, and wonderfully relational. Programs, classes, and services are useful, but there is no substitute for

---

81   Robert E. Coleman, *The Master Plan of Evangelism and Discipleship* (Peabody, MA: Prince Press, 1998).

intentional mentoring. There is no struggle to remember names. In mentoring relationships, or Spiritual friendships, people know one another's names, nicknames, last names, wife's name, children's names, parents' names, even pets names. The gospels list the Apostles by name. They not only know one another's addresses and cell phone numbers, they also know one another's personal struggles and victories. They see both the light side and the dark side of one another, and love one another still without jealousy or condemnation.

Conclusion

This literature review examined some of the predominant writings on transformation along both a spiritual (vertical) and community (horizontal) dimension. With regard to an individual's Spiritual formation, earlier writings are the clearest that the true need is to encounter Jesus, who alone can transform a soul. Intimacy with God is not an objective but a by-product of receiving the love of God. Spiritual disciplines are the Jesus way which, when joined with Jesus truth, results in Jesus life. Just as Jesus, the Great Listener, could hear the voice of His Father, so too can the Spiritually formed. Once a believer is attentive to the leadings of the Spirit, a host of transformational issues can be addressed. The transition from this understanding of inward, spiritual transformation to outward, community transformation has not been easy for church leaders. Willow Creek's *Reveal* Study shed some light on the challenges that churches are facing. It is no surprise that the key struggle is mentoring Christians to die to themselves—their needs and expectations of the church—in favor of "feeding themselves," i.e., engage in Spiritual disciplines. Programs, classes, books, seminars, sermons, and services are all helpful, but the key discovery (or rediscovery) is the classical, biblical method taught by Jesus Himself—mentoring.

If the Church is, as Nouwen says, a fellowship of wounded healers, then mentoring becomes indispensable. There are so many possible ways a disciple's spiritual journey might be stalled, only an intensely personal approach from Spiritual friends attentively listening to God could discern the problem. Then, as Nouwen suggests, as the church journeys with the Divine Healer toward wholeness and freedom, this experience of God becomes a source of life for others.

If ministers would allow their congregations and perhaps their communities greater access to their wounds, this could be a source of healing for everyone.

"[15] The seventh angel sounded his trumpet, and there were loud voices in heaven, which said: "The kingdom of the world has become the kingdom of our Lord and of his Messiah, and he will reign for ever and ever" (Rev. 11:15 NIV).

BIBLIOGRAPHY

Ahn, Che. *Hosting the Holy Spirit: Inviting the Holy Spirit to Abide with You.* Ventura, CA: Renew, 2000.

Bauckham, Richard. *New Testament Theology: The Theology of the Book of Revelation.* Cambridge, UK: Cambridge University Press, 2005.

Bockmuehl, Klaus. *Listening to the God Who Speaks.* Colorado Springs: Helmers and Howard, 1990.

Boff, Leonardo. *Holy Trinity, Perfect Community.* Maryknoll, NY: Orbis Books, 2000.

Buber, Martin. *I and Thou.* New York, NY: Simon & Schuster, 1996.

Chadwick, Harold J. *Madame Jeanne Guyon: Experiencing Union with God through Inner Prayer* (Gainesville, FL: Bridge-Logos Publishers, 2001), ix.

Coan, Titus. *Life in Hawaii: An Autobiographic Sketch of Mission Life and Labors (1835-1882).* New York, NY: Anson D. F. Randolph & Company, 1882.

Coleman, Robert E. *The Master Plan of Evangelism and Discipleship.* Peabody, MA: Prince Press, 1998.

Coulter, Leah K. *Rediscovering the Power of Repentance and Forgiveness, Finding Healing and Justice for Reconcilable and Irreconcilable Wrongs.* Atlanta, GA: Ampelōn Publishing, 2006.

Cordeiro, Wayne. *Doing Church As Team.* Ventura, CA: Regal, 2004.

_____. *The Divine Mentor.* Bloomington, MN: Bethany House, 2007.

_____. *Leading on Empty: Refilling Your Tank and Renewing Your Passion.* Minneapolis: Bethany House, 2009.

Crabb, Larry and Eugene Peterson. *The Safest Place on Earth: Where People Connect and are Forever Changed.* Nashville: Nelson, 1999.

Dallas, Joe. *Desires in Conflict: Answering the Struggle for Sexual Identity.* Eugene, OR: Harvest House, 1991.

Deere, Jack. *Surprised by the Power of the Spirit.* Grand Rapids: Zondervan, 1993.

Dennison, Jack. *City Reaching.* Pasadena, CA: William Carey Library, 1999.

Fee, Gordon D. *The First Epistle to the Corinthians.* Grand Rapids: Eerdmans Publishing, 1987.

Fee, Gordon. *God's Empowering Presence: The Holy Spirit in the Letters of Paul.* Peabody, MA: Hendrickson Publishers, 1994.

_____. *Paul, the Spirit, and the People of God.* Peabody, MA: Hendrickson Publishers, 1996.

Foster, Richard. *Celebration of Discipline: The Path to Spiritual Growth.* New York, NY: HarperCollins, 1998.

_____. *Money, Sex, and Power: The Challenge of the Disciplined Life.* New York, NY: Harper & Row, 1985.

Foster, Richard J. and Emilie Griffin. *Spiritual Classics: Selected Readings for Individuals and Groups on the Twelve Spiritual Disciplines.* New York: HarperCollins, 2000.

Frazee, Randy. *The Connecting Church: Beyond Small Groups to Authentic Community.* Grand Rapids: Zondervan Publishing House, 2001.

Frost, Jack. *Spiritual Slavery to Spiritual Sonship: Your Destiny Awaits You.* Shippensburg, PA: Destiny Image Publishers, 2006.

Gire, Ken. *Windows of the Soul: Experiencing God in New Ways.* Grand Rapids: Zondervan, 1996.

Grenz, Stanley J. *The Matrix of Christian Theology: The Named God and the Question of Being: A Trinitarian Theo-Ontology.* Louisville: Westminster John Knox Press, 2005.

————. *Theology for the Community of God.* Grand Rapids: Eerdmans, 1994.

Guenther, Margaret. *Holy Listening: The Art of Spiritual Direction.* Boston, MA: Cowley Publications, 1992.

Guyon, Jeanne. *Experiencing the Depths of Jesus Christ.* Jacksonville, FL: SeedSowers Publishing, MCMLXXV (1975).

————. *Experiencing Union with God through Inner Prayer & the Way and Results of Union with God.* Gainesville, FL: Bridge-Logos Publishers, 2001.

Guyon, Jeanne. *Intimacy with Christ.* Jacksonville, FL: SeedSowers, MMI (2001).

Haggard, Ted and Jack Hayford. *Loving Your City into the Kingdom.* Ventura, CA: Regal, 1997.

Hawkins, Greg L., Parkinson, Cally, and Arnson, Eric. *Reveal: Where Are You?* South Barrington, IL: Willow Creek Association, 2007.

Hayford, Jack. *The Anatomy of Seduction.* Ventura, CA: Regal, 2004.

————. *The Beauty of Spiritual Language: My Journey Toward the Heart of God.* Dallas: Word Publishing, 1992.

_____. *Fatal Attractions: Why Sex Sins Are Worse Than Others.* Ventura, CA: Regal, 2004.

_____. *Living the Spirit Formed Life: Growing in the 10 Principles of Spirit-Filled Discipleship.* Ventura, CA: Regal, 2001.

_____. *Manifest Presence: Expecting a Visitation of God's Grace through Worship.* Grand Rapids: Chosen Books, 2005.

_____. *Spirit Filled.* Los Angeles: Foursquare Media, 2007.

Heschel, Abraham Joshua. *The Sabbath.* New York: Noonday Press, 1951.

Hunter, George G. III. *Church for the Unchurched.* Nashville: Abingdon Press, 1996.

Hybels, Bill and Mark Mittelberg. *Becoming a Contagious Christian.* Grand Rapids: Zondervan, 1994.

Hybels, Lynne and Bill. *Rediscovering Church: The Story and Vision of Willow Creek Community Church.* Grand Rapids: Zondervan, 1995.

Jaffa, Harry V. *A New Birth of Freedom: Abraham Lincoln and the Coming of the Civil War.* Lanham, MD: Rowman & Littlefield Publishers, 2000.

_____. *Crisis of the House Divided: An Interpretation of the Issues in the Lincoln-Douglas Debates.* Chicago: The University of Chicago Press, 1982.

Johnson, Bill. *A Life of Miracles: A 365-Day Guide to Prayer and Miracles.* Shippensburg, PA: Destiny Image Publishers, 2008.

_____. *Face to Face with God.* Lake Mary, FL: Charisma House, 2007.

_____. *The Supernatural Power of a Transformed Mind: Access to a Life of Miracles.* Shippensburg, PA: Destiny Image Publishers, 2005.

_____. *When Heaven Invades Earth.* Shippensburg, PA: Destiny Image Publishers, 2003.

Kikawa, Daniel I. *Perpetuated in Righteousness.* Kea'au, HI: Aloha Ke Akua Publishing, 1994.

Ladd, George Eldon. *The Gospel of the Kingdom.* Grand Rapids: Eerdmans, 1973.

Brother Lawrence. *The Practice of the Presence of God.* Springdale, PA: Whitaker House, 1982.

Leedy, Paul D. and Jeanne Ellis Ormrod. *Practical Research: Planning and Design:* 8th *ed.* Upper Saddle River, NJ: Pearson, 2005.

Lewis, C. S. *Mere Christianity.* San Francisco: Harper Collins Edition, 2001.

Little, Paul. *Know What & Why You Believe.* Minneapolis: World Wide Publications, 1980.

Lynse, Elana. *Flames of Revival.* Westchester, IL: Crossway Books, 1989.

MacDonald, Gordon. *Ordering Your Private World: Man in the Mirror Edition.* Nashville: Thomas Nelson, 2003.

MacDonald, Gordon. *Rebuilding Your Broken World.* Nashville: Thomas Nelson, 2003.

MacNutt, Francis. *Healing.* Notre Dame: Ave Maria Press, 2002.

Manning, Brennan. *Abba's Child: The Cry of the Heart for Intimate Belonging.* Colorado Springs: NavPress, 2002.

_____. *The Relentless Tenderness of Jesus.* Grand Rapids: Fleming H. Revell, 2004.

McCullough, Donald. *The Trivialization of God*. Colorado Springs: NavPress, 1995.

McIntosh, Gary L. and Samuel D. Rima. *Overcoming the Dark Side of Leadership: The Paradox of Personal Dysfunction*. Grand Rapids: Baker Books, 1997.

McManus, Erwin Raphael. *An Unstoppable Force*. Loveland, CO: Group Publishing, 2001.

Merton, Thomas. *The Seven Storey Mountain*. Orlando, FL: The Trustees of the Merton Legacy Trust, 1976.

Migliore, Daniel L. *Faith Seeking Understanding: An Introduction to Christian Theology*. Grand Rapids: Eerdmans, 2004.

Miller, Donald. *Blue Like Jazz: Nonreligious Thoughts on Christian Spirituality*. Nashville: Thomas Nelson Publishers, 2003.

Moltmann, Jürgen. *The Future of Creation*. Philadelphia: Fortress Press, 1979.

_____. *The Trinity and the Kingdom: The Doctrine of God*. Minneapolis: Fortress Press, 1993.

Mounce, Robert H. *The New International Commentary on the NT: The Book of Revelation*. Grand Rapids: Eerdmans, 1977.

Mullen, Grant. *Emotionally Free: A Prescription for Healing Body, Soul, and Spirit*. Kent, England: Sovereign World, 2003.

Murray, Iain H. *Revival & Revivalism*. Carlisle, PA: The Banner of Truth Trust, 1994.

Newbigin, Lesslie. *Honest Religion for Secular Man*. London: SCM Press Ltd., 1966.

_____. *Sign of the Kingdom*. Grand Rapids: Eerdmans Publishing, 1980.

Oda, Caroline Ward. *Catch the Wave of Transformation: From the Shores of Hawaii*. San Jose: Transformational Publications, 2007.

Ortberg, John. *The Life You've Always Wanted: Spiritual Disciplines for Ordinary People*. Grand Rapids: Eerdmans, 1997.

Osborn, T.L. *Healing the Sick*. Tulsa: Harrison House, Inc., 1992.

Peterson, Eugene, *Christ Plays in Ten Thousand Places*. Grand Rapids: Eerdmans, 2005.

_____. *Christ Plays in 10,000 Places: The 1998 J. J. Thiessen Lectures*. Winnipeg, Manitoba: Christian Press, 1999.

Peterson, Eugene H. *The Jesus Way: a Conversation on the Way that Jesus is the Way* (Grand Rapids: Eerdmans, 2007), 4.

_____. *The Contemplative Pastor* (Grand Rapids: Eerdmans, 1989), 102-105.

Piper, John. *Finally Alive*. Minneapolis: Desiring God, 2009.

_____. *A Hunger for God: Desiring God Through Fasting and Prayer*. Wheaton, IL: Crossway Books, 1997.

_____. *The Pleasures of God: Meditations on God's Delight in Being God*. Sisters, OR: Multnomah Publishers, 2000.

Rainer, Thom S. *Surprising Insights from the Unchurched and Proven Ways to Reach Them*. Grand Rapids: Zondervan, 2001.

Roberts, Ted. *Pure Desire*. Ventura, CA: Regal, 1999.

Scougal, Henry *The Life of God in the Soul of Man.* Harrisonburg, VA: Sprinkle, 2005.

Sherrill, John. *He Still Speaks Today: Releasing the Dynamic Power of God's Word in Your Life.* Seattle: YWAM Publishing, 1997.

Silvoso, Ed. *Anointed For Business.* Ventura, CA: Regal, 2002.

_____. *Prayer Evangelism: How to Change the Spiritual Climate over Your Home, Neighborhood, and City.* Ventura, CA: Regal, 2000.

_____. *That None Should Perish.* Ventura, CA: Regal, 1994.

_____. *Transformation: Change the Marketplace and You Change the World.* Ventura, CA: Regal, 2007.

Sjogren, Bob and Robison, Gerald, *Cat and Dog Theology: Rethinking Our Relationship with Our Master.* Colorado, CO: Authentic Publishing, 2005.

Stevens, R. Paul. *Disciplines of the Hungry Heart.* Vancouver, BC: Regent Bookstore, 1993.

_____. *Marriage Spirituality.* Vancouver, BC: Regent College, 1989.

Synan, Vinson. *The Century of the Holy Spirit: 100 Years of Pentecostal and Charismatic Renewal.* Nashville: Nelson Publishing, 2001.

Torrance, James B. *Worship Community and the Triune God of Grace.* Downers Grove, IL: InterVarsity Press, 1996.

Torrance, Thomas F. *The Christian Doctrine of God: One Being Three Persons* (Edinburgh, Scotland and New York, NY: T & T Clark LTD, 1996), 112, 136, & 168.

Triola, Mario F. *Elementary Statistics,* 9th ed. Boston, MA: Pearson Education Inc., 2005.

Vallotton, Kris. *Developing a Supernatural Lifestyle.* Shippensburg, PA: Destiny Image Publishers, 2007.

Walter, Beryl K.B. *Titus Coan: His Life.* New York: Anson D.F. Randolph & Company, 1882.

Warren, Rick. *The Purpose Driven Church.* Grand Rapids: Zondervan, 1995.

Wijngaards, John. *Experiencing Jesus.* Notre Dame: Ave Maria Press, 1981.

Willard, Dallas. *The Divine Conspiracy: Rediscovering Our Hidden Life in God.* San Francisco: Harper, 1998.

_____. *The Spirit of the Disciplines: Understanding How God Changes Lives.* San Francisco: Harper and Row, 1988.

Wilson, Earl and Sandy, Paul and Virginia Friesen, and Larry and Nancy Paulson. *Restoring the Fallen: A Team Approach to Caring, Confronting & Reconciling.* Downers Grove, IL: InterVarsity Press, 1997.

Wilson, Earl. *Steering Clear: Avoiding the Slippery Slope to Moral Failure.* Downers Grove, IL: InterVarsity Press, 2002.

Wright, N. T. *Surprised by Hope: Rethinking Heaven, the Resurrection, and the Mission of the Church.* New York: Harper-Collins, 2008.

Yamashiro, Danny. *The Spiritual Reshaping of a Christian Hawaii.* Honolulu: Keauhou Press, 2000.

_____. *Successful Evangelism: 100% of the Time.* Honolulu, HI: Keauhou Press, 2007.

Young, William P. *The Shack: Where Tragedy Confronts Eternity.* Los Angeles: Windblown Media, 2007.

Zizioulas, John D. *Being as Communion: Studies in Personhood and the Church.* Crestwood, NY: St. Vladimir's Seminary Press, 1997.

Periodicals
Boice, James Montgomery. *Bible Study Magazine*, May 1989.

Shelley, Marshall Editor. "Leadership" Vol. XXVI, No. 3, "The Apprentices" Carol Stream, IL: *Christianity Today*, Summer 2005), 20.

Stafford, Tim. "The Pentecostal Gold Standard," *Christianity Today*, July 2005, 27.

E-Form
New Hope Christian College website. http://PRCC-hawaii.edu/pages.php?id=33&refer=6; 9/25/08.

Other
Krejcir, Richard J. "Statistic on Pastors." www.churchleadership.org. Francis A. Schaeffer Institute of Church Leadership Development (research from 1989 – 2006), c. 2007.

Otis, George, Jr. Transformations I. DVD. http://www.eaec.org/bookstore/video/transformations-I.htm

Transformations II. Video. http://watch.pair.com/transformations.html

Pinkham, Wess. Description on the perichoretic inter/intra-relationship of the Trinity as heard in lectures to students in the Doctor of Ministry program at The King's Seminary, Van Nuys, CA, 2004-2006.

Riggle, Steven. "Christian Leadership." Lecture: Van Nuys, CA: The King's Seminary, 2005.

Scott, Jim. Teaching Session, Foursquare Regional Conference, Hilo, HI: Nov. 6, 2008.

Stevens, R. Paul. During a regular class discussion, Marketplace Ministries, Regent College, Vancouver, B.C., Dec. 2, 1997.

_____. "Work and Heaven: God as Consummator." Marketplace Ministries Course Notes, Regent College, Vancouver, B.C., Sep.-Dec. 1997, 66.

VITA

Michael Mota Palompo was born in a US Naval Hospital on Sangley Point, Cavite City, Philippines, on March 2, 1958, to Diosdado C. Palompo and Angelina M. Palompo. His father, Diosdado (Desi), is a retired US Navy Senior Chief Musician with the distinction of being the first man of Filipino descent to be appointed leader of a US Navy band. With the devoted support of his wife, Angelina, a former school teacher in their home town of General Trias (Malabon), Cavite, the couple had four other children—Leila, Jerome, Ramon, and Joseph. All four were born in Tripler Hospital in Honolulu, Hawaii from 1960-1966.

In April 1959 the Palompos, with 13-month-old Michael, moved to Hawaii. On August 21, 1959, Hawaii became the 50th state of the United States as the Palompos eyewitnessed the unfolding of this momentous event. On July 16, 1969, the Palompos were stationed at the Naval Training Center in Orlando, Florida, where they were eyewitnesses to another remarkable first—the launching of Apollo 11, when Neil Armstrong and Buzz Aldrin became the first men on the moon as Michael Collins remained in lunar orbit.

On July 18, 1975, Michael became a fully committed follower of Jesus Christ a day after his best friend, Mark Olmos—who would eventually become the best man at his wedding and ministry partner at Hawaii Youth For Christ for fourteen years. As teenagers Michael and Mark founded the John 14:6 Christian Club at Radford High which would eventually become the Radford Campus Life Club. Both Michael and Mark came to Christ through another teenager, Amanda Macaysa, from the Big Island.

Michael graduated with honors in 1976, the bicentennial class, from Arthur W. Radford High School in Honolulu, HI, where he was student council president in his senior year. He then graduated in 1980 from San Francisco State University, BA Psychology, summa cum laude, Phi Beta Kappa. While at SFSU he was Inter-Varsity Christian Fellowship Chapter President from 1979-80. He attended Urbana '79 in Champagne, IL. It was at Urbana he was called of the Lord into "full-time ministry for a lifetime" in response to a New Year's Eve message by Billy Graham. Michael became a Campus Life Director on the full-time staff of Hawaii Youth For Christ from 1980-1996 where he was instrumental in leading hundreds of Hawaii teenagers to Christ. He met Mona Waki at his first YFC summer camp event in 1980, unaware that the Lord had introduced him to his future wife. They were married in 1983 and have three children: Mark (born 1986), Rachael (1989), and Caleb (1998). Michael was baptized in the Holy Spirit in 1994. After graduating with a Master's in Christian Studies (MCS) at Regent College (1996-1998) in Vancouver, BC, Michael pioneered New Hope Central Oahu on Easter 1999 where he continues to minister as Senior Pastor to this day. New Hope Central Oahu is a "Transformation Church" of 700 people seeking the manifest Presence of God with the motto, "Anchored to God's Word, Led by His Spirit." Michael has also been an adjunct instructor at New Hope Christian College since its inception in 1998 where he teaches two courses, Spiritual Transformation and Personal Evangelism and Discipleship.

When he is not working Michael enjoys going on dates with Mona, family outings with the kids (beach, hiking, get-aways, and lots of eating), prayer walking the neighborhood, and going to the movies (preferably sci-fi, action-adventure, or war stories). He is an avid music lover and typically has ambient music constantly playing in the background. Among his all-time favorites in his iTunes playlists: Hillsong, Chicago, and Hans Zimmer. The most fun he has had recently is going on some *very* special trips: Argentina (2006) for International Transformation Network Conference; Study Tour of Israel (2007); Redding, CA (2008) to visit Bethel Church; Portland, OR (2008) to celebrate 25th wedding anniversary with Mona; Austria and Germany (2009) to bring daughter, Rachael, home from college; and mission trip to Uganda (2010) visiting dorm for orphans funded by his church. He absolutely enjoyed two big reunions with over 50 family members at Lake Tahoe (2004) and Big Bear Lake (2007), regarding them as some of the most cherished memories with precious ones. A family reunion is being planned for Hawaii (2012).

Mark, Mike (author), Mona ,Caleb, and Rachael